*Profile of the
Hotel and Catering Indus.*

BY S. MEDLIK
The British Hotel and Catering Industry (Pitman, 1961)

BY J. R. S. BEAVIS AND S. MEDLIK
A Manual of Hotel Reception (Heinemann, 1967)

BY A. J. BURKART AND S. MEDLIK
Tourism: Past, Present, and Future (Heinemann, 1974)
The Management of Tourism (Heinemann, 1975)

Profile of the Hotel and Catering Industry

S. MEDLIK
M.A., B.Com., F.H.C.I.M.A., F.T.S.

*Formerly Professor and Head of Department
of Hotel, Catering and Tourism Management
University of Surrey*

Second Edition prepared with
D. W. AIREY
B.A., M.Sc.

*Lecturer in the Department
of Hotel, Catering and Tourism Management
University of Surrey*

HEINEMANN : LONDON

William Heinemann Ltd
10 Upper Grosvenor Street, London W1X 9PA

LONDON MELBOURNE TORONTO
JOHANNESBURG AUCKLAND

© S. Medlik 1972
© S. Medlik and D. W. Airey 1978
First published 1972
Reprinted 1974
Second Edition 1978
Reprinted 1979
434 91248 4

Printed and bound in Great Britain by
Fakenham Press Limited, Fakenham, Norfolk

Preface

My first study of the British hotel and catering industry appeared in 1961. It had its origin in a thesis, submitted for the Master's degree of the University of Durham, which was reproduced for publication in substantially the same form.[1] That study was to some extent motivated by a reaction against the traditional concentration of the science of economics on goods rather than services, to which Professor Ogilvie pointed more than a quarter of a century earlier in *The Tourist Movement*.[2]

Goods were physical, concrete and capable of measurement; also until not long ago the provision of material things had been inadequate for welfare in most countries. With greater abundance of goods, services had acquired a much greater importance. The human capacity for goods was limited, and as wealth increased, after a point consumers tended to devote a large proportion of their total resources to economic services, as distinct from goods. There was a tendency for a declining proportion of the population to be engaged in the primary and the more basic industries (although the output of these industries had greatly increased), and for an increasing proportion to be engaged in distribution and service industries when material welfare had reached a high level. Men may continue to be consumers of larger quantities of goods in each successive decade, but they also tend to become more and more consumers of services, such as transport, entertainment, and hotel and catering services.

In Britain, as in many other countries, hotel and catering services have grown into an important economic activity. Few industries have had a longer history and exercised a greater influence on the social life of the nation. Few generate a larger volume of output, make a more significant and faster growing contribution to invisible exports, or give employment to more people.

In the decade which passed since my first study of the industry was published, the prospect envisaged then – of being overtaken by events – became a reality. New published statistics tended to show new trends, new legislation exercised its influence on the structure and development of the hotel and catering industry, and the ingenuity, drive and enterprise of hotelmen and caterers shaped the industry of the 1960s. The time clearly came for a new story to be written of the industry on the threshold of the 1970s.

In recent years a deeper appreciation has developed on the part of the Government, of the industry, and of others, of the importance of the contribution of the hotel and catering industry to the nation: of its service in providing facilities for

---

[1] Medlik, S., *The British Hotel and Catering Industry*, London, Pitman, 1961. I was most grateful to Sir Isaac Pitman & Sons Limited, when writing the present book, for giving me permission to adapt material that first appeared in the work published by them.

[2] Ogilvie, F. W., *The Tourist Movement*, pp. vii, 41 *et seq.*

recreation and for the business life of the community, of its role in earning much needed foreign currency, of the part it can play in regional development, and also of its substantial claim on the country's limited resources of land, investment capital and manpower.

The evidence for this is to be found in the establishment of the Economic Development Committee and of the Training Board for the industry, in the provision of selective assistance to hotels, in the creation of statutory tourist boards with a strong interest in the development of the industry, in the first Queen's Awards for export achievement, in the introduction five years ago of selective employment taxation, and in 1971, the first step towards its abolition.

My objects in writing a second book about the industry have been the same as they were in writing the first: to draw attention to a vast field of commercial hospitality with boundless opportunities and exciting possibilities, to contribute to the better knowledge and greater understanding of what constitutes one of the largest economic groups in the country, and to stimulate further the idea of an *industry*.

The book is intended as a text for the student of the industry, and to be helpful to all those with an interest and involvement in the industry; Government, official and other organizations, hotel and catering companies and their suppliers, as well as other bodies and individuals with an interest and involvement in the industry.

In this, the approach has been to provide a simple and reasonably comprehensive outline, rather than a detailed and exhaustive treatment of some or all aspects of hotel and catering services in depth. Suggestions for further reading on particular aspects of the industry are made at the beginning of the six main parts of the book; material used in writing this book and other relevant literature is listed in the bibliography.

In the main, the scope of the book is confined to the hotel and catering industry, in which hotel and catering services are supplied as the principal activities of the constituent establishments. In this respect, the industry tends to correspond to Minimum List Heading 884 in the Standard Industrial Classification (1958) and to Minimum List Headings 884–888 in the Standard Industrial Classification (1968). Catering services, as an ancillary activity to the main purpose of an organization (unless provided by catering contractors) are largely excluded. They are currently the subject of a separate study by the University of Surrey. The hotel and catering industry is seen as part of the service sector of the economy, and as a component of tourism, which constitutes an important element of the demand for its services. However, the industry is related to other services and to tourism only as is strictly necessary to an appreciation of the wider context; the service economy and tourism aspects will be also examined in separate studies.

Most of the matters discussed and the statistics quoted relate to Great Britain, and only occasionally to the United Kingdom. As far as possible, statistical and other data were included to the end of 1970, and the writing of the book was completed in the summer of 1971. At that time, several sources with an important bearing on the contents were not yet available.

Many people have helped in producing this book, but after a close association with the industry in general and with hotel and catering education in particular for more than fifteen years, I cannot hope to acknowledge individually the contribution and influence which men and their writings have had on my formulation of the ideas and concepts expressed here. My indebtedness to them all is none the less gratefully acknowledged.

University of Surrey   S. MEDLIK
Guildford, Surrey
1971

PREFACE TO SECOND EDITION

Such is the speed of change that a completely new edition of the *Profile* has become necessary within a few years of the first, to record the eventful first half of this decade, to see where hotel and catering services stood in mid-1970s, and from there to contemplate their future.

The basic structure of the book, of six main Parts and twenty chapters with the same titles, has been retained. In the main the book continues to be confined to hotel and catering services within the scope of the Standard Industrial Classification 1968. Other catering services have been examined in the meantime by the first British Vending Industries Research Fellow at the University of Surrey between 1972–1974 and documented in two major articles in the *HCIMA Review*[3]; two books devoted to the wider field of tourism have also appeared since the first edition of the *Profile*[4].

The scope of most chapters has been broadened to incorporate much new material and several of them have been rewritten completely. As far as possible, statistical and other data have been included at least to the end of 1975. The new edition was prepared in collaboration with David Airey whose contribution made it possible to go to print early in 1978. We are grateful to several organizations for their agreement to the use of data from their publications.

[3] Koudra, M., Industrial and Welfare Catering 1970–1980, *HCIMA Review*, Vol. 1, No. 1, Autumn 1974, pp. 29–38;
    Koudra, M., Catering Contractors: A Study in Industrial Concentration, *HCIMA Review*, Vol. 1, No. 2, Spring 1975, pp. 97–111.
[4] Burkart, A. J., and Medlik, S., *Tourism: Past, Present, and Future*, London, Heinemann, 1974;
    Burkart, A. J., and Medlik, S. (editors), *The Management of Tourism*, London, Heinemann, 1975.

The 1970s began well for the hotel and catering industry, with a growing demand for its services from home and overseas markets, an hotel building boom which created in a few years more new hotels than in the entire first seventy years of this century, and with a major re-organization of the resources of the industry.

By the end of 1973 the energy crisis and the onset of world-wide recession marked the beginning of a period of uncertain disposable incomes, increased unemployment and unprecedented inflation; overcapacity of hotel accommodation in some locations added to the problems of rapidly rising costs and of financing alterations to meet new legislation on fire precautions; eating out became for many an expensive experience.

But in face of these formidable challenges the industry survived 1974 and 1975 reasonably well. Relative costs of holidays in Britain and overseas contributed much to sustain the domestic market and to generate a further growth in volume and earnings from overseas. The ingenuity, drive and enterprise of hotelmen and caterers, which was seen on p. v to have shaped the industry of the 1960s, also brought the industry through its most difficult period since the Second World War. A rationalization of many catering services made major headway and innovation was clearly in evidence in new forms and in new ways of meeting the market needs and the requirements of viability. From 1976 onwards, parts of the industry, particularly its London hotels, have experienced a new boom.

As we go to print, a more resilient industry is facing the remainder of this decade and viewing with cautious optimism the first years of the next one. Hotel and catering services may be still seen by some as that part of the economy, which makes little difference to the well-being of the country. This new edition has been prepared with the modest hope that it may change that view for some, as well as re-affirm the importance of the industry for others.

S. MEDLIK
D. W. AIREY

Guildford
1978

Contents

		Page
	Preface	v
	Tables	xii
1	Introduction: Hotel and Catering Services as an Industry	1

Part I Historical Development
2	Early Britain and the Middle Ages	21
3	Sixteenth to Early Nineteenth Centuries	27
4	The Railway Age – into the Twentieth Century	36

Part II The Framework
5	Pattern of Location	49
6	Liquor Licensing	59
7	Component Sectors	69

Part III The Market
8	Market and Competition	85
9	Demand for Accommodation	95
10	Demand for Food and Drink	106

Part IV The Firm and the Industry
11	Economics of Operation	119
12	Investment	129
13	Size and Ownership	137

Part V Human Resources
14	Manpower and Employment	151
15	Occupations, Recruitment, and Training	160
16	Conditions of Employment	174

Part VI Organizations
17	Voluntary Organizations of Individuals	189
18	Trade Associations	197
19	Governmental and Statutory Bodies	204

20	Conclusion: The Future of the Hotel and Catering Industry	216
	Appendixes	233
	Bibliography	265
	Index	275

Appendixes

		page
A	Analysis of Catering Turnover 1969	235
B	Annual, Quarterly and Monthly Statistics of Catering Trades 1969–1975	236
C	Overseas Visitors to Britain 1937 and 1946–1968	238
D	Hotel and Catering Industry–Some Major Events I: 1945–1959	239
E	Hotel and Catering Industry–Some Major Events II: 1960–1975	240
F	Standard Regions in England and Conurbations in Great Britain 1971	242
G	Licensed Premises and Registered Clubs in England and Wales and Scotland 1899, 1904, and 1911–1975	244
H	Index of Retail Prices– Meals Bought and Consumed Outside the Home 1974–1976	246
I	British Travel Association/British Tourist Authority Hotel Sleeper Occupancy Surveys 1962–1970	247
J	English Tourist Board– English Hotel Bed Occupancy Surveys 1971–1975	249
K	British Hotels by Size and Location 1 January, 1974	250
L	Bedroom Capacity of British Hotels by Size and Location of Hotels, January 1974	251
M	Leading Hotel Operators in Britain 1976	252
N	Leading Restaurant Operators in Britain 1976	253
O	Leading Public House Operators in Britain 1976	254
	Leading Holiday Camp and Centre Operators in Britain 1976	254
	Leading Catering Contractors in Britain 1976	254
P	Economic Development Committees 1973	255
Q	Industrial Training Boards 1976	256
R	Wages Councils in the Hotel and Catering Industry– Constitution of Employers' and Workers' Sides 1976	257

S	Wages Councils in the Hotel and Catering Industry–Establishments and Scope	258
T	Principal Features of Wages Orders at 30 June, 1976	260
U	New Hotel Construction in Great Britain 1970–1973	262
	Changes in the Hotel Population of Great Britain between 1 January, 1970 and 1 January, 1974	262

Tables

		page
1	Hotel and Catering Industry: Comparison of Principal Definitions	6
2	National Product by Industry Sector 1965, 1970, 1975	9
3	Turnover of the Hotel and Catering Industry in 1969 and 1975	11
4	Travel as an Invisible Export and Import 1965–1975	13
5	Travel as an Invisible Export by Major Market Area 1965–1975	13
6	Overseas Visitor Expenditure in Britain in 1976 by Type of Outlet	14
7	Overseas Visitor Expenditure in Hotels and on Eating Out 1965–1975	14
8	Distribution of Manpower Between Sectors of the Economy	15
9	Ten Largest Employers in Britain in 1975	17
10	Accommodation Position in a Seaside Resort in 1944	43
11	Economically Active Population in Employment in Great Britain 1971	52
12	Hotel and Catering Industry Distribution in Regions in England and in Wales and Scotland in 1971	52
13	Hotel and Catering Industry Distribution in Conurbations in Great Britain in 1971	54
14	Hotel and Catering Industry Distribution in Sub-Regions in England and Wales in 1971	55
15	Liquor Retail Outlets in Britain 1975	62
16	Ratio of On-licences to Registered Clubs 1919–1959	64
17	Ratio of On-licences and Registered Clubs to Population 1919–1959	65
18	Licensed Premises and Registered Clubs 1960–1969	67
19	Industrial and Welfare Catering – the Unit Structure	80
20	Hotel and Catering Industry in Britain 1975 Principal Component Sectors: Summary	81
21	Markets for Hotel and Catering Services	94
22a	British Residents' Holidays of Four or More Nights Away From Home 1951, 1955, 1965–1975	97
22b	British Residents' Expenditure on Holidays of Four or More Nights Away from Home 1951, 1955, 1965–1975	97
22c	British Residents' Holidays of One or More Nights Away from Home 1972–1975	97
22d	British Residents' Expenditure on Holidays of One or More Nights Away from Home 1972–1975	98
23	Accommodation Used on Holidays in Britain 1972–1975	98

	Tables	
24	Demand for Accommodation in Britain by British Residents 1975	100
25	Overseas Visitors to Britain 1969–1975 Visits, Length of Stay, Tourist Nights	102
26	Demand for Accommodation in Britain by Overseas Visitors 1975	102
27	Demand for Accommodation in Britain 1975	103
28	Consumers' Expenditure on Meals and Accommodation 1966–1975	105
29	Catering Establishments and Meals Served 1941–1946	107
30	Expenditure on Food by Catering Establishments 1960–1968	108
31	Household and Total Catering Expenditure on Food 1966–1975	108
32	Expenditure on Food 1966–1975	109
33	Value of Catering Food Purchases by Sector 1968 and 1973	109
34	Estimate of Annual Expenditure on Catering in the Hotel and Catering Industry April 1974 – March 1975 and April 1975 – March 1976	111
35	Personal Incomes, Consumers' Expenditure and Caterers' Expenditure on Food 1966–1975	112
36	UK Alcoholic Liquor Consumption 1966–1975	115
37	Consumers' Expenditure on Alcoholic Drink 1966–1975	116
38	Hotel Costs as a Proportion of Turnover 1971–1973	122
39	Hotel Costs as a Proportion of Turnover in 1973 by Sales Bias of Hotels	122
40	Labour Costs in Restaurants as a Proportion of Sales	123
41	Hotel Occupancy and Operating Costs	126
42	Off-season Costs and Revenue of a Seaside Establishment	126
43	Volume and Operating Costs in Catering	127
44	British Hotels and Bedroom Capacity by Size of Hotel in 1974	139
45	Turnover of Accommodation Units in 1969	140
46	Seating Capacity of Catering Establishments in 1965	140
47	Turnover of Catering Establishments in 1969	141
48	Numbers Engaged in Hotel and Catering Industry 1966 and 1971	151
49	Self-employed and Employees in Hotel and Catering Industry 1966 and 1971	152
50	Hotel and Catering Industry Employment 1966–1975	153
51	Hotel and Catering Industry Full-time and Part-time Employees in Employment by Sector 1975	154
52	Hotel and Catering Industry – Employees in Employment by Region 1975	154
53	Unemployment in Great Britain 1966–1975	155
54	Monthly Unemployment in Great Britain 1975	156
55	Hotel and Catering Industry – Registered Unemployed by Sector in 1975	157
56	Hotel and Catering Industry – Unfilled Vacancies 1975	157
57	Hotel and Catering Industry – Estimated Occupational Breakdown in 1966 and 1971	171

58	Principal Courses for the Hotel and Catering Industry 1975	172
59	New Earnings Survey 1975 – Make-up of Pay	178
60	Catering Wages Councils Changes in Basic Hours of Work 1945–1975	179
61	Guardian Index of Weekly Wage Rates	180
62	Hotel and Catering Industry – Annual Holidays with Pay in 1974	182
63	Hotel and Catering Industry Membership of Professional Bodies 1966–1975	191
64	Catering Wages Act, 1943: Initial Stages of Wages Boards	212
65	Hotel and Catering Industry Comparison of the EDC, ITB and Wages Councils in 1976	215
66	Overseas Visits and Expenditure in Britain 1975–1979 by Major Market Areas	220
67	Forecast Demand for Accommodation in Britain 1980 and 1985	221
68	Food Purchases by the Catering Market 1973–1980	223
69	Forecast Additional Bedroom Capacity Required in Great Britain 1976–1985	223
70	Analysis of Catering Turnover 1969	235
71	Annual, Quarterly and Monthly Statistics of Catering Trades 1969–1975	236
72	Overseas Visitors to Britain 1937 and 1946–1968	238
73	Licensed Premises and Registered Clubs in England and Wales and Scotland 1899, 1904, and 1911–1975	244
74	Price Index for Meals Bought and Consumed Outside the Home	246
75	Hotel Sleeper Occupancy 1962–1970	248
76	English Hotel Bed Occupancy Surveys 1971–1975	249
77	British Hotels by Size and Location 1 January, 1974	250
78	Bedroom Capacity of British Hotels by Size and Location of Hotels 1 January, 1974	251
79	Leading Hotel Operators in Britain 1976	252
80	Leading Restaurant Operators in Britain 1976	253
81	Leading Public House Operators in Britain 1976	254
82	Leading Holiday Camp and Centre Operators in Britain 1976	254
83	Leading Catering Contractors in Britain 1976	254
84	Economic Development Committees 1973	255
85	Industrial Training Boards 1976	256
86	Wages Councils in the Hotel and Catering Industry Constitution of Employers' and Workers' Sides 1976	257
87	Establishments on the List of Wages Councils 1946–1975	258
88	Scope and Wages Orders of Wages Councils 1976	259
89	Principal Feature of Wages Orders at 30 June, 1976	260
90	New Hotel Construction in Great Britain 1970–1973	262
91	Changes in the Hotel Population of Great Britain between 1 January, 1970 and 1 January, 1974	262

1. Introduction: Hotel and Catering Services as an Industry

Economic activities are classified and defined as industries for one or more purposes. In the first place, for purposes of study: in order to examine an activity systematically, it is necessary to define what it covers and how far it extends. Secondly, for statistical reasons: before an activity can be measured, it must be defined. Thirdly, for legislative purposes: legislation may apply to particular activities and not to others. Fourthly, for industrial reasons: particular economic activities provide the framework for the formation of industrial organizations and give rise to market studies. Thus, in economic studies, *products* are the starting points of classification; they may be individual products or groups of them. Corresponding to each product, or group of products, there are segments of economic activity, consisting of *firms* or parts of firms supplying those products to *markets*. *Industries* are made up of firms which produce the same product or group of products.

Economists have traditionally defined an industry as a group of firms producing the same commodity. But the correspondence of such an industry to the industries of the real world is not very close. To define an industry by the commodity produced is in many cases either impossible or at least unsatisfactory. In the first place, industrial products take the form not only of goods or commodities but also of services. Secondly, industries are made up of individual establishments rather than of firms; a firm may consist of more than one establishment and operate in more than one industry. Moreover, the above simple definition of an industry creates problems as the complexity of economic activity increases; firms or even establishments do not confine themselves to one product or service, but tend to diversify their output. Then there are changes in the relative importance of particular industries; new products tend to emerge and others decline.

In practice, there are usually certain activities carried on by a number of organizations which have a bond of interest among themselves, and which come to be regarded as an industry. The bond may be one of the type of product, use of materials or process, or a still looser one – such as their general function and place in the total economic activity. As new bonds are formed and others dissolved, the industrial pattern changes; new industries are acquired, old ones lost.

Since the 1940s, the term 'hotel and catering industry' has come into common usage where the designation 'catering industry' may not be descriptive enough. It embraces the economic activity of undertakings which aim to satisfy the demand for accommodation, food and drink away from home. Statutory recognition of this group in 1943[1] has, no doubt, stimulated its emergence as an entity with common interests, and the concept as we understand it today, probably dates from that year. It has been included as a distinct and separate group in successive official Standard Industrial Classifications,[2] and has set up its own professional body of hoteliers and caterers.[3] It has its own 'Little Neddy', and its own Industrial Training Board.[4] To a greater or lesser extent many products of the group, as well as other characteristics, distinguish its entrepreneurs from others. They all have a common function – to supply those away from home with their basic needs. These are the considerations, which combine this heterogeneous variety of units into a group, described here as an industry.

The exact demarcation of the industry presents many difficulties. The scope of the industry has widened with the emergence of new types of establishment from the seventeenth century onwards, and the distinction between the functions and activities of individual units has become blurred, particularly with the emergence of the substantial separate demand for meals and refreshments away from home, as distinct from the demand for food and drink in conjunction with overnight shelter. Nine major attempts to describe the industry for particular purposes have been made in the recent past; as they provide interesting illustrations of approach, and as many recent statistical data are based on them, the resulting definitions are shown in chronological order below.

The Catering Wages Act (1943)

Enacted with the purpose of regulating remuneration and other conditions of employment in the industry, the Catering Wages Act was concerned with all workers in any undertaking which consisted wholly or mainly in the carrying on (whether for profit or not) of one or more of the following activities:

1. the supply of food or drink for immediate consumption,
2. the provision of living accommodation for guests or lodgers, or for persons employed in the undertaking, and
3. any other activity incidental or ancillary to any of these activities of the undertaking.

On the recommendation of the Catering Wages Commission five Wages Boards were set up for the following sectors within the above definition:

(*a*) Industrial and Staff Canteens,
(*b*) Licensed Non-residential Establishments,
(*c*) Licensed Residential Establishments and Licensed Restaurants,
(*d*) Unlicensed Places of Refreshment,

[1] Catering Wages Act, 1943.
[2] Standard Industrial Classification 1948, 1958, 1968.
[3] The Hotel and Catering Institute in 1949; in 1971 the Institute joined with the Institutional Management Association to form the Hotel, Catering and Institutional Management Association (HCIMA).
[4] Economic Development Committee for Hotels and Catering and the Hotel and Catering Industry Training Board, both established in 1966.

(e) Unlicensed Residential Establishments.[5]

The Standard Industrial Classification (1948)

Within the 'Miscellaneous Services' group of industries the first edition of the Standard Industrial Classification (SIC) designed to promote uniformity and comparability in official statistics of the United Kingdom, included 'Catering, Hotels, etc.' as a separate Minimum List Heading, covering the following:

1. *Restaurants, Snack Bars, etc.*

Restaurants, cafés, tea shops, snack bars, milk bars, soda fountains, etc. The catering activities of the railways (other than hotels), both at stations and on trains are included.

2. *Canteens*

Industrial and staff canteens, school canteens, luncheon clubs, NAAFI canteens and similar establishments not available to the general public. Canteens run by industrial establishments for their employees are, as far as possible, treated as separate establishments and included here.

3. *Lodging and Boarding Houses*

Boarding houses, private hotels, hostels, and establishments letting furnished apartments for short tenancies.

4. *Hotels and Public Houses*

Licensed and temperance hotels, holiday camps, public houses, beerhouses etc.

5. *Social and Political Clubs*

Social and political clubs, including residential clubs, but excluding sports clubs.

Standard Industrial Classification (1958)

The Standard Industrial Classification first issued in 1948 was revised in the light of experience of its actual use over ten years, and a new edition was prepared in 1958. The main changes introduced in the definition of the hotel and catering industry were the exclusion from its scope of certain units, such as

---

[5] Although the Catering Wages Act was subsequently repealed, the Wages Board for Unlicensed Residential Establishments discontinued, and the remaining four Wages Boards converted into Wages Councils, the four bodies continued to operate under the Wages Councils Act, 1959. Subsequently the Wages Council for Industrial and Staff Canteens was abolished in 1976.

industrial canteens operated by employers, school canteens operated by school authorities, restaurants in department stores, and sports clubs, so that only units whose main business was hotel and catering activities were to be enumerated to the industry. The 1958 definition also discontinued the sub-division into component sectors used in the 1948 edition.

Board of Trade Catering Inquiries 1960 and 1964
Department of Trade and Industry/Business Statistics Office
Catering Trades Statistical Inquiry 1969[6]

These large-scale inquiries aimed at providing (*a*) estimates of capital expenditure and stocks as benchmarks for subsequent annual and quarterly inquiries, and (*b*) an analysis of turnover in catering establishments for use in improving data on consumers' expenditure for national income and expenditure purposes, and as a benchmark for the monthly series of turnover indices in catering.

The scope changed to some extent from one inquiry to another. The latest, relating to 1969, covered five main sectors as follows (*see* also Appendix A):
   licensed hotels, motels, licensed guest houses and holiday camps;
   restaurants, cafes, snack bars and fish and chip shops;
   public houses;
   licensed and registered clubs;
   catering contractors/canteens.

Subsequent monthly turnover inquiries have not included clubs and index numbers of catering turnover have been, therefore, available only for four out of the five sectors (*see* Appendix B).

Economic Development Committee for Hotels and Catering (1966)

This Committee, set up to promote the efficiency and growth of the industry, adopted a broad approach to its task and a wide definition of the industry for its working purposes: it is concerned with all hotel and catering activities, whereever they may be found.

The Hotel and Catering Industry Training Board (1966)

The scope of the Hotel and Catering Industry Training Board, established to improve the quantity and quality of training in the industry, was defined initially by an Order of the Minister of Employment and Productivity, and included all hotel and catering activities, except those specifically excluded. The main activities excluded from the scope of the Board by the original Order were air and sea catering, direct catering in approved schools, hospital catering, and other catering operations of the Crown.

[6] The fourth inquiry into catering, to be conducted by the Business Statistics Office on behalf of the Department of Trade and other government departments, has been scheduled for 1978 in respect of business carried out in 1977, with the intention that some provisional results should become available by the end of 1978.

In a House of Lords judgement in 1969 it was held that only activities of industry and commerce were within the scope of the Industrial Training Boards; consequently certain sectors previously included in the original Order were excluded subsequently, in particular clubs and school meals.

Standard Industrial Classification (1968)

The third edition of the Classification issued after another interval of ten years did not alter the broad scope of the industry as shown in the 1958 edition, but sub-divided the industry into five reasonably homogeneous component sectors, each representing a separate Minimum List Heading in the Classification, as follows:

884 *Hotels and other Residential Establishments*
Hotels, motels, holiday camps, guest houses, boarding houses, hostels and similar establishments providing furnished accommodation with food and service for reward but excluding licensed or residential clubs, which are included in Heading 887.

885 *Restaurants, Cafes, Snack Bars*
All establishments supplying food for consumption on the premises to the general public, to which the supply of alcoholic liquor, if any, is ancillary. Included are restaurants, cafes, snack bars, milk bars, coffee bars, refreshment rooms, tea rooms, tea shops, function rooms as separate establishments, fish and chip shops and ice-cream parlours.

886 *Public Houses*
Establishments wholly or mainly engaged in supplying alcoholic liquor to the general public for consumption on premises, to which the supply of food, if any, is ancillary. Included are public houses, beerhouses and other similar establishments licensed for the sale of alcoholic liquor.

887 *Clubs*
Establishments providing food and drink to members and their guests, including residential clubs. Sports clubs are classified in Heading 882 and gaming clubs in Heading 883.

888 *Catering Contractors*
School canteens and industrial canteens and other catering establishments operated by catering contractors. Canteens run by industrial establishments for their own employees are classified with the main establishment.[7]

In all the schemes providing a definition of the coverage of the hotel and

---

[7] Another revised edition of the Standard Industrial Classification is expected to come into operation in 1978.

Table 1
Hotel and Catering Industry: Comparison of Principal Definitions

	Catering Wages Act 1943	SIC 1948	SIC 1958	Catering Trades Inquiry 1969	Economic Development Committee 1966	Industrial Training Board 1966	SIC 1968
Hotels & other residential establishments	Included	Included	Included	Licensed only included	Included	Included	Included
Restaurants	Included	Included	Included	Included*	Included	Included	Included
Fish and chip shops	If consumption on the premises			Included	Included	If consumption on the premises	Included
Public houses	Included	Included	Included	Included	Included	Included	Included
Clubs	Included	Included	Included	Included	Included	Included if proprietary	Included
Industrial and staff canteens	Included	Included	If operated by contractors	Included	Included	Included	Included
Catering in education		If operated by contractors	If operated by contractors	Included if operated by contractors	Included		if operated by contractors
Hospital Catering					Included		
Transport Catering		Rail catering included	Rail catering included		Included	Other than air & sea catering	
Armed Forces					Included		
Institutions					Included		

* Catering by businesses whose main activity was outside the scope of the Inquiry excluded.

catering industry the bases adopted are not occupations but establishments or undertakings, in which hotel and catering activities are carried on, and to which many different occupations contribute.

In most of them a broad line is drawn between units for whom hotel and catering activities represent their main business, and those which are ancillary to the main purpose of the organization. The former are included within the scope of the industry under all the nine schemes outlined earlier in this chapter; the latter are included in some cases if operated by catering contractors (for whom they represent the contractors' main business). This broad distinction finds an expression in the latest edition of the Standard Industrial Classification.

Since most of the available statistical information about the industry is based on the Standard Industrial Classification, it is of advantage to make whatever departure may be necessary from the traditional theory of the firm and industry, and to define the hotel and catering industry in terms of the Standard Industrial Classification for the present purpose. This general approach, defining the industry in terms of its commercial element and excluding from it what are largely welfare forms of catering (unless operated by catering contractors), has been adopted widely in this study. The industry as conceived here consists, therefore, mainly of organizations operated with a view to profit and does not include those in which hotel and catering activities are provided as a service to some other main function of the organizations, such as manufacturing, education, treatment of patients, passenger transport or defence, unless that service is provided under contract by a catering organization. At the same time it must be realized that this approach accounts for only about two-thirds of the establishments in which catering activities are carried on and for only about a half of the men and women engaged in hotel and catering occupations in Britain.

The Importance of the Industry

Before the Second World War hotel and catering services were rarely regarded as an industry in Britain. In the eyes of the Government, of the public and of other industries, the heterogeneous nature of hotel and catering services appeared to defy definition and analysis in economic terms. They had a limited significance in comparison with their post-war position, and there was little cohesion and feeling of belonging to an industry amongst those providing hotel and catering services.

Hotel and catering services have developed as an industry in the last twenty-five to thirty years; several factors have contributed to this, and to bringing the industry into prominence since the war.

The first was the statutory recognition of hotel and catering services in the Catering Wages Act 1943. The setting-up of the Catering Wages Commission and of Wages Boards for the industry, and the numerous reports by the Commission on a wide range of aspects of the industry, going beyond its concern with wages and conditions of employment, led to the emergence of the establishments, and the people engaged in them, as an entity with recognized common interests.

Secondly, the identification of the industry was reinforced by its inclusion in the Standard Industrial Classification 1948 and its successors in 1958 and 1968, and through various specific investigations, such as the Government Catering Inquiries.

Thirdly, the development of international tourism created a growing awareness of the role of hotel and catering services in meeting the needs of tourism, and of their actual and potential contribution to the balance of payments.

Fourthly, the rising standard of living manifested itself in higher disposable incomes and holidays with pay for the British population, giving rise to a new demand for holiday facilities.

Fifthly, the growth and changing pattern of industrial and commercial activity in Britain generated an increasing volume of travel and demand for accommodation and catering facilities away from home; at the same time new concepts of industrial welfare led to the emergence of welfare catering services on a large scale.

Last but not least, the work of voluntary professional bodies, trade associations and other organizations in the industry was supplemented by new organizations for the industry, in particular the Economic Development Committee and the Industrial Training Board, which together with statutory tourist boards with a strong development interest in the industry, provided evidence of official recognition of the industry.

In the following pages the significance of the hotel and catering industry is evaluated in terms of output, as a foreign currency earner and as an employer of labour in the 1960s and 1970s.

Gross National Product

In national income and expenditure statistics, the output of an industry is measured in terms of its contribution to the gross national product (GNP) – the total output of a country, measured over a year, including net property income from abroad, but before providing for depreciation. The contribution of each industry is included net as 'value added' by the industry; that is, the excess of the value of its current output over the value of goods and services purchased from outside the industry and used in production. When capital consumption (that is, what is required to maintain real capital intact) has been deducted from the gross national product, the result is net national product or national income. Actually, in estimates of gross national product by industry, the contribution of each industry to the gross domestic product is shown, before adjustments for stock appreciation and net property income from abroad are made, rather than to the gross national product. The UK national product by sectors of the economy over ten years may be evaluated as in Table 2.

In the ten years to 1975 the contribution of primary and secondary industries to the national product increased in absolute terms, but fell, as a proportion of the total. Over the same period the output of services more than trebled, and accounted for well over one-half of the total national product.

Table 2
National Product by Industry Sector 1965, 1970, 1975

Sector	1965 £ million	%	1970 £ million	%	1975 £ million	%	
Primary	1,776	5·5	2,090	4·5	4,643	4·6	agriculture, forestry, fishing, mining and quarrying
Secondary	13,997	43·1	19,129	41·5	39,663	39·2	manufacturing, construction, public utilities
Tertiary	16,671	51·4	24,863	54·0	56,746	56·2	transport, communication, distribution, insurance, banking, finance, other services
Total domestic product	32,444	100·0	46,082	100·0	101,052	100·0	
Less stock appreciation	318		1,162		5,203		
Less adjustment for financial services	905		1,340		3,623		
Residual error	—		−91		+920		
Gross domestic product at factor cost	31,221		43,489		93,146		
Plus net property income from abroad	435		556		949		
Gross national product at factor cost	31,656		44,045		94,095		
Less capital consumption	2,869		4,445		10,907		
National income	28,787		39,600		83,188		

Source: National Income Blue Book 1965–1975.

Volume of Output

Individual contributions to the national product are published in the National Income Blue Book for thirteen separate groups of activities, but no separate data are available for the hotel and catering industry, which is included with 'Other services', one of the thirteen groups. In the absence of 'value added' information, the output of the hotel and catering industry can be measured in terms of its turnover.

The main indication of the turnover of the industry was produced by the Government Catering Inquiry in respect of 1969, which also provided a benchmark for the calculation of monthly series of subsequent turnover changes in the principal sectors of the industry covered by the Inquiry. The total analysis of turnover in 1969 is included in Appendix A, and the results of the monthly inquiries to 1975 continued by the Department of Industry in Appendix B. These data provide a basis for an assessment of the output of the hotel and catering industry within the scope of this book.

In the preparation of Table 3 a number of adjustments were made to the original data, to bring them as far as possible within the definition of the scope of the hotel and catering industry in the Standard Industrial Classification. Several assumptions were made regarding the change in turnover of individual sectors not covered by monthly inquiries between 1969 and 1975. These adjustments and assumptions are dealt with in the notes accompanying the table, but it is important to bear in mind the tentative nature of the turnover estimates for 1975, as broad indications of magnitude rather than precise quantities.

Of the total turnover of £2,885 million in 1969, over one-half represented alcoholic drink, more than a quarter meals and refreshments, over one-eighth other goods and services (mainly cigarette and tobacco sales) and the remainder residential accommodation.

It is difficult to relate the growth of output in value added terms to the growth in turnover, but some tentative conclusions may be drawn. Between 1969 and 1975 the contribution of the tertiary sector to the national product increased from £22,200 million to £56,700 million – about 155 per cent; in the same period the contribution of 'other services' (which included the hotel and catering industry) increased from £5,000 million to £10,500 million – about 109 per cent, in the six years. The turnover of the hotel and catering industry between 1969 and 1975 increased from about £2,900 million to £5,800 million or 100 per cent in six years. All data shown are in terms of current prices.

Changes in output in terms of current prices are made up of changes in the physical volume of goods and services produced, and of changes in price. The real growth of an industry can be seen only in terms of *volume at constant prices*. The National Income Blue Book gives an indication of index numbers of output at constant factor cost for the major groups of activities, based on 1970 = 100. In 1975, the index number for the total gross domestic product was 107, and for miscellaneous services, including the hotel and catering industry, 104. The major growth of output occurred in chemicals (index number 116), public utilities

(120), in the tertiary sector in insurance, banking, finance and business services (index number 131) and in professional and scientific services (index number 120). The slow rate of growth in miscellaneous services as a whole in the period suggests that most or all of the increase in turnover in the hotel and catering industry between 1969 and 1975 occurred through increases in prices and not through an increase in the volume of business in real terms.

Table 3

Turnover of the Hotel and Catering Industry in 1969 and 1975

	Turnover in 1969 (£ million)	Increase to end 1975 (%)	Turnover in 1975 (£ million)
Licensed hotels and holiday camps	407·5	116	880
Unlicensed residential establishments[a]	—	—	—
Restaurants, cafés, snack bars and fish & chip shops[b]	623·4	78	1,110
Public houses[c]	1,349·0	111	2,833
Licensed clubs [d]	64·2	78	114
Registered clubs[e]	371·8	111	784
Catering contractors canteens[f]	68·9	66	114
Total[g]	2,884·8		5,835

Source: Based on Department of Trade and Industry/Business Statistics Office *Catering Trades 1969* and subsequent monthly Inquiries.

[a] Not covered by 1969 Inquiry.

[b] All fish and chip shops included irrespective of extent of consumption on the premises.

[c] Public houses include hotels managed for brewery companies.

[d] Licensed clubs were not covered by monthly statistics; percentage change to end 1975 assumed same as for restaurants.

[e] Registered clubs were not covered by monthly statistics; percentage change to end 1975 assumed same as for public houses.

[f] Contractors canteens were not distinguished from other canteens in monthly inquiries; percentage change to end 1975 assumed same as for all canteens.

[g] According to monthly statistics of catering trades the total turnover of the four principal sectors covered by the monthly statistics was £2,533 million in 1969 and their total increase to end 1975 was 201 per cent. If the overall change of 201 per cent were applied to the total turnover of £2,885 million in 1969, the total turnover of the industry in 1975 would have been £5,798 million.

Invisible Exports

Invisible exports generate income to a country from the provision of services to people living abroad, as distinct from visible exports, which represent the sale of physical goods abroad. The significance of invisible earnings is beginning to be understood in Britain, very belatedly, and still not fully in all its implications. An example of this belatedness is the fact that, whereas official statistics of physical exports have been collected for centuries, no formal record of invisibles existed until after the war; this lack of understanding continued into recent times, as the Selective Employment Tax and other discriminatory measures between goods and services demonstrated in the 1960s. A major realization of the importance of invisibles came in 1967 with the publication of the Report of the Committee on Invisible Exports, *Britain's Invisible Earnings,* which concluded:[8]

1. Britain, as far back as the statistical records go and probably even further, has had a continuous deficit on visible trading account. Only 7 out of the past 175 years have shown a trading surplus (8 in the last 180 years if 1970 is included).

2. Over the same extended period, Britain has had a continuous surplus on her invisible trading accounts. If Government spending abroad is excluded from the figures, this invisible surplus has always been big enough to offset the deficit on visible trade.

3. It is clear, therefore, that Britain is and has been for well over a century and a half as much a commercial and financial nation as a manufacturing nation.

Earlier in this chapter we have seen that services account for a large and growing proportion of the gross national product.

The Report of the Committee on Invisible Exports demonstrated that invisible trade is a large and increasing element in world trade, and that it is dominated by the United States and Britain, which still account between them for one-third of the world total. In Britain more than £1 in every £3 earned from abroad comes from invisibles; the share of invisibles in Britain's trade with the rest of the world increased from one-quarter after the war to well over one-third at present.

Travel as an Invisible Export

Travel as an invisible export of Britain increased more than five-fold between 1965 and 1975. In the last two years, travel receipts (i.e. expenditure by overseas visitors in Britain, excluding international fare payments) exceeded British residents' expenditure abroad considerably (*see* Table 4).

---

[8] Committee on Invisible Exports, *Britain's Invisible Earnings,* p. 19.

Table 4
Travel as an Invisible Export and Import, 1965–1975
(£ million)

	1965	1966	1967	1968	1969	1970	1971	1972	1973	1974	1975
Receipts	193	219	236	282	359	432	486	546	681	837	1,123
Payments	290	297	274	271	324	382	439	527	682	683	878
±	−97	−78	−38	+11	+35	+50	+47	+19	−1	+154	+245

Source: International Passenger Survey.

The increase in the number of visitors to Britain between 1946 and 1968 is shown in Appendix C, and between 1969 and 1975 in Table 25. The number increased from 2·9 million (excluding visitors from the Irish Republic) in 1965 to 8·8 million (including visitors from the Irish Republic) in 1975. The value of these visits, by major market areas, between 1965 and 1975 is shown below.

Table 5
Travel as an Invisible Export by Major Market Area 1965–1975
(£ million)

	1965	1966	1967	1968	1969	1970	1971	1972	1973	1974	1975
N. America	61	71	79	92	126	150	171	188	205	215	267
W. Europe–EEC	78	90	94	90	106	125	132	146	199	240	316
W. Europe–Non EEC				30	41	48	53	64	82	113	152
Other areas	54	58	63	70	86	109	130	148	195	269	376
Total	193	219	236	282	359	432	486	546	681	837	1,123

Source: International Passenger Survey. Includes estimates for the Irish Republic, and from 1975 (in total only) for the Channel Islands.

Hotel and Catering Services as an Exporter

About one-third of the money spent by overseas visitors in Britain goes to hotels and eating out. The British Tourist Authority estimate for 1976 was as in Table 6.

On this basis, the export earnings of the hotel and catering industry over the period 1965–76, can be estimated as shown in Table 7. Whilst it took some four years to double the performance of the mid-1960s, the 1974 figure of £285 million was almost doubled in two years.

Between 1969 and 1975 the invisible earnings of the hotel and catering in-

Table 6
Overseas Visitor Expenditure in Britain in 1976 by Type of Outlet

	£ million	%
Accommodation:	472	29
of which hotels[a]	358	22[b]
Eating out	195	12
Hotels and eating out	553	34
Internal transport	147	9
Entertainment, sightseeing, etc.	163	10
Shopping	651	40
Total	1,628	100

Source: BTA Estimate

[a] It is assumed that this broadly corresponds to hotels and other residential establishments as covered in SIC 1968.
[b] Approximate figure.

Table 7
Overseas Visitor Expenditure in Hotels and on Eating Out 1965–1975
(£ million)

1965	1966	1967	1968	1969	1970	1971	1972	1973	1974	1975	1976
66	74	80	96	122	147	165	186	232	285	381	553

dustry increased from over 4 per cent to some 6·5 per cent of its turnover. The hotel and catering industry is a major exporter, having contributed nearly £400 million to the balance of payments in 1975. Its contribution increased at the rate of 23 per cent between 1967–8, 34 per cent between 1974–5, and 45 per cent between 1975–6; a higher rate of growth than most other forms of export. In 1975 the hotel and catering industry contributed 3·5 per cent of Britain's invisible earnings. Its performance has been recognized by the Queen's Awards for Export Achievement to a number of hotel companies.

Services in the Economy

We have seen that services and invisible exports play a growing role in the British economy. A high proportion of manpower in the service, as compared with the goods sector, is the third distinctive feature of advanced economies. Industry in the narrow sense, having replaced agriculture as the main source of employment, is in turn succeeded by services. Two main explanations have been put forward for this development, which has been described as the 'tertiary revolution'. First, that the demand for goods expands less rapidly than the demand for services after a certain level of income is reached; the income elasticity of services changes relative to the income elasticity of manufactured goods. Secondly, the general tendency for labour productivity in services is to be lower than in other sectors.

Table 8
Distribution of Manpower Between Sectors of the Economy
(percentages)

BRITAIN 1924–1974

	1924	1937	1951	1964	1974
Primary Sector	14	10	9	6	4
Secondary Sector	38	38	43	44	41
Goods	52	48	52	50	45
Tertiary Sector – Services	48	52	48	50	55

UNITED STATES 1929–1974

	1929	1947	1965	1974
Goods	53	49	42	37
Services	47	51	58	63

Definition of Sectors
Primary – agriculture, forestry, fishing, mining and quarrying.
Secondary – manufacturing, construction and public utilities.
Tertiary – transport and communications, distributive trades, banking finance, hotels and catering, and all other services.

Sources: A research project on the growth of advanced economies sponsored by the Social Science Research Council of New York, quoted by George K. D., in *Industrial Organisation*, Allen & Unwin, London 1971 for data to 1964–5; *Department of Employment Gazette* June 1975 and December 1976, and *Year Book of Labour Statistics 1975* for 1974 data.

Table 8 illustrates the experience of Britain and of the United States over a period of some fifty years. In this illustration the estimates cover total manpower, including employers and self-employed, and transport is included in the services sector.

If we distinguish between three sectors (primary, secondary and tertiary as defined above), in Britain the share of the primary sector fell throughout the period; the share of the secondary sector was static in the inter-war years, rose substantially during the war, and less so after the war; a significant decline has occurred since 1964. The two sectors, taken together, registered a fall in the inter-war years, whilst an increase took place in services; these changes were reversed during the war and early post-war years when there was a marked increase in manpower in goods; by 1951 the relative shares were again much the same as they were in 1924; since 1951 there has been again a fall in the goods sector and an increase in the share of services.

Over a similar period the US experience was different; the fall in the share of the goods sector and a corresponding increase in the service sector was more or less continuous. Britain has now reached the position when services account for a higher proportion of manpower. That they absorb over a half is significant, but there has been relatively little change in the last forty to fifty years, whilst in the US, the services 'took over' unmistakably shortly after the war. The different experience in Britain may be due to two main factors. First, the share of services was already very high in the 1920s, when it included, for example, a significant element of private domestic services, which diminished after the war. There was, therefore, a major change in the composition of the services sector without much change in its total size. Secondly, there was the artificial influence of the war which reversed the inter-war trend for a time.

It has to be remembered that over the whole period since the 1920s the goods sector increased its share of output through increased productivity – at all times the increase in output was greater than in manpower; the reverse was true of services. And here is one explanation why in 1966 the introduction of the Selective Employment Tax in Britain was to give a particular incentive to more economical use of labour in those industries where the tax was payable without refund. The fact that this need applied to a greater or lesser extent to all sectors of the economy, that this stimulus was badly needed in manufacturing too, seems to have been overlooked.

The advent and growth of the service economy has major implications for the economy; for example, most jobs in the service sector are held by women, most incomes in the service sector tend to be more variable, many jobs in the service sector provide a greater involvement and satisfaction, few services sector employees are organized in trade unions. It may be that a service economy may be a more stable economy.[9]

Hotel and Catering Services as an Employer

The manpower share of the hotel and catering industry is analysed in Chapter 14; the industry accounted for almost 3 per cent of the occupied population of Britain and nearly 5 per cent of women at work, if self-employed as well as employees are included.

The ten largest employers in 1975 based on broad industry groups are shown in Table 9. These accounted for well over ten million employees or more than two-fifths of all employees; all but two of the ten were services.

---

[9] For a fuller discussion of the importance of services to the British economy, see *Britain– Workshop or Service Centre to the World?* A University Lecture by this author.

Table 9
Ten Largest Employers in Britain in 1975

		(000s)
1	Retail distribution	1,880
2	Educational services	1,776
3	Construction	1,273
4	Medical and dental services	1,218
5	Insurance, banking, finance and business services	1,088
6	Local government service	996
7	Hotels and catering	816
8	National government service	612
9	Wholesale distribution	543
10	Motor vehicle manufacturing	455

Hotels and catering as defined by the Standard Industrial Classification (1968)
Source: Department of Employment Gazette, July 1976.

The hotel and catering industry ranked as the seventh largest employer of labour in this list and fourth in industry and commerce, exceeded only by retail distribution, construction, and insurance, banking, finance and business services. In 1975 the industry also ranked as the fifth largest employer of women and the second largest employer of women in industry and commerce, after retail distribution.

Importance of Sectors and Regions

In 1975 the hotel and catering industry had an annual turnover approaching £6,000 million; it earned almost £400 million or nearly 7 per cent of its turnover in foreign currency; it accounted for close on 3 per cent of the working population and ranked as the fourth largest employer in British industry and commerce. However, this total evaluation of the significance of the industry conceals some important sectoral and regional differences, which emerge if we consider the position in 1975 from information earlier in this chapter and in Chapters 5, 9 and 14.

In recent years, hotels and other accommodation units registered the highest increase in turnover, to some £880 million in 1975 (close on one-sixth of the total turnover of the industry), they account for over one-quarter of the demand for accommodation away from home and most of the business demand in Britain. Their accommodation facilities cater for more than one-third of the overseas demand, and earn over 20 per cent of the expenditure by overseas visitors in Britain (over £350 million; together with restaurants, some £550 million). They account for about 255,000 employees, about one-third of the labour force of the industry. Their main geographical concentration is in the south-east and south-west England, which account together for almost one-half of all employees in hotels and other accommodation units, and in Scotland. London hotels are by far the most important foreign currency earners.

In 1975 restaurants and similar eating establishments had an annual turnover of about £1,100 million, which increased by over 75 per cent between 1969 and 1975. They are the second most important sector of the industry in terms of foreign currency earnings, and account for about 160,000 employees, about 20 per cent of the industry, of whom more than 60,000 are in the south-east.

The turnover of public houses represented over £1,300 million in 1969 and over £2,800 million in 1975, an increase of 110 per cent over the six years, and almost one-half of the total turnover of the industry. In 1975 they employed 230,000 people, two-thirds of them women. Almost one-third of all public house employees were in the south-east and by far the lowest number was in East Anglia.

Clubs had a combined turnover of about £900 million in 1975, of which licensed clubs accounted for about 13 per cent and registered clubs for about 87 per cent, and employed nearly 100,000 people. Although women outnumber men in them, as they do in all sectors of the industry, together with hotels, clubs have the highest proportion of men employed in them of all sectors of the industry. The highest concentrations of club employees are in the south-east and in the north of England.

Catering contractors have the smallest turnover – about £114 million in 1975 – and, if their turnover grew at a similar rate to all canteens, they also showed the lowest growth in turnover of all sectors of the industry between 1969 and 1975. They employ close on 70,000 people, of whom three-quarters are women. Their highest concentration of employment is in the south-east and West Midlands; these regions accounted together for well over one-half of all employees in 1975. The lowest contractor employment was in East Anglia.

Part I
Historical Development

Additional Reading for Part I

A. J. Burkart and S. Medlik: *Tourism – Past, Present, and Future,* Part I.

Sir Noel Curtis-Bennett: *The Food of the People.*

L. J. Lickorish and A. G. Kershaw: *The Travel Trade,* Chapter 2.

A. J. Norval: *The Tourist Industry,* Chapter I.

J. A. R. Pimlott: *The Englishman's Holiday.*

2. Early Britain and the Middle Ages

The beginning of catering and hotel-keeping can be traced back to ancient civilizations. Such is the resemblance between these and more modern times, and so gradual has been the development since the first days of hospitality that the early times warrant more than a passing mention in an historical outline. However, this study is concerned with Britain, and records of the earliest phases of hospitality in Britain are scant. Before the Roman conquest the roads were grass trackways, probably used to a great extent by semi-nomadic tribes whose shelter was tents. In the time of the Druids there appears to have been an order of people, called beatachs, brughnibhs, or keepers of open houses, established for the express purpose of hospitality. In Ireland the prince of the territory provided persons, called the bruighs, with land and stock to keep beds, stabling, and such amusements as backgammon boards.

Roman Britain and After

The Romans originated several kinds of establishment. Along their magnificent system of highways they set up posting houses known as mansiones or stabulae; these inns were also known as diversoria. In addition all towns had the alehouse or bibulium, which was simply a drinking shop; there were taverns at Chester, Londinium, Eboracum (York) and elsewhere, which served food as well, also various sutlers' booths were attached to the commissariats of the legions.

When the Romans left England a long period of anarchy and barbarism followed. The Roman cities and inns were destroyed or left to decay. The roads remained, but they seem to have been used to a decreasing extent, without any repair for centuries after. In fact, no one made any more hard roads until the turnpikes of the eighteenth century. The Nordic invasions and internal political wars constituted a period of upheaval and turbulence, which lasted until the eleventh century. Due to the poor state of roads, dangers of travel and little internal trade, travelling was undertaken only when absolutely necessary. When the King or other great personage travelled, hospitality was commanded from the nearest castle or manor, and the retinue was billeted in the best houses of the town or village. Other rare travellers resorted to private hospitality or stayed in abbeys and monasteries, which took upon themselves the duties of hospitality. The more important travellers were entertained within the Abbey itself, the 'ordinary' people at hostels and hospices built for the purpose at the gates.

The historian notes[1] that 'Saxon and Dane each came of a thirsty race, and many an acre of barley went to fill the ale-horn'. They had long been familiar

[1] Trevelyan, G. M., *History of England*, p. 86.

with brewing, and it seems that from the end of the sixth century ale-houses were quite common, although for a long time they were mostly crude shelters, situated at the cross-roads and in the more populated centres.

Early Middle Ages

In the eleventh century England emerged into an era of comparative peace and development. But the bad roads were generally impassable for loaded wagons and the transport of goods was difficult. The travellers were people on foot and on horseback, and carriers transported goods by pack horse. Moreover, travel remained very dangerous: since roads were infested with outlaws and robbers, travellers moved in groups and sought shelter by night. However, several factors contributed to some increase in the volume of travel already before, and particularly after the Norman conquest. Pilgrimages were undertaken by thousands of people who made long and arduous journeys to the sacred shrines in various parts of the country. The series of crusades which started towards the end of the eleventh century accelerated the process of greater contact with other nations and within the country itself. Finally, there was a slow revival of trade, and fairs assumes some importance.

Religious houses and private persons continued to provide most of the accommodation for pilgrims and other travellers for some time. The monastic institutions, which at first received all freely as an informal service, established separate dormitories and refectories, and certain monks were detailed to entertain the guests. There were several orders of monks whose main function was the harbouring of pilgrims. Also, in parishes much frequented by pilgrims and other travellers, special guest houses or refuges for strangers were established. Although they were usually connected with a monastery or church, this was not always the case – often the provider was a nobleman. There pilgrims and strangers were taken in, in addition to the poor and the sick. The private houses of the nobles and of the gentry accommodated large numbers, too. Some travellers availed themselves of the right of salt and fire, and applied to the castles of the great, where they dined in the huge hall but sat at the lower table with the dependent classes. Many others were accommodated in the guest chambers of the clergy. In addition to the types of accommodation mentioned so far, private householders were taking in not only acquaintances but also strangers.

Inns, Taverns, and Ale-houses

The origin of the English inn may be traced to this practice of receiving travellers by private householders. There is little doubt that the inn largely evolved from the private house. Any householder might receive a stranger for the night, particularly in rural communities. In the course of time, one such householder often came, either through the superiority of his accommodation or by reason of lack of competition, to receive all travellers who needed shelter in that particular village; he became an inn-holder. This usually happened gradually, without any distinct change marking the transition from the private householder to the innkeeper.

Inns were still not common in the twelfth and thirteenth centuries; many travellers, especially the 'better class', preferred to stay with acquaintances or in the monasteries, and this retarded the development of the inns. But already, when there were inns in existence, there was an interesting discrimination against travellers on the part of religious houses. The nobility were received amiably because it was through their bounty and protection that the monasteries existed; the poor were also received, out of charity. But the middle classes, the men who on the one hand had no special claim to favour, and on the other hand were able to pay their way, had to go to those whose business it was to care for them – to the innkeepers. And similarly the lord of the manor soon had no desire to compete with the innkeeper; for the middle classes – the merchants, small landowners, packmen and others – there was the inn. Under Norman rule it was called the *common inn,* to distinguish it from the town houses which were used as residences for the men attending courts and called simply *inns*.

The accommodation in the earliest inns would not differ from that which might be offered by the private householder. Meals were eaten in the large hall, where tables were removed and beds spread for the night. Only the houses of the well-to-do, and later the better inns, had an additional chamber for guests. A stable was usually attached to the hall at one end. In some of the early inns the travellers had to bring their own food, but soon they were able to buy what they wished to eat, chiefly bread, meat, and beer. If a traveller brought a horse and paid for his keep, he paid no extra for his bed, but the traveller on foot paid a small sum for his lodging. Where a traveller of better class would receive accommodation in a small chamber, he would pay for the food and lodging, as well as his fire and candle. Even then he would not usually occupy the chamber alone, or even a bed alone.

Before the fourteenth century inns were found mainly in London and the large towns; in the provinces, taverns and ale-houses were most common. All of them were at first little more than sheds, and not till the late fourteenth and early fifteenth centuries were solid structures of stone built. For some time then, buildings actually built as inns still followed the layout of private houses, with a large hall, the centre of all activity, and a common dormitory. The accommodation provided was very simple. But the inn was already firmly established by the fourteenth century.

The taverns were closely associated with the inns at all times, and in the smaller communities the two were often indistinguishable. But by the fourteenth century a differentiation had emerged. The tavern was a local rendezvous and a place of recreation, restricted to providing casual refreshment of food and drink within certain hours. It could not be used to harbour guests, and was usually kept by a vintner. Its nearest modern equivalent is the licensed restaurant and the better type of publican's on-licensed house. The tavern supplied, therefore, the wants of the inhabitants of the place; it might provide incidental refreshment to the traveller but its primary purpose was different. The ale-house was similar to the tavern but sold beer rather than wine and offered more meagre amenities. The inn was restricted by custom or common law licence, to the reception and entertainment of travellers by day or night. 'Tippling' was forbidden, and it was not 'a place of idle resort'.

At first ale was supplied to these establishments from the manor and the proprietor was rarely permitted to brew his own; later, beer and ale were brewed in almost every home, and by most owners of inns and hostelries, as well as in ale-houses.

Other Medieval Catering

In addition to the catering establishments mentioned above, there were several others, some of which bear a close resemblance to modern large-scale catering; e.g., the Royal Household, the manor, the guild and the workshop. The former two were mentioned previously in connection with entertainment of strangers, but it should be realized that travellers constituted neither the only nor necessarily the main body at the tables. The court, its officials and servants ran into hundreds and even thousands, quite apart from any travellers. We are told that 'the household accounts of Richard II show that every day ten thousand people sat down to meat at his charges, the royal kitchens serving out the messes to them by the hand of three hundred servitors'.[2]

The great barons and the manorial lords had their catering problems, too. The large numbers of retainers were fed from their master's kitchen and ate their meals in the same great hall as the lord and lady. It was only when the demands made upon the households became too excessive, and a series of bad harvests followed, that the 'free-for-all' meals were restricted. The custom should also be mentioned of supplying food and drink to the 'villeins' or manorial tenants when they undertook 'boonwork' for their lord, which was work on certain days in time of pressure, such as harvests, and distinct from the ordinary 'week-work'.

The guilds held many feasts each year in their halls, for which excuses were found on every holiday and Saint's day and on days when new members were admitted. Finally, some catering also took place continually in towns where many journeymen and apprentices 'lived in' and their meals in their master's household represented a part of their remuneration.

Early Legislation

Inns and other catering establishments invited legislation designed to regulate them at quite an early date. Publicans were compelled by law to put up a sign, although with other trades this was optional. In the fourteenth century concern was expressed at the excessive number of taverns. The statutes for the regulation of the City of London in the reign of Edward II mentioned that 'divers persons do resort unto the city', some of whom became innkeepers and tavern-keepers. In the reigns of Edward II and III many ale-houses and taverns were closed and

[2] Curtis-Bennett, Sir N., *The Food of the People*, pp. 38–41.

only a limited number allowed.[3] At this time, the people petitioned Parliament about excessive prices, and the King interfered accordingly with the forces of supply and demand. In 1349 Edward III promulgated a statute compelling all hostelers and herbergers to make reasonable charges, under penalty of refunding to the swindled guest double the sum taken from him. Four years later another and stronger law was passed to put an end to the 'great and outrageous cost of victuals kept up in all the realm by innkeepers and other retailers of victuals, to the great detriment of the people travelling across the realm'. Mayors and justices were charged to inquire in all places of the 'deeds and outrages of hostelers and their kind' and to deal with them summarily. The scandal appears to have been settled by the innkeepers themselves – competition stepped in and did what the law found most difficult to do.[4] A close parallel with modern authority existed already in the Middle Ages in two respects. Firstly, taverns and ale-houses were not allowed to be opened for the sale of wine and ale after the tolling of the curfew. Secondly, the predecessor of our Food and Drugs legislation was designed in the fourteenth and fifteenth centuries to counter adulteration of wine, and the practice of the cheaper cookshops, particularly common in London, of preparing pies and other dishes from tainted meat.

Close of the Middle Ages

As the Middle Ages drew to a close, inns were beginning to increase in importance. There were a number of factors, which contributed to this. Private hospitality was gradually ceasing. The influence of the Church in social life began to wane and with it the influence of the monasteries, as the numbers of pilgrims became smaller. Travel was on the increase, despite the upheavals of the Wars of the Roses, and with the boom in English raw wool a new merchant class began to emerge, to whom travel was a frequent necessity. And thus the old methods of hospitality began to pass away.

The hospitia of religious houses, which had for centuries furnished shelter and provender, were slowly on their way out; as the demand of travellers increased, the number of inns was also rising. The quality of most still left much to be desired, and that was one of the main reasons why some travellers continued to prefer monastic hospitality, as long as it was available. Nevertheless, towards the end of the Middle Ages, England had a proper system of public hospitality, and the English inns had reached the first stage in their development.

Position in Scotland

The farther north one proceeded the fewer inns one encountered, due to the sparseness of population and the relative poverty of the northern counties. In Scotland the development was by no means parallel to that in England. There were numerous taverns where all classes and types mingled, and where food was

[3] French, R. V., *Nineteen Centuries of Drink in England*, pp. 87, 108.
[4] Jusserand, J. J., *English Wayfaring Life in the Middle Ages*, p. 61.

provided as well as drink. Ale-houses existed too, but there were few establishments comparable to the English inns. The main reason, beside the smaller amount of travel, was the widespread hospitality of private citizens, which continued for a longer time than in England. Friends were entertained by private citizens as a matter of course, but in addition many private houses would entertain strangers for payment. Many citizens brewed ale and also entertained travellers, and many tavern-keepers, and later coffee-house proprietors, also had a few rooms to let. The old Scottish inns which did exist were small and compared unfavourably with their English counterparts. 'Accommodation was prepared for the horse rather than the rider, which explains why the Scottish innkeeper held for so long his title of stabler,' states Marie Stuart in her study.[5] The title of 'innkeeper' was not used in Scotland until the beginning of the nineteenth century. It is interesting to note in this connection that as early as 1529 a decree was made giving the stablers a monopoly in the retailing of oats and hay, any other person dealing in them being punished with banishment and confiscation of goods.

A statute of 1425 attempted to curtail private hospitality in Scotland. Travellers were liable to a penalty of forty shillings if they took abode with friends when there was an inn available. The only exception was made for a nobleman accompanied by his retinue; he could stay where he pleased but his servants and horses had to be quartered in the 'common hostillaries'.

[5] Stuart, M. W., *Old Edinburgh Taverns*, p. 9, *et seq.*

3. Sixteenth to Early Nineteenth Centuries

The Growth of Inns

In the two centuries following the Middle Ages the inn received a twofold stimulus. The first was provided by the dissolution of the monasteries, when 608 religious houses, including the forty-eight of the Knights Hospitallers, were suppressed by an Act of Parliament in 1539. In the second place, the new type of hostelry was more in accord with the changing social and economic system generally, which had by then put an end to feudalism, and in the Tudor period of settled peace started to foster national and international trade. The roads were the same rough ways, and travel was still medieval in character. At the beginning of the sixteenth century horseback was still preferred to journeys by wagon, but towards the end of the century carriers' wagons and other wheeled carriages became more numerous. Elizabeth herself set the fashion by her journeyings about the realm, and the beginnings of a posting system for the hire of horses date back to her reign.

The Tudor inn was generally built on a much larger scale than the medieval inn, with a galleried courtyard, and another yard for stabling and wagons. Separate chambers became common, and the better class of traveller expected linen sheets and tablecloths. In London there were inns which could lodge more than a hundred guests; in such inns all guests were accommodated in chambers, because the hall was needed for reception and eating, but most travellers were still allocated to the rooms as they came, sharing not only the room but also the bed with strangers. In particular, the large terminal inns attained a high standard of efficiency, and in London they established an interesting pattern of location: Smithfield inns catered for northern traffic; Holborn received traffic from the west, and Bishopsgate that from East Anglia; southern traffic terminated at Southwark where 'The Tabard' of Chaucer's *Canterbury Tales* was the most famous inn.

In the latter half of the century William Harrison speaks in his *Description of England* (1577) of the 'great and sumptuous inns' of the highway town, capable of entertaining two or three hundred people (and their horses) at one time, and of the healthy rivalry between the innkeepers. By this time carpets had been introduced, and the walls of the best rooms were hung with tapestry or embossed leather. Tudor inn architecture, with its quadrangle layout, lent itself well to the performance of plays; after the decline of churches and abbeys (which had regularly given performances of religious plays), inn yards were the scenes of many Elizabethan plays, and contributed considerably to the development of the modern theatre.[1]

---

[1] Burke, T., *English Inns*, p. 12.
  Richardson, A. E., *The Old Inns of England*, pp. 7, *et seq.*

An increase in density of population followed the years of Tudor peace and prosperity, and the rapidly growing volume of trade, with its resultant increase in traffic, called for better and faster transport. The stage coach provided the answer, and although the roads showed little improvement over the preceding century, improvement in transport was achieved by changes of horses from day to day, or from place to place. At the close of the Civil War, a stage coach service was well established on some of the trunk roads leading out of London, the main ones being to Winchester, Plymouth, Exeter, Chester, Lancaster, Kendal, Preston, York and Newcastle. Many innkeepers operated a stage coach themselves, and demand grew for more inns at stopping places. In addition to new buildings, many private mansions became inns. Competition, which led to continual improvement in the speed and frequency of stage coach services, was also evident among innkeepers, who were anxious to do their best for travellers. It was mainly the regularization of traffic which improved the inns; it is true that complaints were still heard as to the quality of food and beds, but the moral character of the inns improved, and from the sixteenth century onwards this country established a reputation for the number and quality of its inns. Fynes Moryson is quite definite in his *Itinerary* (1617) about the supremacy of the English inn, having travelled through the main European countries for some ten years: '. . . the world affoords not such Innes as England hath, either for good and cheape entertainment after the Guests owne pleasure, as for humble attendance on passengers, yea, even in very poor villages . . .'[2]

Some Early Statistics

In 1577 a general inquiry was made, through the Mayors and Justices of the Peace under an Order in Council, to ascertain the exact number of inns, alehouses and taverns throughout England, with a view to levying a tax on them towards the cost of repairing Dover harbour. The returns, which have been preserved (for twenty-seven English counties, six boroughs and the Cinque Ports), give a total of 16,347, of which about 1,600 were classed as inns, about 400 as taverns, and the remaining 14,000 as ale-houses. But these estimates apparently excluded the cities of London and Westminster, and several of the more populous counties, such as Gloucestershire and Wiltshire. If 8,000 or 9,000 are added to cover these areas, from which the returns are lacking, the total would be about 25,000 establishments in which drink was sold in England.[3] At this time the population of England was at the most five million, which means about one outlet per two hundred of population.

The Changing Pattern

The sharp distinction which had been drawn in the past between the inn on the one hand and the tavern and the ale-house on the other became blurred to some

[2] Quoted in Sarkies, E. L., *The Importance of the Hotel Industry*, p. 62.
[3] Richardson, A. E., op. cit., p. 6.

extent by the middle of the seventeenth century, as the law against ale-house and tavern accommodation had been either relaxed or had fallen into abeyance. This had contributed considerably to the growth of inns as important social institutions, used not only for social purposes but also for transaction of business and local government, between the sixteenth and nineteenth centuries. The change in the character of the inn was not universal, but many, whilst being more than taverns, and apart from providing lodging and stabling, depended to a great extent, like taverns, on their tap rooms.

In towns, taverns were becoming more and more popular, and many were frequented by the aristocracy and men of letters. In the sixteenth century the habit started of dining at taverns or 'ordinaries' as they were called. The 'ordinary' was actually the name for the meal consisting of a hot meat dish, bread, cheese and ale.

The Coffee-house Era

In France the introduction of coffee gave rise to the café, and in Britain to the coffee-house, from which evolved the club. The coffee-house era, which followed closely the first appearance of coffee in England, was of importance not only to the catering trade but also to the political and social life of the nation. The first coffee-house was opened in Oxford in 1650 at a time when there were 350 ale-houses in the town; the first London coffee-house appeared a few years later, and by the end of the century their number in London exceeded 2,000. Prior to their emergence, taverns and ale-houses were the main places of social intercourse, but in London especially, coffee-houses rapidly took their place. People could hear the news there when it was hard to come by, and the chance of hearing news reinforced the attractions of the novel drink. As early as 1660 Charles II had been complaining of the freedom of speech enjoyed there, though it was not until several years later that he started unsuccessful attempts to suppress them; but in spite of repeated attempts of his (and of efforts of vintners, brewers and tavern-keepers, and also of women), to discredit them, coffee-houses thrived and enjoyed immense popularity.

No attempt was made by early coffee-houses to discriminate between customers; they were absolutely democratic in all respects and open to any man, rich or poor, who paid his penny at the bar and was prepared to obey the rules. At the beginning they usually consisted of one room with one large table to accommodate the patrons. Up to the Restoration no intoxicants were sold, although alternatives to coffee were offered in many establishments in the form of tea and other herbal drinks and chocolate, and light refreshments such as cakes, tarts and jellies were also served.

Coffee-houses were also quite common in the country. The earliest ones, outside Oxford and London, were at Cambridge, Bristol and Exeter. Most towns had at least one, and many several, but most provincial coffee-houses came into being only towards the end of the seventeenth and beginning of the eighteenth centuries. Only in thriving commercial centres in regular contact with London, or in a great port like Bristol, did they ever assume the importance or character of London's seventeenth-century houses. Very few of the smaller market towns had any similar to those in the capital. This applied to the countryside generally, as the inn remained there the social centre of the community; also there was a much more law-abiding community there than in London, removed from the centre of Government, and ignorant of the real state of affairs in the capital, which would have been conducive to discussion in the coffee-houses. Defoe said after his visit to Shrewsbury that those houses, which did have the name, were mostly but ale-houses and used the name only to acquire 'a better air', as he put it.

Scotland had its coffee-houses, too, but few began as temperance houses. In Edinburgh they had a strong political character and were required to enter into bond or recognizance not to tolerate unapproved newspapers. The first appeared in the city in 1673, and Marie Stuart described eloquently how they had been adapted to Scotland: '. . . it appears that the city's coffee-houses merely borrowed their name from those fashionable London resorts while satisfying Scottish tastes by functioning as ale-houses.' She stated that Edinburgh might have been slow in developing her inns but that she was 'quick i' the uptak' to adopt and adapt the London's coffee-houses to her own usage. Their more political tone, as compared with the taverns, brought them early into disfavour with the authorities.[4]

Emergence of Inland Resorts

The late sixteenth and seventeenth centuries saw yet another development of importance in the present context – the origin of the inland resort, promoted by the vogue for medicinal waters. Continental spas had been famous for some two hundred years before the English began to look for them at home. Bath and Buxton had been used for healing and relaxation by the Romans, but the revival of their springs for therapeutic bathing and drinking dates to the decades before the Civil War. Many of the spas were holy wells in the Middle Ages – pools and springs where men prayed; their transformation into healing springs and social centres owes much to the Royal patronage of James I and Charles I, although their visits were only a seal on something which had started in the preceding century. The first spas were Tunbridge Wells, Epsom, Bath and Buxton; the others followed much later. The journey to the spas was made either by stage or private coach and added to the volume of travel and demand for inn accommodation *en route,* as well as to the business of innkeepers in the spas themselves, although many well-to-do people stayed with friends, or had their own mansions there.

Liquor Licensing – The Beginning

No account of the development of catering at the beginning of the modern era would be complete without reference to the beginnings of liquor licensing, which dates back to the middle of the sixteenth century. Until then establishments

[4] Stuart, M. W., op. cit., pp. 166, *et seq.*

selling liquor did not require a special licence, although ale-houses to a greater and taverns to a lesser extent had been subject to a varying degree of mainly local control for a few centuries before. By an Act of 1494 keepers of ale-houses were admonished to be of good behaviour, and if their houses were conducted in a disorderly manner, to the annoyance of neighbours, the Justices of the Peace could close them at their discretion and debar the keeper from selling ale. Their discretion extended to the taking of sureties (recognizances).

In 1552 an Act of Parliament required all keepers of ale-houses to be bound by recognizance, and introduced licensing by local justices. The Act provided for the issue by two justices of a licence to carry on the trade and, although it was repealed later, its principles survive to this day. The result of giving discretion to local justices was control over the number of licences, and with statutory help, licences were soon limited to two in most boroughs. The Act also established a uniform fixed code of conduct: 'closing time' for drinking was nine o'clock in summer and eight o'clock in winter, drinks were sold at prices fixed by the justices of the locality, and ale-houses and taverns were open to inspection.

The motives for the introduction of liquor licensing were several. In the first place, the financial possibilities of licensing could not have escaped the notice of the Government; secondly, drinking implies social gathering and conviviality, and the houses in which this took place had been suspect for political and social reasons at different periods of history; thirdly, drinking constituted competition with the Church on Sundays, and concern for better Sunday observance had been felt for a long time.

The Age of the Stage Coach

Two descriptions by historians indicate the extent of the transformation of Britain's roads between the beginning of the eighteenth and the middle of the nineteenth centuries.

Trevelyan writes[5] that:

'. . . the roads in winter were often quagmires wherein loaded pack-horses sank to the girth, and waggons could not be moved at all. On portions of the main roads, indeed, tollbars were being set up by private companies, with Parliamentary powers to tax the traffic and keep the surface in repair. But during the Seven Years' War most of the mileage, even on the main roads of England, was still free to those who could force their way through the mud. The heavy coaches lumbered along in the ruts in a very different style from that in which their light-timbered successors in the years following Waterloo scoured the same roads remade by Macadam.'

According to Curtis-Bennett:[6]

'Transport was abominable at the beginning of the eighteenth century and the roads a disgrace to a civilized country. The turnpike Acts did much to improve them, but we owe our road system today mainly to three great road-makers,

[5] Trevelyan, G. M., op. cit., pp. 527–8.
[6] Curtis-Bennett, Sir N., op. cit., p. 131.

John Metcalf, the famous "Blind Jack of Knaresborough", who laid out hundreds of miles of roads in Yorkshire, designed bridges and viaducts and supervised their building without being able to see a stone or a stick since he was six years old, William Telford, the surveyor, and Robert McAdam, engineer.'

In the eighteenth century most progress towards faster travel came through frequent changes of horses, and (later) through improvements in vehicle design and construction. The effect of the improving road system was only felt in the late eighteenth and especially in the first half of the nineteenth centuries; during this time the stage coach brought about a rapid expansion of travel, and had to meet the new demands of the industrial revolution and of the increase in trade. In addition to the stage coach there was the mail coach, which represented first-class travel; its standard was between the stage coach and the private carriages of the nobility and the gentry. The stage coach was also growing in importance in Scotland, and made irregular journeys between Edinburgh and London from the early eighteenth century.

Development of Inland Resorts

The eighteenth century was the age of watering places. Bath enjoyed undisputed supremacy; Epsom and Tunbridge Wells were the other principal resorts. London had Sadlers Wells, Islington Spa, Clerkenwell and later Hampstead, which had, however, only a short span as a watering place in the literal sense, perhaps twenty years. By the end of the century most spa gardens in London had been replaced by tea gardens, which in turn gave place to modern parks. To the early eighteenth century dates the development of Matlock, Bath, Harrogate and Scarborough, known for their famous inns. Midland spas were established as resorts still later than their southern and northern rivals: Malvern, Droitwich, Cheltenham and Leamington became spas only towards the end of the eighteenth and beginning of the nineteenth centuries, by which time the waters were frequently no longer of principal interest; leisure and recreation were their attractions. Generally there were two lines of development in inland resorts – the scientific and the social. The former was prominent in the case of Buxton, Harrogate and Droitwich, the latter in Tunbridge Wells, Malvern, Cheltenham and Leamington; Bath was a combination of the two. The transition from a purely healing resort to a pleasure resort, which took place in most cases, so that but a few resorts retained both the medicinal and social attractions to the same degree, reflected the changing social customs of the day.

Inn Prosperity

Although there was a great variation in the standards of hospitality, the large inns, particularly, offered a high degree of comfort and service by the end of the eighteenth century. In the first half of the nineteenth century, coach travel and inn prosperity reached their peak and the coaching inns represented the best accommodation available, both at the termini and at places where horses were changed. In the seventeenth and eighteenth centuries, inns rarely had a common dining-room; the better class guests ate in private rooms and the poorer travellers, including the servants, in the kitchen. This class differentiation, which was created by the distinction between those who travelled on foot and those who travelled inside the stage coach, prevailed until the beginning of the nineteenth century. At this time the old Tudor custom of a common table was revived in inns for coach breakfasts and dinners, and only those travelling privately by their own post-chaise, and residents, still dined in private.

With the industrial revolution a new class of traveller and a new type of inn emerged – the Commercial Inn – which had a common dining-room and private rooms. At about the same time, the new holiday habit brought increasingly large numbers to inns as temporary residents, and some inns became Family Inns. Enterprising innkeepers frequently adapted themselves to both kinds of traffic – hence the Family and Commercial Inn.

The First Hotels

The word 'hotel' came into use in England at the introduction in London, after 1760, of the kind of establishment, then common in Paris, called 'hôtel garni', or a large house, in which apartments were let by the day, week or month. Its appearance signified a departure from the customary method of housing guests into something more luxurious and ostentatious. Hotels proper, with managers, liveried porters, page-boys and receptionists, arrived generally only at the beginning of the nineteenth century. Until the middle of that century their development in England was relatively slow. They were making great progress in Switzerland, where at the time the idea of a *resort hotel* originated. The absence of good inns in Scotland to some extent accelerated the arrival of the hotel there; by the end of the eighteenth century, Edinburgh, for example, had several hotels where the traveller could procure elegant and comfortable rooms.

Beginnings of Seaside Resorts

A most interesting description of another eighteenth-century development is given by the social and economic historian Lecky:[7]

> 'Sea-bathing in the first half of the eighteenth century is very rarely noticed. Chesterfield, indeed, having visited Scarborough in 1733, observed that it was there commonly practised by both sexes, but its general popularity dates only from the appearance of a treatise by Dr Richard Russell, "On glandular consumption", and the use of sea-water for diseases of the glands, which was published in Latin in 1750, and translated in 1753. The new remedy acquired an extraordinary favour, and it produced a great, and on the whole very beneficial change in the national tastes. In a few years obscure fishing-villages along

[7] Lecky, W. E. H. L., *A History of England in the Eighteenth Century*, Vol. II, p. 199.

the coast began to assume the dimension of stately watering places, and before the century had closed Cooper described in indignant lines, the common enthusiasm with which all ages and classes rushed for health or pleasure to the sea.'

The growth of many seaside resorts, due to the enthusiasm for the sea described above, and manifesting itself in the early bathing machines and huts, was encouraged by other factors, too. Some existed previously as spas; Scarborough, for instance, was a spa long before it became a fashionable seaside resort. Others developed with defensive measures against Napoleon, e.g. Eastbourne, Hastings and Torquay. Royal patronage established a number of them: Brighton, which was a small fishing village at the beginning of the century, had the patronage of George IV, and in a hundred years it became the most fashionable resort in Europe. Weymouth enjoyed the patronage of George III, and the Princesses brought the nobility to Worthing, Bognor and Southend.

The standard pattern of resort development, from the patronage of Royalty to that of the working classes over a period of about two hundred years or even less, had only reached an intermediate stage in the first half of the nineteenth century; after Royalty and the aristocracy came the middle classes. The inn, which had earned such a reputation for accommodating travellers, was rarely to be found on the seaside, catering for the new holiday maker. As in the spas, Royalty, the nobility and the gentry usually had their own mansions; several hotels were built in the resorts; the seaside landlady accommodated others in her lodging house, which became a boarding house, and in the nineteenth century (with the wealth of the industrial revolution and its desire for respectability) often a private hotel.

Eighteenth-century Coffee-houses

The first half of the eighteenth century was the heyday of the coffee-house, the origin of which was described in the last chapter. New ones were still being opened, and their numbers ran into thousands. In Queen Anne's reign they probably exceeded inns and taverns in London in number and importance. The single room with one large table gradually changed into one with 'tables set apart for divers topics' or into several rooms in most coffee-houses; some had boxes or partitions. In England, even after the Restoration, many continued as temperance establishments.

Many coffee-houses became famous as meeting places of members of literary, artistic and commercial circles, and gradually particular professions, e.g. lawyers, stockbrokers and jobbers, banking, insurance and shipping men, adopted one or more favourite houses in London, and particularly in the City, and much of their business was done there. Soon discrimination began to be shown in the more fashionable houses; undesirables were excluded; it was this move towards exclusiveness which led to the creation of clubs, as many coffee-houses became 'subscription coffee-houses', which were really the first clubs. The growth of clubs was so rapid that in London at the beginning of the nineteenth century there were as many clubs as there were coffee-houses at the beginning of the eighteenth century.

The Liquor Trade

Throughout the coffee-house era the tavern was undergoing a gradual process of transformation. Until the seventeenth century the tavern-keeper or licensed victualler was not a mere dram-seller, i.e. a retailer whose primary and almost exclusive business it was to supply alcoholic liquor to the public, but a victualler, i.e. a retailer of food and drink with or without alcoholic liquor. With the spread of the coffee-houses some setbacks were suffered by the taverns. But they had already started changing in character since the beginning of the seventeenth century, and the licensed victualler gradually became a publican, whose primary and practically sole business was the retailing of alcoholic beverages. The victualling trade offered relatively small profits, not easily earned, whilst the sale of liquor was a simple trade which held out the inducement of easy profits; this was probably the main influence on the development of taverns at this time, and lax administration of the licensing system led to an increase in their numbers. The initial control over the number of licences was loosened, it was not difficult to obtain a licence, and, in many districts, licences were granted without regard to local needs. The efforts of the state to restore the victualling trade by a series of Tippling Acts from as early as the reigns of James I and Charles I met with little success.

A great deal of heavy drinking took place in the eighteenth and early nineteenth centuries, particularly in London and in the rising centres of industry. There are frequent references in literature to aqua-vitae (simple distilled spirit). Although spirits were known in England from Tudor times, they were not widely drunk, but in the late seventeenth century the distillation of gin became an important trade in London, and gin drinking rapidly spread amongst the lower classes. Gin shops sprang up in every part of London. Whilst the sale of beer had been controlled since the day of Edward VI, no restriction was placed on the sale of spirits. In 1725 a report from a committee of Middlesex magistrates stated that there were in the Metropolis, exclusive of the City of London and Southwark, 6,187 houses and shops wherein 'geneva or other strong waters' were sold by retail; this was for a population of some 700,000, so that there was one outlet for just over a hundred people.[8]

[8] French, R. V., op. cit., pp. 274, *et seq*.

4. The Railway Age – into the Twentieth Century

The first railway to be built with a view to conveying passengers was opened in 1830. For a time afterwards the road held its own and the few railway lines did not perceptibly affect the increasing amount of traffic on the much improved highways. But soon a new map of the lines of communication was in the making. The railway made its own road, it touched many towns away from the main coaching routes and, at least for some time, many were by-passed. The new means of transport had a revolutionary effect on everybody's life. It was quicker, cheaper and more comfortable than transport by road. Before half a century had passed since the opening of the first line, the railway created 'a smaller world'. In the second half of the century it emptied the main roads and by the end of it the road traffic was mainly local and served to feed the railways.

Inns and Hotels

We have seen the appearance of the hotel in the late eighteenth and early nineteenth centuries at a time when the inn was at the peak of its prosperity. With the growth of the railway the importance of the inn began to decline and the reign of Queen Victoria saw a long eclipse of innkeeping. The terminal and posting inns were disappearing, as their position, based as it was on the halting and incoming traffic, rarely coincided with the new routes and termini. Until the development of motor transport in the twentieth century many inns became local ale-houses, private houses or farmhouses. Those which fitted in with the new pattern of traffic were in a minority.

Hotels followed to a great extent the same pattern of location as the coaching inns – along the lines of traffic – and thus took over the role of the terminal and posting inns. The terminal railway hotels were the giants of hotel architecture of the day. Gilbert Scott's imitation Gothic Midland 'Grand', adjoining St Pancras station, with its 450 rooms, the 'Great Eastern' at Liverpool Street, the 'Euston Hotel', both with 250 rooms each, and the old Georgian 'Great Northern' at King's Cross, took the place of the Smithfield inns. Philip C. Hardwick's Victorian 'Great Western Royal' at Paddington (which could then accommodate 200 guests) served some of the western traffic, which once had terminated in the inns of Holborn, and Edward Myddleton Barry's Victorian 'Charing Cross Hotel' with its 450 rooms retreated a little, as it were, to perform the function of 'The Tabard' and other Southwark inns. They were followed by many railway hotels in the provinces – the 'Central' at Glasgow, the 'Midland' at Leeds, by hydros in watering places, and others outside important railway stations. *Ruff's Hotel Guide* (1902) lists some seventy hotels owned or controlled by the railway companies. Large hotels in town centres also emerged at an early date; in London the Langham Hotel opened with 450 rooms, and the Hotel Russell with 300 rooms.

Increased travel by the well-to-do, by railway and steamship, stimulated the European capitals and resorts into building luxury hotels. A strong impetus was provided also by the great international fairs and exhibitions. The ancient picturesqueness was abandoned, replaced by luxurious decoration and furnishings, and improved service and amenities. The closing years of Queen Victoria's reign marked the end of an epoch, which saw vast national wealth built up and Britain's prestige raised to a level it had never before attained, and it also witnessed the beginning of the Ritz era in hotel-keeping. The Hotel Victoria, which was opened in London, off Trafalgar Square, in 1887, could accommodate 500 visitors. The Irish businessman, D'Oyly Carte, opened the Savoy in 1889 and shortly after, César Ritz (the Swiss who came to be called 'the hotelier of Kings and the King of hoteliers') took over the management. Next on Ritz's list was the Carlton (1899), and soon a network of Ritz hotels spread, promoted by the Ritz Development Company. The Hotel Cecil was opened next to the Savoy in 1896, and the new Claridges in 1898.

The Railway and the Resorts

The introduction of the railways had a profound influence on the development of seaside resorts. Some, such as Blackpool, owed their development directly to the railway; as the railway did not reach it until 1846, Blackpool (which can nowadays accommodate half a million people at one time) did not emerge as a seaside resort of importance until more than half a century after those on the southern coast. Much the same is true also of Southport and of Bournemouth in the south. Among the towns which had grown fastest between 1840–50 were two purely 'seaside residence and recreation towns', Southport and Torquay. After 1851, each successive Census showed more resorts of this class. The railway age was directly responsible not only for the increase in the number of resorts, and for making the sea accessible to the masses for the first time; the new means of transport greatly influenced the size and character of the resorts, and the location of hotels and other facilities. Hotels, for example, were built within easy 'coaching' distance of the railway station, a factor which created the present concentration in particular locations.

The early part of the nineteenth century experienced a decline of inland spas as pleasure resorts; although the population of some continued to increase, this was mainly due to their becoming places of residence and retirement. The second half of the nineteenth century saw the revival of the inland spas, with the progressive introduction of scientific treatment, and many residential towns were brought back into use for healing. This was particularly so in the case of Harrogate, Bath, Droitwich, Buxton and Matlock.

Clubs and Restaurants

In the nineteenth century the club, as a place for meeting, eating, drinking and conversation, became firmly established as a specifically English institution, which has since flourished in this country with an individuality and abundance unrivalled in any other part of the world. The earliest clubs were proprietary; some elected a committee for a temporary period in order to recruit membership, and having succeeded, the committee resigned. But members' clubs became increasingly common. Towards the end of the century some clubs lost their masculine exclusiveness by opening certain rooms or annexes to women, and some clubs for both sexes and for women only were established. Another development was the residential club, which offered accommodation to members, in addition to other amenities.

About a century after the term had first been used in Paris to denote an establishment where meals and refreshments were supplied, the restaurant entered London. This name was at first applied, during the last decades of the nineteenth century, to the dining-rooms of large hotels and to a few large, separate, high-class establishments, which began to cater on a more elaborate scale for the fastidious diner. Its popularity grew with after-theatre suppers and the spread of 'dining out'. Many people, who had rarely dined in public before, acquired a new taste. Men who had been content to use their clubs were among its customers, and so, for the first time dining out, were women. To this time is also ascribed the introduction of the common dining-room with separate tables, first in restaurants, and then in inns and other establishments. The modern 'grill-room' is a later offshoot of hotels and restaurants, owing its existence largely to the travelling American, who, with his own idea of comfort, felt that he did not wish to dress every night but that otherwise he would be out of place in a fashionable restaurant.

Eating out was still an expensive luxury for most people in these years, but this was also changing rapidly. At the other end of the social scale, cafés and tea shops, (designed to provide cheap refreshment and often operating in groups) were soon brought within the reach of all. The first ABC shop was opened in London in 1884, the first Lyons teashop in 1894, and within a few years both companies operated a chain of them. The turn of the century also saw many manual and clerical workers change from home-packed lunches and patronize teashops and the cheaper commercial restaurants.

Liquor Licensing

Liquor licensing passed through an eventful period between the end of the Napoleonic Wars and the end of the century, and had a pronounced effect on the licensed trade. At the close of the Wars, an active period of legislation produced a number of licensing Acts designed to deal with the unsatisfactory heritage from the eighteenth century. The Ale-house Act of 1828 repealed and codified the vast number of statutes then in existence and formed the basis of subsequent liquor licensing; indeed, this Act constitutes a dividing line between the past and the present. Only two years later an attempt was made to reduce the amount of spirit drinking by permitting the general sale of beer by retail. But the effect was disastrous and a great increase in drunkenness followed. There was a vast spread of disorderly little shops; between October when the Act came into force, and the end of the year nearly 25,000 licences had been issued. During the year following this Act, more than 30,000 beer shops were opened and this process brought the total in existence to some 50,000 by the middle of the century. As the trade in beer alone was not profitable enough, many combined it with the more profitable spirit trade.[1]

Although certain amendments were made by subsequent legislation, the position was not substantially altered until 1869, when the issue of beerhouse licences was definitely transferred to the magistrates who could use discretionary powers. The effect was the inauguration of a real policy of restriction on the number of licences, which consequently tended to increase in value. A far-reaching effect was the encouragement given to brewers to invest in the retail trade on a large scale, and to compete with one another for the control and ownership of licensed houses. This gave a distinct stimulus to the 'tied-house' system, which is almost universal in England today, and which has so much influenced the organization of the licensed sector of the industry. This was then the transition of the inn, tavern and ale-house into the Victorian 'pub', and there is no doubt that all three were its predecessors.

The Twentieth Century[2]

The beginning of the twentieth century was a period of rapid social and economic change, in which political controversy led to new social legislation and inventions acted as powerful stimuli to industry and trade. The motor car entered into competition with the railway: the 8,500 private cars in this country in 1904 had increased to 132,000 by 1914. This was the beginning of the boom period of motor transport, which restored the traffic to the road and gave new impetus to holiday making. Other travel developments also took place: the turn of the century saw the foundation of the Cyclists' Touring Club, the National Cyclists' Union, the Polytechnic Touring Association, the Co-operative Holidays Association, Sir Henry Lunn's; these were soon followed by other organizations, bringing holidays to the less well-to-do. In 1903 the Trust Houses were founded as one of the Public House Trust Companies, set up at about the same time in different counties, to acquire free licensed houses, and to secure in them 'disinterested management'. The traveller and the holiday maker found many new hotels and guest houses opening at this time, and the gradual growth of road traffic meant the beginning of a new era of innkeeping.

[1] French, R. V., op. cit., pp. 274, *et seq.*
[2] Much information included in this chapter was derived from 'The Story of the Association', *B.H.R.A. Journal,* November 1957–May 1958.

First World War

The First World War caused considerable disorganization and loss of manpower to an industry in which personal service demands a high labour contribution; the internment of enemy aliens who formed a high proportion of those in hotel and catering occupations aggravated the position still further. Many hotels were requisitioned from the early days of the war, and others were used as billets for the armed forces. As rationing of foodstuffs was not introduced until February 1918, most control measures concentrated on catering establishments. After the restriction on the number of courses to be served, which was introduced in 1916 and proved so ineffective that it was soon rescinded, more resolute measures were designed in order to preserve the diminishing food supplies as the war proceeded: one meatless day a week in 1917, limitation of the weekly quantities of some foodstuffs, and the keeping of a register of meals served and food used were followed by local rationing schemes for hotels and restaurants early in 1918; anyone eating outside his own home was required to surrender meat coupons for any meat served. In the closing months of the war restrictions were imposed on the use of fuel and power, and price regulations were introduced for the sale of spirits.

The First World War also saw a precursor of the British and Civic Restaurant of the Second War with the opening of a 'National Restaurant' in London, but the scheme to open others throughout the country was abandoned, as the war ended. One of the most important developments of the war was the widespread introduction of the industrial canteen. The concept of feeding the worker was by then already a few hundred years old. In the Middle Ages, the feeding of his employees was looked upon as part of the normal responsibilities of any employer, whether he were the manorial lord, the tenant farmer or the master craftsman; the employee was normally part of his employer's household. But the spirit of a master's responsibility for the welfare of his workmen almost disappeared with the domestic system of manufacture during the seventeenth and eighteenth centuries, and it did not revive on any significant scale with the Industrial Revolution. Only a few enlightened employers provided canteen facilities during the nineteenth century. The industrial canteen as we know it today owes its origin to those pioneers, but its emergence on any scale was given impetus by the war. In the Report on Factories and Workshops for 1918, the Chief Inspector of Factories stated that before the First World War started there were barely a hundred regular factory canteens, whereas before the end of 1918 there were probably nearly a thousand operating, or in the process of being built, while no important munitions factory was without a canteen. This development was not so much a revival of the medieval responsibility as a new recognition of the need of the worker for adequate nourishment, which received stimulus under the Defence of the Realm Act.

Between the Wars

But as soon as the war was over, industry fell back into apathy as regards employee feeding, and many firms which had started canteens during the war had closed them at the end of it. Sir Noel Curtis-Bennett attributes this to three main causes: first, lack of enterprise on the part of canteen managers and catering supervisors in 'selling' the idea sufficiently forcefully to both management and personnel, secondly, lack of support from directors and managers who still tended to look upon a factory canteen as an unnecessary luxury and nuisance, and thirdly, indifference on the part of the workers themselves. Industrial catering remained almost stagnant in the twenties. Whilst a greater realization of the importance of the personnel factor in industry tended to support industrial welfare generally, progressive experiments suffered a setback in all but a few firms with the General Strike of 1926 and with the economic depression. Only when the conditions improved, did the canteens begin to be considered as a practicable welfare service in the late thirties.[3]

The close dependence of the hotel and catering industry on general economic prosperity resulted in serious difficulties; curtailment of holiday and tourist traffic and unemployment in the industry, in the early thirties. However, the industry withstood the onset of the depression comparatively well, and was again rapid in its recovery.

Although the early years following the war saw attempts to introduce prohibition in this country (campaigns resulted in four temperance bills being introduced in Parliament in 1922-23), they could do little to affect the prosperity in the post-war boom. Several potent factors were contributing to it in the twenties; some of which were again present, even more prominently, in the post-depression years. First, in the early twenties there was a widespread reaction to the restrictions and privations of the previous war, which brought with it the desire for travel and enjoyment. Secondly, rapid development of transport, by car, motor coach and by air, brought new custom to hotels, which had to adapt themselves to the increasing restlessness of holiday makers, and to the increased volume of business travel. Although the motor coach and car touring holiday was known already before the war, they gained great popularity in the inter-war years. The number of private cars in use in Britain reached two million by 1939, and there were over 50,000 buses and coaches in 1937. Civil aviation came to be regarded as a commercial proposition and received Government backing in many countries, including Britain. Within a comparatively short time daily services were operating between London and the principal European cities, and regular transatlantic services were inaugurated in 1939. Finally, there were social changes, with a gradual breaking-down of social barriers and class distinctions, and the rising standards of living of the lower-income groups in this country and overseas had considerable bearing on the development of British hotel and catering services. Wide introduction of holidays with pay in the years immediately preceding the Second World War resulted in eleven out of the eighteen-and-a-half million workpeople earning under £250 p.a. having holidays with pay by 1939.[4]

---

[3] Curtis-Bennett, Sir N., op. cit., pp. 230, *et seq.*
[4] Catering Wages Commission, *First Annual Report*, p. 8.

At the same time new forms of holidays were emerging: camping, youth hostels and holiday camps. The Butlin organization opened the first large-scale holiday camp at Skegness in 1937, and it is estimated that by 1939 there were about two hundred permanent holiday camps owned by various firms, catering for some 30,000 people weekly during the season.[5] Although between the wars a number of well-known hotels ceased to operate, several of the present leading hotels were opened within a few years in London: the Park Lane and the Mayfair Hotels, Grosvenor House, the Cumberland, the Dorchester, and the Strand Palace in its present form, were all opened between 1927 and 1932. This building and expansion was by no means confined to London; the railway companies and other firms opened some of their modern hotels in the inter-war period.

A new type of catering establishment made its appearance in the thirties: the milk bar, supplying milk drinks, ice-cream and milk dishes. Within a short time of the opening of the first milk bar in Fleet Street in 1935, there were several hundred of them in England and Wales – over 400 in the summer of 1936, and over 900 in August 1937. But by this time only about one-third of them had retained their distinctive character and confinement to milk products; the remainder supplied also other food.[6]

The Second World War

In the summer of 1939 Britain's holiday trades enjoyed their last peaceful season. The outbreak of the Second World War resulted in more dislocation than the hotel and catering services had ever experienced before. The obvious suitability of the hotels, and other room-letting establishments, for the accommodation of Civil Departments of the Government and the armed forces made it inevitable that they should be requisitioned for Government use. At the outbreak of the war, holiday resorts and inland spas became reception areas for evacuated Civil Service Departments and training centres for the Services, and were used for garrison troops and other purposes. Some two hundred hotels were requisitioned in the first two weeks of the war. In February 1942 *The Times*[7] estimated that, in London alone, about 5,000 fewer hotel bedrooms were available than before the war, and that eight large hotels, each containing from 100 to 400 bedrooms were then in Government occupation. Some of these buildings have not been used as hotels since.

The Catering Wages Commission estimated[8] that by the end of 1943 there were 1,832 hotels under requisition – 1,417 in England, 178 in Wales and 237 in Scotland – and that this represented between 15 and 20 per cent of the total number of hotels in the country. The differing criteria adopted by the requisitioning

---

[5] Brunner, E., *Holiday-Making and the Holiday Trades*, p. 5.
[6] Colam, E. E. F., *Practical Milk Bar Operation*, pp. 1–2.
[7] *The Times*, February 10, 1942.
[8] Catering Wages Commission, *The Rehabilitation of the Catering Industry*, pp. 2–3.

departments for classifying hotels as distinct from boarding houses on the one hand, and boarding houses as distinct from private houses on the other hand, make any precise assessments impossible, and particularly in the case of boarding houses no statistics are available. A number of holiday camps and hostels were also taken over; by the end of 1943 only eight of the twenty-eight Co-operative Holidays Association hostels were available as holiday accommodation, twenty-five of the thirty-eight properties belonging to the Holiday Fellowship had been requisitioned, and so had about one hundred of the three hundred hostels belonging to the Youth Hostels Association in England and Wales.

Statistical information about the number of establishments which suffered war damage is very limited, but it is certain that in large towns and in certain coastal holiday resorts, particularly on the eastern and southern coasts, damage was extensive. After the collapse of France and because of the threat of invasion, the Government decided to encourage the evacuation of the civilian population from a large number of towns on the eastern and southern coasts. Hoteliers and caterers suffered more than the rest of the trading community in the evacuation areas; their old customers had been urged to leave the areas, new ones had been forbidden to enter or take up residence, and curfews had been imposed. Much the same was the case in other areas where severe restrictions were placed on entry, notably in the Highlands of Scotland.

Few statistics are available as to the amount of sleeping accommodation provided by hotels, boarding houses and apartment houses before the war, but there is no doubt that the reduction in accommodation as a result of the war was very substantial. For example, in one medium-sized holiday resort on the south-east coast, in which there were sixteen licensed hotels, thirty-six unlicensed hotels and about 1,000 boarding and apartment houses in 1938, the position in Spring 1944, as given in the Report of the Catering Wages Commission on the Rehabilitation of the Industry,[9] was as follows:

Table 10
Accommodation Position in a Seaside Resort in 1944

	Licensed Hotels	Unlicensed Hotels	Boarding & Apartment House
Functioning	5	6	100
Occupied but not functioning	–	1	100
War damaged	5	15	334
Requisitioned	6	11	109
Empty	–	3	357
	16	36	1,000

[9] Catering Wages Commission, ibid., p. 1.

It is not suggested that this was typical of the country as a whole, but it is believed to have been a fair example of what had happened in the holiday towns on the south-east and east coasts of England – towns which depended on this industry for their livelihood. How far the position had deteriorated during the flying bomb attacks is not known, but there had been further deterioration in the situation.

In contrast to the First World War, food rationing for the general public was introduced at an early date, and this provided some inducement to eating at catering establishments, especially since the pre-war plans envisaging the surrender of coupons for meat meals were never brought into operation. On balance, the Ministry of Food felt that it would suffice to restrict supplies to caterers without rationing their customers. In 1940 restrictions were placed on the number and nature of courses to be served in catering establishments. As the situation became more critical, new sumptuary regulations were introduced. The Meals in Establishments Order, which was introduced in June 1942, imposed further restrictions on the number of courses to be served at a meal, introduced a maximum price of five shillings for a meal, except in establishments which were authorized to make a 'house charge', and prohibited the consumption of meals in public, after midnight in London, and after eleven in the evening elsewhere.[10]

Probably the most important development of the Second World War in the present context was the emergence of communal feeding on an unprecedented scale. The first British Restaurant was opened in October 1940, the idea behind the scheme being to ensure that the best use was made of the limited food supplies available, so that all civilians could obtain at least one hot meal a day. Its spread throughout the country was rapid: by May 1941 there were 489 in operation outside the area of the London County Council, a further 169 had been approved by then and were being prepared. By June 1942 the number of British Restaurants had increased to over 1,500 and the peak was reached in 1943 with 2,160 establishments. In addition to British Restaurants, which were established under the control of the Ministry of Food, the London County Council operated 195 Londoners' Meal Service Centres, local authorities controlled their own feeding centres and evacuee centres, some were operated by voluntary organizations, and many school canteens served the general public.

Industrial catering developed beyond recognition.[11] It was stimulated by the Factories (Canteens) Order of 1940, whereby every factory employing 250 or more workers, in which munitions or allied goods were manufactured or repaired, was obliged to provide a dining-room where wholesome meals at reasonable prices could be obtained. By the end of 1941, Special Orders were issued to include building and civil engineering sites, docks and mines. The scope was further extended, by the Factories (Canteens) Order, 1943 (which revoked the 1940 Order), to factories supplying civilian needs. In April 1942 there were

[10] Hammond, J. R., *History of the Second World War*, United Kingdom Civil Series, Food, Vols. I and II, *passim*.

[11] Curtis-Bennett, Sir N., op. cit., pp. 247–279, *passim*.

already 7,528 canteens and by the end of that year 9,509; in December 1943 they numbered 11,535. In these numbers are also included colliery canteens, which were established under the 1941 Orders; within a comparatively short time canteens were in existence in about 90 per cent of the collieries throughout the country employing fifty or more workers. By the end of the war the numbers of industrial and staff canteens of all kinds reached 25,000.

After the Second World War

Unlike the decades after the First World War, the period after 1945 has witnessed a rapid and continuous growth in hotel and catering activities in Britain. This growth has also been accompanied by very significant changes in the industry.

A number of factors have contributed to these developments. Real incomes and living standards have increased steadily, particularly among the lower income groups, at least until the early 1970s. Leisure time has continued to grow, both as a result of an increase in the average length of paid holidays and a decrease in the length of the average working week. By 1975 average actual hours of work per week stood at about 40 hours compared with around 60 hours in the early part of the century. Female employment has increased significantly. Whereas 34 per cent of all employees in employment in 1950 were female, this figure was 40 per cent in 1975. The education sector has enjoyed a rapid growth at all levels. Workers' organizations have played an increasingly important role in influencing conditions within and outside the work place. There has been a major expansion of the public sector and of Government control and intervention in all areas of economic and social activity. The motor car and air transport have replaced the railway and the steamship as the major forms of passenger transportation. Holiday organization has become a far more sophisticated and significant operation with the development of the air inclusive tour. Finally there have been some remarkable changes in the relative prosperity of different countries, particularly with the re-emergence of Western Germany and Japan as major economic powers.

The implications and effects of these post-war changes for the hotel and catering industry in Britain are contained in the following chapters of this book. It is sufficient here to say that some of the factors have been of major significance in expanding the demand for hotel and catering services; others have been important in that they have created new kinds of demand for accommodation and catering away from home; all have been important in presenting the industry with a challenge. In meeting this challenge, hotel and catering services have established themselves as a major industry in Britain as already outlined in Chapter 1.

Part II
The Framework

Additional Reading for Part II

Hotels and Catering EDC: *Hotel Prospects to 1980*, Volume 1, Chapters 1 and 2.

Hotels and Catering EDC: *Hotel Prospects to 1985*, Research Findings, Chapters 1 and 2.

Koudra, M.: Industrial and Welfare Catering 1970–1980, *HCIMA Review*, Volume 1, No. 1.

Koudra, M.: Catering Contractors: A Study in Industrial Concentration, *HCIMA Review*, Volume 1, No. 2.

Monopolies Commission: *Beer*, Chapters 2–5.

Pickering, J. F., *et al.: The Small Firm in the Hotel and Catering Industry*, Chapters I–III.

5. Pattern of Location

The hotel and catering industry provides an outstanding example of location in relation to the market. The factors which influenced the location of a number of major British industries in the past had little bearing on the location of the hotel and catering industry; neither the availability of raw materials nor of sources of power exercised much influence on hoteliers and caterers as regards the location of their activities. By their very nature, hotel and catering services must be supplied direct to the consumer in person; they are consumed at the point of sale, and are also produced or provided there. In this respect the hotel and catering industry is in a similar position to many other services which must be provided in the places where the demand exists. The market is the dominant, and often the only influence on location. Thus we find that the industry is widely dispersed over the whole country; there are areas of concentration, but the presence of at least one or two establishments in almost every locality is an important characteristic of the industry, as well as being often a significant feature of the locality. In turn, location is the key influence on the viability of the business, so much so that a prominent entrepreneur could have said with conviction and much justification that there are only three rules for success in the hotel business: location, location, location.

Accommodation Services

Innkeeping and hotel-keeping are the two parts of evolutionary process, which has kept pace with the development of the means of travel. We have seen in the historical outline that from the early days accommodation units followed transport development. Inns were situated along the roads and at destinations, serving transient and terminal traffic. The rapid spread of the railways marked the emergence of railway hotels in the nineteenth century. In the twentieth century motor transport created a new demand for accommodation along the highways, as it gradually but unmistakably represented the return to the road for a substantial proportion of passenger traffic; the modern hotel and motor hotel, both post-war developments in Britain, have been a distinctive response to the new impetus of the motor car. Within a century passenger transport, as well as accommodation units, completed a full cycle in their development and location.

A similar though less pronounced location of hotels arose in relation to passenger shipping; Dover and Southampton, for example, are ports in which demand is exercised by outgoing and incoming passengers from and into Britain. But travellers to the ports frequently come from places at relatively short distances and then there is little need for overnight stay. Similarly, incoming travellers tend to make for their final destination rather than stay in ports, and long-distance shipping services often arrange the disembarkation of their passengers after a night on board the ship in the harbour. These and similar considerations have, therefore, limited hotel development in relation to passenger shipping.

Air transport began to exercise a very significant influence on hotel location in Britain relatively recently. Before 1960 few hotels were located in the vicinity of airports, although many were near air terminals. However, the growth of air traffic brought about a major growth of accommodation capacity in both types of location. For example, in London it extended the concentration of hotels westward towards the air terminals, and a substantial new hotel complex of several thousand beds has come into being north of Heathrow Airport since 1960. Gatwick Airport and several provincial airports encouraged a similar, although smaller, development of accommodation capacity in other parts of the country.

Although closely related to transport development, the influence of holidays may be regarded as a separate influencing factor on the location of facilities. The movement to spas and resorts for healing and recreation represented less transient traffic; it brought into existence different types of establishment, accommodating visitors for longer periods of time; it created concentrations of hotels, guest houses and boarding houses around the British coast and in many inland resorts; it gave rise to the holiday camp as a distinctive type of facility in response to particular market needs. The initial holiday flow has grown into an annual movement of such dimensions that holiday visitors are accommodated in localities where the inhabitants may represent only a small proportion of those present at the time.

The third major influence on hotel location has been the location of industry and trade. Whilst again not separable from transport development, industrial and commercial activities have often created demand for transit and terminal accommodation in industrial and commercial centres throughout the country. Although they rarely gave rise to distinctive types of unit, they explain the availability of accommodation capacity in locations not frequented by holiday visitors.

Catering Services

Demand for catering services, as distinct from accommodation, is generated by the resident population as well as by visitors to the locality; the former often exercise a decisive influence on the extent and range of catering services in a given area. We have seen earlier that the demand for meals and refreshments away from home has been to a great extent a product of urbanization, which has stimulated different sectors of the industry to a different extent. It has been supported by increased travel, for pleasure as well as business, which has brought additional custom to catering units as well as hotels. The location of catering establishments has often therefore been determined by the density of population and, more particularly, by market density, i.e. the availability of spending power per given area. The concept of market density explains the concentration of catering services in general terms, not only in cities and large towns with all-year-round demand, but also, for example, in resorts where, although not constantly high, market density is high during the holiday season.

The geographical distribution of licensed establishments has been influenced also by secondary factors; in the case of public houses by the discretionary powers of local licensing authorities, who may indirectly also stimulate the growth of registered clubs in a particular area. Although liquor licences are granted primarily with the needs of the public in view, the licensing law varies to some extent between England, Wales and Scotland, and between London and the rest of England; its application is by no means uniform. Therefore, whilst theoretically the distribution of liquor licences should, on the whole, follow market density, this is not necessarily the case. The concentration of clubs is sometimes high in areas where licensing laws are most restrictive in themselves or where they are most restrictively applied. This aspect is considered further in the next chapter.

Catering contractors represent the main sector of the hotel and catering industry, the location of which has been directly conditioned by other considerations. As they operate to provide a service ancillary to some other main function of organizations engaged, for example, in industry, commerce or education, the first influence has been the geographical distribution of such organizations which tends to correspond broadly to the distribution of population. Next it is the extent to which these organizations provide catering services. Finally, the distribution of catering services under contract is determined by the penetration of the market by catering contractors in competition with those provided by direct management.

Measurement of Concentration

An indication of the distribution of the hotel and catering industry throughout Britain can be obtained from the Census of Population. If numbers of persons enumerated as engaged in the hotel and catering industry are expressed as a proportion of the economically active population of a given area, a location factor can be calculated as a measure of the concentration of the industry in the area, by comparing the proportion of those engaged in the industry in the area with the proportion so engaged in the country as a whole.

If x per cent of all economically active persons in a given area are engaged in the hotel and catering industry, and y per cent of all economically active persons are engaged in the hotel and catering industry in the country as a whole, the location factor for the industry in the area is x/y.

If an area has its exact proportionate share of the hotel and catering industry, its location factor is equal to 1. If the location factor is greater than 1, the area has a greater concentration of the industry than the average for the country as a whole; if the location factor is less than 1, the concentration of the industry in the area is less than average. The location factors thus provide a measure of comparison between different areas.

The basis for calculating the location factor for the hotel and catering industry in this chapter is the data in the 1971 Census, given in Table 11, which shows that y can be taken as 2·90 per cent, i.e. the percentage of all economically active persons engaged in the hotel and catering industry in Great Britain.

Table 11
Economically Active Population in Employment in Great Britain 1971

	All Industries and Services	Hotels etc.	Restaurants etc.	Public Houses	Clubs	Catering Contractors	Total Hotel and Catering	Industry %
Males	15,031,550	93,460	71,360	60,320	22,950	15,670	263,760	1·75
Females	8,701,060	137,170	110,820	99,150	39,900	37,720	424,760	4·88
Total	23,732,610	230,630	182,180	159,470	62,850	53,390	688,520	2·90

Source: Office of Population Censuses and Surveys, London, General Register Office, Edinburgh, Census 1971, Great Britain, Economic Activity, Part II (10% sample), Table 18, London, HMSO, 1975.

The location factors for the Standard Regions in England, used for regional organization by Government departments and for other purposes, and for Wales and Scotland as a whole are given in Table 12. The location factors for the seven conurbations of Great Britain are given in Table 13. The areas covered by each region and each conurbation are shown on the accompanying map and described in Appendix F.

Table 12
Hotel and Catering Industry Distribution in Regions in England and in Wales and Scotland in 1971

Region	All Industries and Services (1)	Hotels etc.	Restaurants etc.	Public Houses	Clubs	Catering Contractors	Total Hotel and Catering Industry (2)	(2) as % of (1) (x)	Location factor (z)/(y)
North	1,354,260	16,050	9,660	9,890	8,570	1,590	45,760	3·38	1·17
Yorkshire and Humberside	2,083,800	14,290	17,880	13,700	8,250	2,980	57,100	2·74	0·94
North-West	2,951,070	24,610	22,210	19,120	8,930	5,040	79,910	2·71	0·93
East Midlands	1,493,910	7,770	9,860	10,830	3,470	2,850	34,780	2·33	0·80
West Midlands	2,351,050	13,410	12,060	18,960	5,820	4,760	55,010	2·34	0·81
East Anglia	714,320	6,760	4,590	4,640	1,000	1,010	18,000	2·52	0·87
South-East	7,987,880	73,780	66,620	50,680	15,070	27,090	233,240	2·92	1·01
South-West	1,552,980	27,770	13,700	11,680	2,540	3,420	59,110	3·81	1·31
Total England	20,489,270	184,440	156,580	139,500	53,650	48,740	582,910	2·84	0·98
Wales	1,079,230	12,540	8,590	6,730	4,870	1,670	34,400	3·19	1·10
Total England and Wales	21,568,500	196,980	165,170	146,230	58,520	50,410	617,310	2·86	0·99
Scotland	2,164,110	33,650	17,010	13,240	4,330	2,980	71,210	3·29	1·13
Total Great Britain	23,732,610	230,630	182,180	159,470	62,850	53,390	688,520	2·90	

Source: ibid.

Pattern of Location

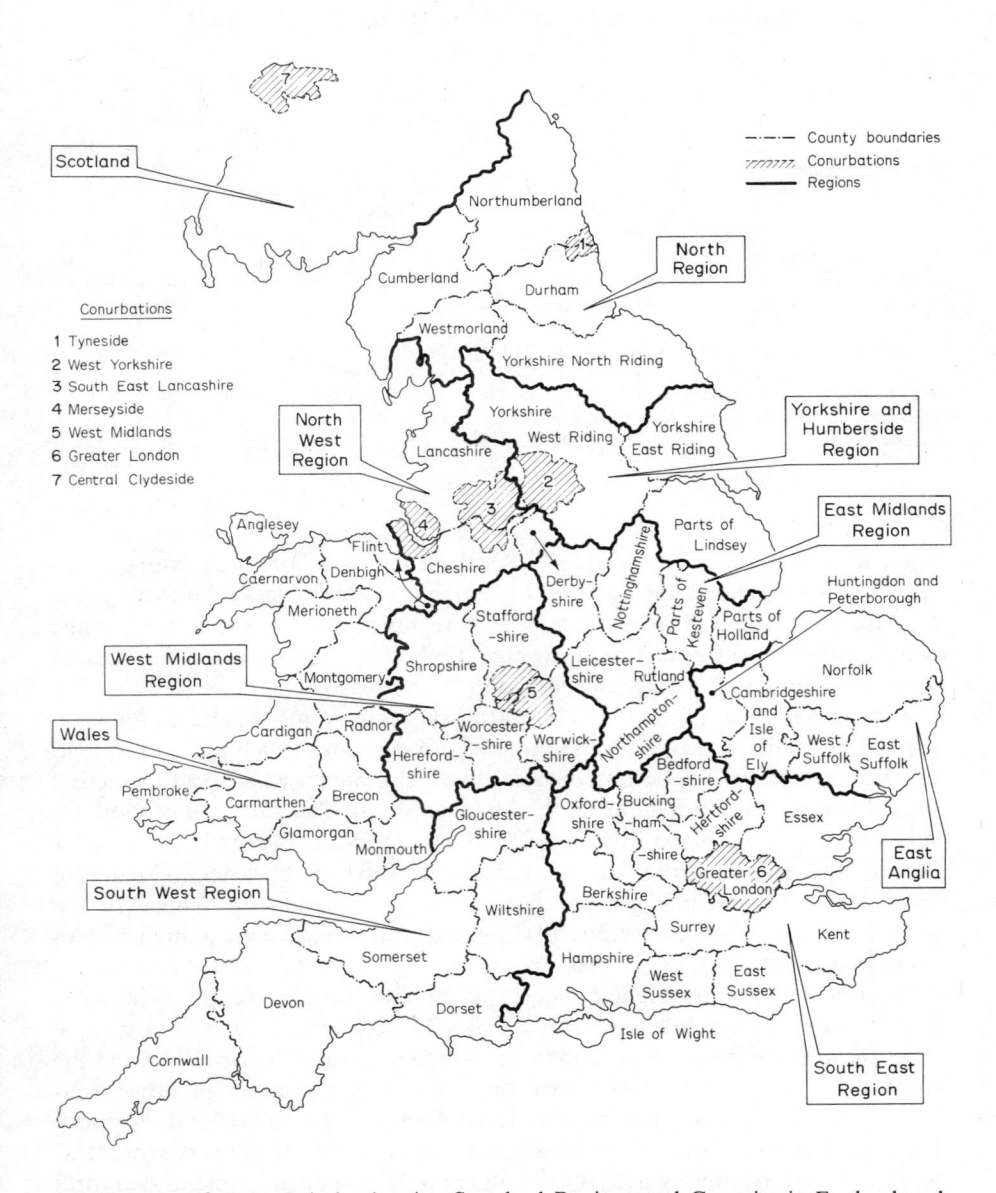

Outline map of Great Britain showing Standard Regions and Counties in England and Wales and Conurbations.

Table 13
Hotel and Catering Industry
Distribution in Conurbations in Great Britain in 1971

	Economically active population engaged in							(2) as % of (1)	Location factor (x)/(y)
Conurbation	All Industries and Services (1)	Hotels etc.	Restaurants etc.	Public Houses	Clubs	Catering Contractors	Total Hotel and Catering Industry (2)	(3)	(4)
Tyneside	378,720	3,000	2,710	2,770	2,330	650	11,460	3·03	1·04
West Yorkshire	810,970	3,380	6,760	4,950	2,540	1,300	18,930	2·33	0·80
South East Lancashire	1,123,140	6,270	7,270	5,890	3,070	2,260	24,760	2·20	0·76
Merseyside	562,190	3,560	3,550	4,260	1,670	940	13,980	2·49	0·86
West Midlands	1,197,850	4,340	5,760	8,910	2,580	2,840	24,430	2·04	0·70
Greater London	4,085,530	34,520	38,650	22,350	9,470	17,160	122,150	2·99	1·03
Central Clydeside	740,430	4,390	6,200	5,130	1,250	1,290	18,260	2·47	0·85

Source: ibid.

It can be seen that both Wales and Scotland have a higher than average concentration of the hotel and catering industry; it is slightly less than average for England as a whole. Three of the English regions have a higher than average concentration and five less than average. Only two of the seven conurbations have a higher than average concentration.

The measurement of industry concentration becomes more meaningful when applied to smaller areas, as variations within larger areas such as regions, tend to offset each other. The pattern of location which emerges when location factors are calculated for sub-regions, is shown in Table 14. The sub-regions used are sub-divisions of Standard Regions of England and Wales (46 for England, 5 for Wales); this approach provides the location factors for the hotel and catering industry for 51 separate geographical units of England and Wales. In the accompanying map sub-regions of England and Wales with a higher than average concentration are shaded.[1]

It can be seen that the highest concentration of the hotel and catering industry occurs in the main holiday areas of Britain. The concentration is almost three times the average in the Fylde, and twice as high in parts of North Wales and the south-west; it is significantly above the average in a number of other well-known holiday areas, such as the Lake District, Yorkshire and northern Lancashire coasts, Kent and the Sussex coast. By contrast, the lowest concentration of hotel and catering activities occurs mainly in industrial and agricultural

---

[1] The original source of the basic data used for the calculations should be consulted for the definition of the sub-regions:
Office of Population Censuses and Surveys, Census 1971, England Wales, Economic Activity Sub-regional Tables (10% sample), London, HMSO, 1976.

Table 14

Hotel and Catering Industry
Distribution in Sub-Regions in England and Wales in 1971

Region	Sub-region	All Industries and Services (1)	Hotels etc.	Restaurants etc.	Public Houses	Clubs	Catering Contractors	Total Hotel and Catering Industry (2)	(2) as % of (1) (x) (3)	Location factor $\frac{(x)}{(y)}$ (4)
North	Industrial North East: North	661,580	4,520	4,400	4,940	4,580	940	19,380	2.93	1.01
	South	375,710	2,690	2,310	2,540	2,960	310	10,810	2.88	0.99
	Rural North East: North	55,300	1,200	380	370	210	110	2,270	4.10	1.41
	South	104,840	3,040	1,050	890	290	110	5,380	5.13	1.77
	Cumberland and Westmorland	156,830	4,600	1,520	1,150	530	120	7,920	5.05	1.74
Yorkshire and Humberside	North Humberside	196,690	1,400	1,430	1,330	750	260	5,170	2.63	0.91
	South Humberside	137,140	1,150	1,010	800	570	90	3,620	2.64	0.91
	Mid-Yorkshire	172,480	3,140	2,470	1,390	390	330	7,720	4.48	1.54
	South Lindsey	54,920	1,290	610	490	200	70	2,660	4.84	1.67
	South Yorkshire	349,740	1,830	2,080	2,190	1,370	660	8,130	2.32	0.80
	Yorkshire Coalfield	286,430	1,240	2,830	2,000	2,140	200	8,410	2.94	1.01
	West Yorkshire	886,400	4,240	7,450	5,500	2,830	1,370	21,390	2.41	0.83
North-West	South Cheshire (High Peak)	215,340	1,840	1,950	2,160	470	310	6,730	3.13	1.08
	South Lancashire	265,790	1,090	1,820	1,930	1,240	330	6,410	2.41	0.83
	Manchester	1,151,220	6,790	7,750	6,090	3,140	2,480	26,250	2.28	0.79
	Merseyside	747,620	5,120	4,790	5,290	2,160	1,340	18,700	2.50	0.86
	Furness	47,310	940	470	240	160	40	1,850	3.91	1.35
	Fylde	112,470	5,840	1,810	850	610	120	9,230	8.21	2.83
	Lancaster	48,100	1,130	770	220	130	30	2,280	4.74	1.63
	Mid-Lancashire	148,860	690	1,380	760	340	170	3,340	2.24	0.77
	North-East Lancashire	214,360	1,170	1,470	1,580	680	220	5,120	2.39	0.82
East Midlands	Nottingham/Derbyshire	769,310	3,960	5,170	5,820	1,780	1,200	17,930	2.33	0.80
	Leicester	349,120	1,890	1,910	2,160	790	980	7,730	2.21	0.76
	Eastern Lowlands	172,850	1,050	1,400	1,380	390	320	4,540	2.63	0.91
	Northampton	202,630	870	1,380	1,470	510	350	4,580	2.26	0.78
West Midlands	Central	466,730	3,980	2,700	4,590	1,220	810	13,300	2.85	0.98
	Conurbation	1,197,850	4,340	5,760	8,910	2,580	2,840	24,430	2.04	0.70
	Coventry Belt	315,470	1,980	1,610	2,440	1,180	650	7,860	2.49	0.86
	Rural West	137,160	1,780	1,020	1,280	260	140	4,480	3.27	1.13
	North Staffordshire	233,840	1,330	970	1,740	580	320	4,940	2.11	0.73

(*Cont. overleaf*)

(Cont.)

| Region | Sub-region | Economically active population engaged in ||||||| (2) as % of (1) (x) | Location factor (x)/(y) |
		All Industries and Services (1)	Hotels etc.	Restaurants etc.	Public Houses	Clubs	Catering Contractors	Total Hotel and Catering Industry (2)	(3)	(4)
East Anglia	South-East	161,830	1,420	1,060	1,050	210	140	3,880	2·40	0·83
	North-East	252,290	3,340	1,750	1,620	250	380	7,340	2·91	1·00
	North-West	139,430	980	720	910	280	230	3,120	2·24	0·77
	South-West	160,770	1,020	1,060	1,060	260	260	3,660	2·28	0·79
South-East	Greater London	4,085,530	34,520	38,650	22,350	9,470	17,160	122,150	2·99	1·03
	Outer Metropolitan	2,120,730	10,520	12,480	14,820	2,800	5,680	46,300	2·18	0·75
	Outer South-East									
	Essex	149,780	1,430	1,100	1,120	240	290	4,180	2·79	0·96
	Kent	222,350	3,950	2,640	2,020	260	270	9,140	4·11	1·42
	Sussex Coast	352,820	8,060	3,930	2,660	380	1,070	16,100	4·56	1·57
	Solent	695,280	12,690	5,660	4,890	1,380	1,800	26,420	3·80	1·31
	Beds. and Bucks.	127,560	740	730	890	160	230	2,750	2·16	0·74
	Berks. and Oxon.	233,830	1,870	1,430	1,930	380	590	6,200	2·65	0·91
South-West	Central	293,670	3,980	2,430	2,500	400	680	9,990	3·40	1·17
	Southern	316,320	9,430	3,370	2,630	590	650	16,670	5·27	1·82
	Western	185,500	7,680	2,430	1,470	200	230	12,010	6·47	2·23
	Northern	757,490	6,680	5,470	5,080	1,350	1,860	20,440	2·70	0·93
Wales	Industrial South Wales	749,520	4,670	5,440	4,200	3,850	1,230	19,390	2·59	0·89
	North-East Wales	90,710	330	470	690	340	90	1,920	2·12	0·73
	North-West Wales	121,420	4,970	1,880	950	380	170	8,350	6·88	2·37
	Central	35,250	760	260	140	90	50	1,300	3·69	1·27
	South-West Wales	82,330	1,810	540	750	210	130	3,440	4·18	1·44

Source: Office of Population Censuses and Surveys, *Census 1971, England and Wales, Economic Activity Sub-regional Tables (10% sample)*, Table 3, London, HMSO, 1976.

Pattern of Location

Outline map of England and Wales showing distribution of the hotel and catering industry in sub-regions.

areas with few or no attractions for the tourist and the holiday maker; this occurs especially in parts of Yorkshire, Lancashire, the Midlands, East Anglia and South Wales.

There is no doubt that areas of high concentration of certain hotel and catering facilities enjoy advantages. First, the facilities themselves may be an attraction to visitors who bring spending power to the areas and who tend to spend at a higher rate than they do when they are at home. Secondly, the hotel and catering industry is a source of employment and hence of livelihood of many communities. Thirdly, it provides amenities for local residents.

To the hotel and catering industry itself, high concentration may bring external economies which arise when a group of firms in the same industry is concentrated geographically: scope for specialization in the provision of services of different types and standards, a supply of labour with a knowledge of the industry, a growth of subsidiary industries and services.

But there are also drawbacks, particularly those arising from low diversification of economic activity and from the seasonal nature of many hotel and catering services. These are discussed in Chapter 14 in connection with employment.

6. *Liquor Licensing*

In this chapter the hotel and catering industry is viewed from the point of view of liquor licensing, which divides the whole group into establishments in which alcoholic liquor is supplied and those in which it is not. This approach is necessarily based on the framework of statute law, within which retail liquor distribution takes place. This is in England and Wales the Licensing Act 1964, a consolidation measure which made no significant changes in the law; the last previous reforming Act was the Licensing Act 1961. In Scotland liquor licensing is governed by the Licensing (Scotland) Act 1976, which implemented many of the recommendations made in the 1973 report of the Committee on Scottish Licensing Law (Clayson Committee).

A detailed consideration of the law relating to the distribution of alcoholic liquor is outside the scope of this study and is available from numerous other sources;[1] but a brief general outline of the licensing system is necessary in order to establish a basis for statistical analysis, and to provide an indication of the effect of licensing legislation on the structure and organization of the hotel and catering industry.

Retail liquor distribution in Britain takes place through two main channels: licensed premises and registered clubs. Both are essentially on the same side of a line of demarcation, which divides the whole industry into two major parts. Licensed premises are on-licences including licensed clubs, or off-licences.

Licensed Premises: The System

Premises in which alcoholic liquor is to be supplied, and which are not registered clubs, must be granted, in England and Wales, a Justices' Licence (in Scotland, a Licence by the Licensing Board). The object is to maintain a control over the number and distribution of outlets in any one district, and to ensure good order on the premises. These functions are carried out in England and Wales by the Licensing Justices, and in Scotland by the Licensing Boards of Islands and District Councillors appointed by the Councils.

In England and Wales there are two kinds of clubs: licensed (usually proprietary) clubs which need a Justices' Licence, and registered, or members', clubs which are registered with the magistrates' court. In Scotland there are no licensed or proprietary clubs.

In England and Wales there are five types of Justices' Licence applicable to retailers:

(*a*) on-licences, which permit the sale of all or some classes of liquor for

[1] *See* for example, Bull, F. J., and Hooper, J. P. G., *Hotel and Catering Law*, and relevant Acts of Parliament.

consumption on the premises, and also sanction sale for consumption off the premises for which the licence is granted;
(b) residential licences, permitting liquor sale only to residents and their friends;
(c) restaurant licences, for sale of liquor only to persons taking substantial meals on the premises;
(d) residential and restaurant licences, a combination of (b) and (c) above;
(e) off-licences, which authorize sales of all classes of liquor, but only for consumption *off* the premises for which the licence is granted.

Different classes of liquor may be sold with each type of licence:
(a) on-licences including residential and restaurant licences:
  (i) spirits or liquor of all descriptions, or
  (ii) beer, cider and wines only, or
  (iii) beer and cider only, or
  (iv) cider only, or
  (v) wine only;
(b) off-licence:
  (i) liquor of all descriptions, or
  (ii) beer, cider and wine only.

In Scotland there are seven types of licence[2]:
(a) hotel licence, for residential premises;
(b) restricted hotel licence, similar to the joint residential and restaurant licence in England and Wales;
(c) restaurant licence, similar to the restaurant licence in England and Wales;
(d) public house licence;
(e) off-sale licence, the Scottish equivalent of the English off-licence;
(f) refreshment licence, allowing cafe-style premises to serve alcoholic drinks with food and non-alcoholic beverages;
(g) entertainment licence, for places like cinemas and dance halls with the sale of liquor restricted to patrons.

The hotel licence and the public house licence are in effect equivalent to the full on-licence in England and Wales. The licensing board can exclude spirits, but not wine, from the list of authorized drinks.

Since 1961 club premises in England and Wales conducted as commercial ventures owned by individuals or limited companies by whom the stock of liquor is also owned and sold retail to members have been put on the same legal basis as licensed premises. Such clubs need to hold justices' on-licences, to which the justices may attach conditions governing the tenure of the licences, and any other matters they think proper in the interests of the public.

As sale for consumption on the premises is a decisive criterion for including an establishment within the scope of the hotel and catering industry, it is clear that establishments in England and Wales possessing all types of licence except the

---

[2] Prior to the Licensing (Scotland) Act 1976 there were only five types of licence. These, known at that time as certificates were issued by the Licensing Court.

off-licence, and in Scotland all types of licence except the off-sale licence, do so qualify. Establishments with off-licences alone, in England and Wales, and with off-sale licences alone, in Scotland, are outside the scope of the industry[3].

Registered Clubs: The System

The legal position of registered clubs differs considerably from that of licensed premises, and has been significantly clarified in the last decade. In the proprietary club, which was the oldest form of club, all the property, including liquor, belonged to the proprietor, to whom members paid a subscription and in return they had by contract a licence to use the club. The actual club management was generally entrusted to a committee, partly nominated by the proprietor and partly elected by the members. The supply of liquor to a member constituted, in the legal sense, a 'sale' to him by the proprietor, and a magistrates' licence was required. In a members' club, on the other hand, all the property, including liquor, belongs to the members jointly: their subscriptions are paid to a common fund, and an elected committee manages the club. The members' right to use the club is founded on their joint ownership, and the supply of liquor to a member is not regarded a 'sale' in law, but merely a transfer to a member of a portion of the collective interest of all members; therefore, a magistrates' licence is not required.

From 1903, any club in which intoxicating liquor was supplied to members, has had to be registered. Since proprietary as well as members' clubs had to be registered, proprietary clubs usually had a purely elective committee to satisfy the registration provisions, which stipulated that a club might be struck off the register if the supply of liquor was not under the control of the members, or of a committee appointed by them. If these provisions were complied with, there was no legal objections to the actual property in the liquor being in the proprietor but he would still require a magistrates' licence 'to sell'. Consequently the usual practice was for the liquor to be purchased by the committee on behalf of the members so as to put the club (in this respect alone), on the same footing as a members' club, and to obviate any necessity for a magistrates' licence. An Excise licence for clubs was introduced in the Finance Act 1959, so that as from January 1, 1960, all clubs, in addition to registering, had to obtain an Excise licence. Therefore, licensed premises as well as registered clubs had to hold an Excise licence, but licensed premises had to obtain first a magistrates' licence, whilst clubs only had to register.

The Licensing Act 1961 drew a clear distinction between a licensed and a members' club in England and Wales. The Finance Act 1967 abolished the

---

[3] Premises for which a justices' licence is not required are: messes and canteens for the armed services, seamen's canteens, theatres either under Royal Patent or theatre licence duly granted, passenger aircraft, passenger vessels, and railway passenger vehicles in which passengers can be supplied with food.

requirement for a separate Excise licence in respect of registered clubs as well as of licensed premises.

Statistics of Licensed Premises and Registered Clubs

Statistics of retail liquor licences and of registered clubs in England and Wales are compiled by the Home Office, and published annually in *Liquor Licensing Statistics for England and Wales*. In Scotland the statistics are compiled by the Scottish Home and Health Department and are included in an annual Command paper, *Civil Judicial Statistics*.

Table 15

Liquor Retail Outlets in Britain 1975[a]

England and Wales		*Scotland*[b]		*Great Britain*
Full on-licences	64,614	Public houses[c]	4,002	
		Hotels[c]	2,755	71,371
Residential	2,532			2,532
Restaurants	9,599	Restaurants	587	10,186
Residential & restaurants	2,763	Restricted hotels	317	3,080
Licensed clubs	2,802			2,802
Total on-licences	82,310	Total on-sale	7,661	89,971
Registered clubs	24,931	Registered clubs	2,404	27,335
Total hotel & catering industry	107,241	Total hotel & catering industry	10,065	117,306
Off-licences	31,644	Off-sale certificates	4,182	35,826
Total retail outlets	138,885	Total retail outlets	14,247	153,132

Source: Home Office, *Liquor Licensing Statistics for England and Wales 1975*; Scottish Home and Health Department, *Civil Judicial Statistics* 1975.

[a] At 30 June 1975.

[b] For Scotland statistics in this table are based on types of licence (certificate) available prior to the coming into operation of the Licensing (Scotland) Act, 1976, which introduced two further new types of licence in addition to the above.

[c] The public house and the hotel certificate in Scotland were, in effect, equivalent to the full on-licence of England and Wales; both types of certificate authorized the holder to sell liquor for consumption either on or off the premises. The need for separate public house and hotel certificates arose from the fact that public houses in Scotland had no permitted hours on Sundays; as a result better statistics of individual types of unit were available for the hotel and catering industry in Scotland than in England and Wales where the same full on-licence may be granted to an hotel and to a public house.

Statistics from these two sources provide an interesting illustration of changes in the number of outlets over a period, and are shown in Appendix G from the end of the last century to 1975. Licensed premises in England and Wales decreased in the six decades to 1960 from over 100,000 to under 70,000, i.e. by about one-third, and in Scotland in the five decades to 1960 from under 7,000 to over 6,000, i.e. by about one-tenth. This trend was due to a determined effort to control the number of outlets with regard to public need on the part of licensing authorities, and to a process of rationalization on the part of brewers. In England and Wales the decrease was largely due to a reduction in the number of beerhouses; in Scotland there was an overall reduction in the number of public houses, which was to some extent offset by an increase in the number of licensed hotels.

In the same period, in which a substantial reduction took place in the number of licensed premises, the number of clubs in England and Wales increased more than three and a half times, and more than doubled in Scotland.

The trends in the 1960s, influenced significantly by new legislation, are discussed later in this chapter.

Although the types of licence in England and Wales and the types of certificate in Scotland do not correspond exactly to each other, and the dates to which the statistics relate are different, it is possible to relate the statistics of both to provide an approximate pattern for the whole of Great Britain in 1975 (*see* Table 15).

In 1975 there were in Britain 153,000 retail outlets for the supply of alcoholic liquor. Of these some 35,800 were licensed for sale for off-consumption only and, therefore, could not be regarded as part of the hotel and catering industry, which comprised some 117,300 licensed establishments: 90,000 on-licensed premises and 27,300 registered clubs (which may be regarded as effectively on-licensed in this context). Of the 90,000 on-licensed premises, about 14,000 were hotels, 11,000 restaurants, 2,800 licensed clubs, and 62,000 public houses.

Factors of Club Growth

It is possible to discern some of the factors which have contributed to the increase in the number of clubs since the beginning of this century. First, it must be viewed as a reaction to the strict liquor licensing laws in the country. Registered clubs are regarded as private premises in the eyes of the law, and enjoy many advantages as compared with licensed houses; for instance, they can, within limits, adjust their permitted hours to suit their members, and they can allow many activities on their premises which would require another licence, or special permission of the magistrates in case of licensed premises, or which are entirely, prohibited there. Secondly, the comparative ease in the formation of a registered club is undoubtedly another factor; registration cannot be refused in England and Wales, provided that certain minimum formalities are complied with, and even in Scotland the procedure is less complicated than that for obtaining a liquor licence. Thirdly, until 1959, financial provisions were overwhelmingly in favour of clubs. Licensed houses in England and Wales alone had to return to the State the scarcity value of the licence, known as the 'monopoly value', in the form of a levy assessed as the difference in the capital value of premises licensed and unlicensed. The club duty which clubs had to pay was often less onerous than the annual Excise licence duty paid by licensed houses, which might also have to contribute to a Compensation Fund, out of which compensation was paid for licenses declared redundant. Last but not least, the social value of the club is considerable. It provides the opportunity to associate with those whose company is desired, and the committee controls the admission of members. Membership of many a club is valued for reasons of social status, as well as for the contacts which it provides; much of the attraction may well lie in a high rather than a low subscription.

By the Finance Act 1959, the financial provisions relating to licensed houses and registered clubs were brought more into line with each other. The Act recognized that it was no longer logical to charge licensed premises with 'monopoly value', which had to be paid by them on the grant of a licence. The growth of clubs destroyed the scarcity of a licence, so that most licensed houses no longer possessed the monopoly on which the payment of the annual licence value represented a levy, and the payment was abolished. The Act also introduced a radical reform of the system of liquor licence and club duties, which put licensed houses and clubs on a more equal footing; the system of duties based in most cases on annual values of licensed premises and on liquor purchases in clubs was changed to a simple payment in the nature of a registration fee.

Pubs versus Clubs

From the tables in this section emerges the diminishing ratio of on-licences to registered clubs, which gave rise to concern to the Amulree Commission and subsequently about the effectiveness of the liquor distribution control. With the exception of such abnormal periods as the war years, before the licensing legislation of the early 1960s the ratio was decreasing continually with the reduction in the number of licences and the increase in the number of clubs (Table 16).

Table 16
Ratio of On-licences to Registered Clubs 1919–1959
(England and Wales)

Year	1919	1920	1921	1924	1929	1933	1948	1959
Approximate ratio	10:1	9:1	8:1	7:1	6:1	5:1	4:1	3:1

The same trend emerges from the following Table 17, in which numbers of on-licences and of registered clubs are expressed in relation to the population.

Table 17

Ratio of On-licences and Registered Clubs to Population 1919–1959
(England and Wales)

Year	1919	1953	1954	1955	1956	1957	1958	1959
On-licences per 10,000 of population	22·1	16·6	16·5	16·4	16·2	16·0	15·8	15·4
Registered clubs per 10,000 of population	2·3	4·6	4·7	4·8	4·8	4·9	5·0	5·1

These ratios indicate the trend, but only represent the national average, which conceals wide regional variation. The pronounced local impact could be observed if the numbers of on-licences and of registered clubs are analysed for individual counties and county boroughs. There were three on-licences to each registered club in England and Wales at the end of the 1950s. But in some parts of the country the club movement has been particularly strong and has occupied a special place in the life of the people. This has been the case in the industrial north – Yorkshire, Durham and Northumberland, south Lancashire and Midlands, South Wales (particularly in the county of Glamorgan) and Monmouthshire; clubs, although of a different character, were also numerous in the Home Counties and in many seaside resorts. In these areas the ratio of on-licences to registered clubs was at the end of the 1950s much lower than the national average; in some counties and county boroughs it was in the region of two on-licences to each club, and in two county boroughs, both seaside resorts–Bournemouth and Southport – the number of clubs exceeded that of on-licences.

A measure of the importance of registered clubs lies in their share of the national turnover of alcoholic liquor. This was estimated in the 1950s to have been well in excess of 10 per cent, as compared with some 7 per cent before the war. The Monopolies Commission reporting in the late 1960s estimated that in 1967, 20 per cent of the beer in the country was supplied through registered clubs, which represented well over a half of all beer reaching the consumer through 'free trade' outlets (i.e. premises not owned by brewers). In the main club areas of the country the share of clubs in liquor distribution generally, and of beer in particular, is likely to have been much greater.

The Amulree Commission, reporting in 1931, considered that the club movement at its best was a most valuable element in the structure of our society, but it also expressed the view that in all parts of the country many clubs had been brought into existence solely for the purpose of supplying intoxicants, and that such clubs, for all practical purposes, fulfilled the same function as public houses.

In the thirty years between 1929 and 1959, the ratio of on-licences to registered clubs in England and Wales decreased from 6:1 to 3:1, and by the end of the 1950s licensing by magistrates controlled liquor distribution even less effectively than it did in 1931 when the Commission reported. This gave much concern not only to those who administered the law, but also to licensees facing growing competition from clubs, on an unequal footing.

Three courses were open, if the situation which had developed was to be remedied. The first was to extend the law relating to licensed premises to cover registered clubs; such a move would have virtually abolished the club as a private institution and placed it in the same position as licensed premises; this was hardly conceivable. The second course was to ease the restrictions on licensed premises through amendments in the law and through more liberal use of the discretionary powers by the justices; changes of this nature would have secured greater equity as between the two sectors of the industry, given less cause for grievance to the licensees, and probably less reason for the licensing system to be by-passed. The third course consisted of a combination of the first two – of increased control of clubs coupled with some relaxation of control over licensed premises. This course would bring the law into line with the changing social system, remedy most of what was unsatisfactory, and would be widely acceptable.

This third course was adopted in the Licensing Act 1961, which drew a clear distinction between proprietary and members' clubs; it placed the former on the same footing as licensed premises, and preserved the genuine members' club as a private institution although its registration ceased to be a pure formality. It also relaxed the law relating to licensed premises by introducing three new forms of licence, which may be refused only on specific grounds, and by easing the control of licensing justices over licensed premises, as well as the rules of conduct in them.

In Scotland the licensing law was also amended at the time, by the Licensing Act 1962, but there is no provision for licensed (or proprietors') clubs. Although clubs have been also on the increase there, their control under Scottish law was still stricter than was the case with their English counterparts.

The effects of the new licensing legislation on the structure of the industry are shown in Table 18.

The immediate effect of the licensing legislation of the early 1960s was a reversal of the previous downwards trend in the number of on-licences in England and Wales (as a result of the inclusion of licensed clubs in this category, and of the introduction of the three new types of licence), and a substantial reduction in the number of registered clubs. Subsequently the number of on-licences began to grow and the number of registered clubs also resumed its growth, but the ratio of the two types of outlet remained relatively constant. In Scotland the numbers of both types of outlet continued their previous growth, but this was almost entirely due to certificates other than that for public houses, and registered clubs increased in number proportionately faster; the total effect has been a gradually declining ratio of certificates to clubs.

The continuing trend for unlicensed establishments to become licensed also emerges from Appendix S, which shows in particular a significant increase in licensed hotels and restaurants (the number of establishments on the list doubled

Table 18
Licensed Premises and Registered Clubs 1960–1969

Year	1960	1961	1962	1963	1964	1965	1966	1967	1968	1969

ENGLAND AND WALES

On-licences	69184	68936	68037	67450	66931	66570	66373	65916	65541	65048
Residential			550	709	837	963	1087	1191	1365	1504
Restaurant			1318	2130	2841	3520	4116	4590	5160	5739
Residential & restaurant			942	1180	1358	1506	1650	1769	1917	2055
Licensed clubs			1153	1940	2045	2199	2318	2377	2438	2488
Total on-licences	69184	68936	72000	73409	74012	74758	75544	75843	76421	76834
Registered clubs	23773[a]	24418[a]	21459	20663	21010	21405	21872	22368[b]	22705	23176
Approximate ratio	2·9:1	2·8:1	3·4:1	3·6:1	3·5:1	3·5:1	3·5:1	3·4:1	3·4:1	3·3:1

SCOTLAND

Hotels	1987	2056	2096	2138	2196	2265	2319	2404	2449	2509
Restricted Hotel			60	111	142	149	170	184	212	226
Restaurant			44	106	148	175	201	221	274	307
Public houses	4186	4206	4218	4212	4222	4213	4222	4230	4198	4111
Total Certificates	6173	6262	6418	6567	6708	6802	6912	7039	7133	7153
Registered clubs	1297	1326	1379	1421	1497	1554	1607	1686	1793	1890
Approximate ratio	4·8:1	4·6:1	4·6:1	4·6:1	4·5:1	4·4:1	4·3:1	4·2:1	4·0:1	3·8:1

GREAT BRITAIN

On-licences & certificates	75357	75198	78418	79976	80720	81560	82456	82882	83554	83987
Registered clubs	25070	25744	22838	22084	22507	22959	23479	24054	24498	25066
Approximate ratio	3·0:1	2·9:1	3·5:1	3·5:1	3·6:1	3·6:1	3·5:1	3·4:1	3·4:1	3·3:1

[a] Licensed clubs are included in these figures up to 1961; until the Licensing Act 1961 the number of licensed clubs was not shown separately.

[b] In 1967 of these some 1,200 registered clubs were in Wales; the proportions (over 5 per cent) were about the same throughout the decade.

in the twenty years between 1949 and 1969), and a substantial decrease in the number of unlicensed places of refreshment (the number of establishments on the list decreased by a third over the same period).

The Monopolies Commission Report on the Supply of Beer was published in 1969. The Commission found the restrictions on competition involved in the tied house system operated by the brewer-suppliers to be detrimental not only to efficiency in brewing, wholesaling and retailing and to the interests of independent suppliers, but also to the interests of consumers. Having considered alternatives to the tied house system, within the present licensing laws, the Commission did not consider any of them effective and practicable. It then considered the economic and social effects of relaxing the licensing laws and, in the sole recommendation of the Report, recommended that by way of remedy for the defects it found in the tied house system the licensing system in England and Wales should be substantially relaxed, so that any retailer satisfying certain minimum standards could sell alcoholic drinks for consumption on or off the premises.

The Government reaction to the Report was at first cautious. In a written reply in the House of Commons on May 20, 1969, the President of the Board of Trade said that the Commission had made a strong case for relaxing the existing limitations on competition on economic grounds, but that he thought that a change in the licensing laws called for a thorough examination of the social implications.

In 1970 a Government Committee under the chairmanship of Lord Erroll was set up to review the licensing laws in England and Wales, which reported in 1972. A similar committee set up in Scotland under the chairmanship of Dr C. Clayson reported in 1973. From this and other indications it would appear that Britain may be moving further towards a more liberal licensing system with its consequential effects on the structure of the industry. However, whilst many of the recommendations of the Clayson Committee were included in the Scottish licensing legislation of 1976, no action followed the Erroll Committee report, and Licensing in England and Wales continues to be based on the 1961 Act.

7. Component Sectors

In the case of a heterogeneous industry consisting of units of many different types it is useful to sub-divide it into component sectors, for the purposes of further study. In the preceding chapter an attempt has been made to provide a survey of the licensing framework, within which a substantial proportion of the establishments in the hotel and catering industry operate, and to indicate the size and composition of that part of the industry through which retail distribution of alcoholic liquor takes place. Although the supply of alcoholic liquor influences the character of the establishment in which it takes place, it is not necessarily fundamental to a classification of the industry into its component sectors.

Basis of Classification

In the analysis of an industry into its component sectors, establishments are grouped into reasonably homogeneous divisions according to their most important characteristics, which are normally determined by their respective functions.

A departure from the ideal has to be made in the case of an industry in which many establishments engage in a combination of activities. This is certainly so with establishments providing hotel and catering services, where there is a two-fold explanation for the lack of clear-cut specialization. In the first place, only when the density of traffic and the market density are high, do establishments of a particular type emerge, as only then are they economically possible. But secondly, even then the fact that some hotel and catering services are often in joint demand, such as food and accommodation, or drink with a meal, makes it necessary and desirable that they should be provided together. Thus any classification of the hotel and catering industry into its component sectors is bound to be a rough one.

The difficulties inherent in any attempt at homogeneous grouping can be, to some extent, overcome by the creation of a large number of sectors within the industry, probably as many as twenty or more, each comprising establishments of a very distinct type. However, there is little to recommend this in the present study. Even if this approach were adopted, the fact that many establishments engage in a combination of activities, and that it is frequently difficult to determine the main one with any accuracy, would still present problems of some magnitude. There is, therefore, much to be said for a broad division of the industry into a small number of sectors, each comprising units sharing important common characteristics and carrying on broadly comparable activities. Of the schemes outlined in Chapter 1, that adopted in the Standard Industrial Classification 1968 meets the needs of this study by dividing the industry into five sectors:

(a) hotels and other residential establishments;
(b) restaurants;
(c) public houses;
(d) clubs;
(e) catering contractors.

In this chapter each of the five sectors is described briefly, and its size estimated in the light of available statistics.

Hotels and Other Residential Establishments

The Standard Industrial Classification 1968 defines the accommodation sector of the industry as consisting of hotels, motels, holiday camps, guest houses, boarding houses, hostels and similar establishments providing furnished accommodation with food and service for reward; it excludes licensed or residential clubs, which are classified to the club sector. We are, therefore, principally concerned with establishments meeting the accommodation demand of travellers and temporary residents.

Three main demarcation problems present themselves. The first is between the accommodation sector of the industry, and the provision of accommodation on a tenancy basis. In order to qualify for inclusion in the scope of the industry, an establishment must provide some food and service for its residents for reward. Although this distinction may be sometimes difficult to draw in practice, it does exclude establishments whose primary function is the letting of flats and similar accommodation, whether furnished or not, and whether for holiday or other use, which places them in the property ownership and management sector, rather than in the hotel and catering industry.

The second difficulty arises with an establishment with a small amount of sleeping accommodation to let, which merges into something else because the provision of meals and refreshments constitutes its principal activity, to which the letting of a few beds is merely ancillary, and which may be variously called an hotel, an inn, a public house, or the like. In most countries a minimum accommodation capacity is adopted in defining an accommodation unit, although the minimum requirement varies. In Britain the Catering Wages Commission met this problem by establishing four letting bedrooms or accommodation for eight guests, whichever is less, as the line of demarcation between residential and non-residential units, any establishment satisfying this minimum requirement being regarded as a residential one. In Scotland four letting bedrooms were regarded as the minimum accommodation necessary for the grant of the Hotel Certificate to allow the sale of liquor in an establishment situated in a town. Although this approach may not attach due importance to the principal activity of the business, it does provide a basis which, as a result of statutory recognition, has been widely accepted in Britain.

The third problem is to find a point at which the private house, letting rooms to visitors, should be regarded as being a guest house or a boarding house, and thus a part of the accommodation sector of the industry. On this issue, the

Catering Wages Commission felt that the minimum accommodation of four bedrooms or for eight guests should be *ordinarily available* as sleeping accommodation for guests or lodgers. Another line of demarcation is provided by the Fire Precautions (Hotels and Boarding Houses) Order 1972, which covers premises providing sleeping accommodation for more than six persons, guests or staff.[1]

The variety of establishments within this sector is considerable. Moreover, as there are no rules of law prohibiting the use of various designations unless certain conditions are satisfied, the name given to the establishment does not necessarily provide a reliable guide to its nature. The legal definition, which has been embodied in the Hotel Proprietors Act 1956, describes an hotel as 'an establishment held out by the proprietor as offering food, drink and, if so required, sleeping accommodation, without special contract, to any traveller presenting himself who appears able and willing to pay a reasonable sum for the services provided and who is in a fit state to be received'.[2]

Thus, in law, all residential establishments fall into one of two classes: hotels, within the meaning of the Act on the one hand, and others, which are usually for convenience described as 'private hotels'. The distinction is of importance mainly in determining the proprietor's duty to receive travellers, and his responsibility for guests' property. The Act does not preclude the use of the name 'hotel' and its use does not, *ipso facto*, make an establishment an hotel in the legal sense. It is up to the proprietor to decide whether he wishes to consider his establishment as an hotel in the legal sense and to accept the duties and obligations arising out of it, or whether he wishes to be regarded as a private hotelier in the eyes of the law. He is absolutely free to describe his establishment as he chooses and, whatever name he gives to it, to conduct it as he chooses. If he decides to conduct it as an hotel within the meaning of the 1956 Act, subject to certain exceptions he must receive all travellers and accept responsibility for their property; he also has a lien on his guests' property in respect of unpaid bills. A private hotelier on the other hand, has no such obligations, neither can he detain his guests' property.

Whilst probably most establishments described as 'hotels' are, in fact, hotels in the legal meaning of the word, by no means all of them are. Thus the usage of the word does not exactly coincide with its legal meaning. However, subject to this qualification, the hotel usually provides accommodation, meals and refreshments for irregular periods of time for those who may reserve their accommodation in advance but need not do so and the word tends to denote, therefore, an establishment which meets the demands of the modern traveller. In this sense its usage corresponds to that in other countries.

It is interesting to note here that under the scheme of hotel appointments operated in this country by the motoring organizations, hotels classified by stars undertake to receive guests without prior reservation. The absence of stars does not imply inferiority in position, atmosphere, equipment or standard; the

[1] Order made under the Fire Precautions Act 1971.
[2] Hotel Proprietors Act 1956, s. 1(3).

classification is intended to indicate the type of hotel rather than to show degrees of merit, but one reason why an establishment may be 'approved' by the motoring organizations, but not classified by stars, may be that it caters only to a limited extent for visitors without previous reservation.

The establishment which is known in some countries, particularly in Austria, Germany and Switzerland, as a *pension*, is in Britain variously described as a private hotel, a guest house or a boarding house. Catering facilities are usually restricted to residents, whilst the true hotel is normally also open for meals and refreshments to non-residents. The pension also differs from the hotel in its choice of customers, many of whom usually stay longer, and for definite periods, such as a week or a fortnight. Particularly the small establishment, which is almost universal in this category, has the character of an extended household.

Hostels are even more sharply distinguished from hotels by the length of stay of their residents, which tends to be still greater than in the case of a boarding house. The same is true of lodging houses; in practice many of these become boarding houses for a part of the year, only to revert to their character as lodging houses for the remainder of the year. As far as hostels are concerned, accommodation in them is in many cases provided by (or by arrangement with) an organization with which the resident is associated; for example, by an employer for his employees or by an educational institution for its students.

Although the accommodation of holiday makers in hostels or camps is known in other countries (for instance in the United States, where country clubs and vacation motels have been popular for many years), the holiday camp, as it is known in Britain, represents an establishment distinct from similar ones in other countries, and from other residential establishments in this country. Since the early days of primitive tent accommodation, it has developed into permanent structures usually consisting of central buildings and chalet accommodation for visitors; it offers recreational facilities and a wide variety of entertainment for the holiday maker within its own grounds.

Motels represent the most recent addition to this sector of the industry in providing chalet-type accommodation, usually centred round a solid building with catering facilities, for motorists. Whereas much of the accommodation may not differ greatly from that offered by the holiday camps, their facilities are geared to the needs of motorists, and they cater almost exclusively for highly transient custom.

Estimates of the size of the accommodation sector of the hotel and catering industry are available from several sources.

The study by consultants for the Hotels and Catering Economic Development Committee *Hotel Prospects to 1985* covered a wide variety of establishments of four or more bedrooms, including hotels, motels, guest houses and public houses offering overnight accommodation. The study identified at 1 January 1974 13,668 licensed and 19,991 unlicensed units, with a capacity of 311,000 bedrooms in the former and 187,000 bedrooms in the latter.[3] As liquor licensing statistics indicate a continuing trend for unlicensed establishments to become

[3] Hotels and Catering EDC: *Hotel Prospects to 1985*, Research Findings.

licensed[4], a further growth has occurred in licensed hotels since 1974.

In October 1975 there were 23,913 establishments on the list of the Licensed Residential Establishment and Licensed Restaurant Wages Council.[5] An analysis of liquor licensing statistics suggests that some 11,000 of this figure were licensed restaurants[4], leaving about 13,000 licensed residential establishments. However, this number on the one hand includes some residential clubs, and on the other hand leaves out some small hotels with no employees covered by the Wages Council.

Information covering a wider range of accommodation units is now also provided by the fire authorities, since the Fire Precautions (Hotels and Boarding Houses) Order 1972, issued under the Fire Precautions Act 1971, requires hotels and boarding houses with sleeping accommodation for more than six persons to apply to the fire authorities for a fire certificate. According to reports of Inspectors of Fire Services, by 1975 applications had been received for a total of 40,144 premises. Whilst it was estimated that there were still many premises, for which applications had not been made, the statistics from this source also indicate an annual reduction of several thousand premises, as a result of establishments reducing their accommodation to bring them outside the scope of the Order, of changes in the use of premises, and of those going out of business.[6]

Hotel Prospects to 1985 appear to provide the best estimate of accommodation capacity in Britain. On the basis of these estimates and in the light of subsequent developments, by the end of 1975 Britain had in the region of 34,000 hotels, of which about 14,000 were licensed and some 20,000 unlicensed.

Restaurants, Cafes, and Snack Bars

The large number of non-residential catering establishments which supply food for consumption on the premises, in which the supply of alcoholic liquor (if any) is merely ancillary, are conveniently grouped into a separate sector of the hotel and catering industry. They are variously called restaurants, cafés, refreshment rooms, tea rooms, tea shops, snack bars, milk bars, coffee bars and the like; many fried-fish shops fall within this category, and the Standard Industrial Classification 1968 also includes in this sector function-rooms operated as parts of restaurants, or as separate establishments. The common characteristic of all these units is that they supply food to the general public who consume it on the premises, and that they do not provide sleeping accommodation.

According to their mode of operation they may be divided into service or self-service establishments; in the former, food is served at tables, in the latter category, the customer collects his own food, and seating accommodation is either provided at tables or the food is consumed at the counter. The fare may range

---

[4] *See* Chapter 6 and Appendix G.
[5] *See* Appendix S.
[6] Reports of Her Majesty's Chief Inspector of Fire Services and Inspector of Fire Services for Scotland for 1975 and 1976.

from a variety of cooked dishes on the one hand to light refreshments on the other, according to the type of establishment. In the region of one-third of units within this section of the industry are licensed for the sale of intoxicating liquor.

Most difficulties of demarcation arise because a combination of catering and other activities is being carried on, and because of the similarities between the catering establishment and a retail shop. Such difficulties arise, for instance, in connection with fried-fish shops, which fall into three broad groups: (*a*) shops from which all sales are taken away for consumption off the premises, (*b*) shops similar to those in the first category, but which also provide facilities for consumption on the premises, and (*c*) shops which sell for consumption only on the premises. Many fried-fish shops fall within the first category; the number in the last category is negligible. Hence the remainder – between one-half and two-thirds – combine sales on- and off-consumption. The view has been adopted, for example by the Wages Councils, that only types (*b*) and (*c*) can be considered to be a part of the industry; and then, as regards the second category, only those with substantial sales, consumed on the premises. If this line of demarcation is accepted, probably no more than one-half of all fried-fish shops can be regarded as catering establishments.

Although restaurants, cafés, snack bars and allied units have many characteristics of retail trading (many of them, of course, combine the sale of meals and refreshments with retail sales, particularly of bakery goods, confectionery, tobacco and other products), the catering establishment in its pure form differs in several important respects from a retail shop:

(i) the goods sold are consumed on the premises, whilst the goods bought in a retail shop are taken away by the purchaser;
(ii) the buyer himself determines the quantity of goods bought in a shop but, as far as meals are concerned, the unit of sales is variable and is determined by the seller, usually by size of portion;
(iii) the caterer also determines the quality; the customer rarely has any choice in the matter, because he mostly orders his meal without seeing it before his order has been placed. The main exceptions here are, for example, cold buffet and self-service sales;
(iv) the caterer is not only a retailer, he is also a producer who subjects most of the raw materials he uses to a process, and sells them in a different form from that in which he received them; and
(v) last but not least, the caterer's mode of operation is different from the retailer in other respects: his cycle of operation from receipt of raw materials to the sale of the finished product is short, and his stocks are relatively small.

It is generally accepted that restaurants, in common with retail shops, represent one of the most volatile sectors of the economy. The ease of entry into the restaurant business, its frequent closures and changes in ownership and its responsiveness to demand in providing catering services readily where the demand becomes apparent, are some of the reasons why an assessment of the size of this sector of the industry can be made only in broad terms. Three main sources provide an indication.

The 1969 Catering Trades Inquiry enumerated 29,755 restaurants, cafés and snack bars, and 14,282 fish and chip shops with or without consumption on the premises.[7]

The Hotels and Catering EDC Supplies Study estimated the total number of restaurants in 1973 at 35,000 outlets.[8]

The Wages Councils lists included a total of 23,913 licensed residential establishments and licensed restaurants in 1975, of which about 11,000 were, by reference to liquor licensing statistics, licensed restaurants and the remainder were licensed hotels.[9] The list of the Unlicensed Place of Refreshment Wages Council, consisting entirely of restaurants and similar establishments, included 20,171 establishments in 1975.[10]

Some of the differences between estimates from these sources are due to:
(a) the 1969 Inquiry excluding catering by businesses whose main activity was outside the scope of the Inquiry, for example, catering in cinemas, theatres and dance halls;
(b) the Wages Councils figures for UPR establishments including some fish and chip shops with consumption on the premises, but excluding those with no employees covered by the Council.

Available statistics provide evidence of four main trends in numbers of establishments in this sector:
(a) a continuing decrease in numbers of unlicensed places of refreshment and an increase in the number of licensed restaurants with a restricted licence;
(b) a gradual but substantial reduction in the number of fish and chip shops and an increase in the number of other take away outlets of various kinds.

In broad terms in 1975 the total number of restaurant-type establishments was probably in the region of 35,000, including some 5,000 fish and chip shops with significant sales for consumption on the premises.

Public Houses

Public houses represent a reasonably homogeneous group of establishments wholly or mainly engaged in supplying alcoholic liquor to the general public for consumption both on and off the premises, to which the supply of food, if any, is merely ancillary. Under the designation 'public houses' are also included the remaining beerhouses, which have most characteristics of public houses and are frequently described as such; they are distinguished from the true public house

---
[7] *Catering Trades 1969*, Statistical Inquiry, p. 16.
[8] Hotels and Catering EDC: *The Catering Supply Industry*, p. 2.
[9] *See* Chapter 6 and Appendix G.
[10] *See* Appendix S.

mainly by the terms of their licence, which restricts them to the sale of beer, cider and sometimes wines.

The most important economic characteristic of the public house is the requirement of a magistrates' licence, which enables it to carry on its activities. Whilst this requirement is common also to other establishments, such as hotels and restaurants, if they wish to sell alcoholic liquor, in no other section of the industry is it universal. The business of a public house cannot be carried on without a licence, and in this sense there is a restriction on entry into this sector of the hotel and catering industry, as it exists whenever a statutory authority makes a licence a pre-requisite of carrying on an activity.

Another important characteristic of most public houses is their tie to a brewery company, which provides an integration of production with retail distribution of alcoholic liquor. The system, described in detail in Chapters 8 and 13, has led to a concentration of the ownership of the greater part of the public house sector of the industry in the hands of a small number of firms, a concentration not paralleled in any other sector of the industry.

In 1931 the Amulree Commission considered as a most urgent requirement the transformation of the public house 'into a place where the public can obtain general refreshment, of whatever variety they choose, in decent, pleasant and comfortable surroundings'.[11] This 'ideal' as it was described, has been in recent years to a great extent realized, and there are indications that the provision of refreshments other than liquor has been on the increase in public houses in postwar Britain. Whilst the supply of liquor may still constitute the principal activity in most of them, some catering is carried on in most public houses; it ranges from sales of light snacks at the counter in some, to extensive meal service in separate dining-rooms in others, and to this extent many publicans can be again considered licensed victuallers. In recent years most brewery companies have developed food service in their public houses; in many managed houses, managers' wives have carried on catering on their own account. Other brewers have created chains of eating houses from selected public houses, and even set up new ones. Catering companies have been entering the public house field with similar intentions. Several groups have been marketed with a brand image. The distinction between the restaurant and the pub has been blurred.

In arriving at the total number of public houses two main problems present themselves, in spite of the availability of accurate licensing statistics. First, the statistics only differentiate fully in Scotland between licences granted to different types of establishment, such as public houses, hotels and restaurants; in England and Wales, because of different types of licence provided, they do not. Secondly, the exact number depends on the definition adopted: on whether public houses with a limited number of letting bedrooms are counted as public houses or as hotels, and to a lesser extent where the line is drawn between public houses with extensive catering facilities on the one hand, and restaurants on the other. Accordingly, the number of public houses has been variously quoted in different sources ranging between 62,000 and 73,000. If most units with bedroom accom-

[11] Amulree Report, p. 45.

modation are regarded as hotels, the number of public houses is at the lower end of this range; the higher the minimum bedroom capacity is set for the hotel sector of the industry, the higher the number of units remaining in the public house sector.

Clubs

Clubs, as a sector of the hotel and catering industry, comprise establishments providing food and drink (and sometimes also accommodation) to members and their guests. Club membership may be the only common ground between the users, but many have been established by and for persons associated together for the promotion of cultural, political, social or other objects, for members of sports clubs and for employees of firms.

We have seen that clubs owe their origin to the eighteenth-century coffee-houses, and more specifically to the desire of those who assembled in them to restrict admission. This exclusiveness is the chief characteristic of clubs, which distinguishes them from other establishments and makes it desirable to regard them as a separate sector of the industry: the relationship between a club member and the club premises is different, for example, from that which exists between a member of the public and the public house which he frequents.

The legal position with regard to the supply and consumption of liquor in clubs has evolved from the beginning of the century in a different way from that of licensed premises, and in the last decade in particular, differently between England and Wales on the one hand, and Scotland on the other. Only in England and Wales is there a licensed club operated as a business where the profit accrues to the owner who may be an individual or a company, operating one or more clubs; such establishments are proprietary clubs and require a justices' licence to operate. Common to the whole of Britain is a registered club, which is a non-profit-making organization belonging to members, and providing a service to members; such establishments are genuine members' clubs and require merely to be registered.

Within the legal framework outlined in the previous chapter the nature and characteristic of clubs vary considerably. They may be residential (with letting bedrooms), restaurants with entertainment, or merely bars; they range from those with substantial numbers employed to those in which the management and operation of the club are shared by members with no staff being employed. Their revenue normally consists of more than one element: some charge entrance fees to those becoming members, most levy subscriptions, and all derive the greater part of their income from supplying services to members.

Most of the English licensed clubs tend to resemble licensed restaurants, and a high proportion of their income is derived from the sale of meals; the sales mix of registered clubs approximates more closely to that of public houses in that a high proportion of their income is derived from the supply of drink.

The size of the club sector can be defined from the licensing statistics with some accuracy. The detailed annual statistics to 1975 are given in Appendix G and in Chapter 6. In 1975 there were 2,800 licensed clubs and 27,300 registered clubs in Britain. Both types of club have continued to increase in number.

Catering Contractors

The four industrial sectors described so far, hotels, restaurants, public houses and clubs, cover organizations whose main activity is in providing accommodation, food and drink. Substantial catering services are also provided in organizations whose main activity is in some other field, to which catering is ancillary. The principal fields where catering activities are provided as a service to some other main function of the organizations are:
- (a) employee catering, in manufacturing, commerce and other fields;
- (b) catering in education, in different forms and levels of the educational system;
- (c) hospital catering, for patients and staff;
- (d) institutional catering, in various other organizations;
- (e) transport catering, for passengers in transit;
- (f) services catering, for army, air force and navy personnel.

Most of these forms are provided both in the public and private sectors. They share certain characteristics in common: they are an ancillary activity to the main purpose of the organization, and are not provided by the main organization with a view to profit; meals and refreshments are largely supplied to particular groups of user and not to the general public.

Two main approaches may be discerned in providing catering services in these circumstances: under direct management, or under contract. In the former case, the parent organization operates the catering service under its own management (as one of its operating services), with its own personnel, employees of the parent organization. In the latter case, the parent organization contracts with a specialist catering organization for the provision of its catering services. For the organizations which run their own catering, it is an ancillary function; for the catering contractors catering is their main activity.

Those organizations which operate their own catering units as a service do so on a non-profit-making basis and, in fact, subsidize them to a varying extent. Catering contractors as firms operate on a profit-making basis. It is rare for them to work on a lump sum contract, the client paying an all-in figure and contractor deriving a profit from operating within the agreed price. The majority of contracts are 'cost plus', the client paying the contractor a fee for operating the catering service, in addition to paying the operating costs.

Direct management normally provides for a closer direct control and supervision by the parent organization, and for more flexibility in operation. The major reason for the employment of a catering contractor is to relieve the parent organization of an unfamiliar service, which enables it to concentrate on its main activity, and to draw on the contractor's wider resources in the approach to its own catering services.

Ancillary catering services may be, therefore, considered in one of two ways:

viewed one way, there are many organizations, which undertake catering as an activity ancillary to the main one; viewed another way, ancillary forms of catering are a distinctive activity serving a variety of other organizations. If viewed as the latter, they emerge as sectors of the hotel and catering industry.

However, in defining the scope of the hotel and catering industry, the Standard Industrial Classification 1968 draws a broad distinction between businesses whose main activity is in the hotel and catering industry, and includes ancillary forms of catering as a separate sector only if operated by contractors as defined on the lines adopted in this chapter. Employee catering services operated by industrial establishments themselves for their own employees, and other ancillary forms of catering operated directly by the parent organization, are classified with the main establishment and not as part of the hotel and catering industry.

The contract approach to providing catering services has appeared in a number of countries, and has been well established in Britain for several decades.[12] It is most prominent in employee catering but, particularly in recent years, it has entered into fields where it was either insignificant or non-existent before. The post-1918 experience in employee catering was not repeated after 1945; employee catering received support from managements as an integral part of staff welfare; the quality produced by expert management did much to make it attractive to the worker whose education and earnings were higher than a generation earlier. School meals and other welfare forms of catering also developed significantly in post-war Britain. Whilst few data exist to show the trends in contract catering, it is clear that until recently the sector has grown in a growing market.

As an indication of its importance in a field in which it is most important, i.e. in employee catering, the Catering Trades Inquiry of 1969 listed over 18,000 canteens, of which 4,000 were then operated by catering contractors.[13] This Inquiry also suggested that catering contractors operated the larger units. There are indications that the number of contractor-operated units has grown since then.

In its Report on industrial catering [14] the Commission of Industrial Relations estimated that there were about 24,560 establishments employing about 220,000 industrial or office catering employees in 1970. Of these, 18·4 per cent of catering units were run by catering contractors, employing almost 26 per cent of the labour force. In industrial catering alone, they were found to operate nearly 24 per cent of the units, and to employ 29 per cent of the labour force. These data

[12] For example, as early as 1942 the National Society of Caterers to Industry (the association of catering contractors operating canteens) formed with several trade unions a national joint industrial council for the voluntary negotiation of wages and conditions of employment. This arrangement was later superseded by the creation of statutory Wages Boards, and the association became a part of the Caterers Association of Great Britain, forming its Industrial and Staff Canteen Division in 1948. But the existence of a trade association indicates the developed state of contract catering in Britain at an early date.

[13] *See* Appendix A.

[14] Commission on Industrial Relations, *Report No. 27, The Hotel and Catering Industry*, Part 2, *Industrial Catering*, Chapter 2 and Appendix 2.

also reflect the tendency for contractors to operate the larger than average units, particularly in their main field of interest, in industrial catering. They are more prominent in the private than in the public sector.

A more comprehensive study[15] covering both welfare as well as industrial catering has estimated that in the early 1970s there were about 76,000 units in industrial and welfare catering activities. A breakdown of these is given in Table 19.

Table 19
Industrial and Welfare Catering – the Unit Structure
(number of units)

Sector		Public	Private	Total	Operated by Catering Contractors
Industrial catering	(1971)	5,000	20,000	25,000	4,500
Schools	(1972)	33,281	3,067	36,348	
Further and Higher Education	(1970)	1,134	—	1,134	
Hospitals	(1971)	2,760	150	2,910	500
Homes	(1971)	5,000	5,000	10,000	
Armed Forces	(1971)	450	—	450	
NAAFI	(1972)	338	—	338	
Penal establishments	(1972)	150	—	150	
Approximate Total		48,000	28,000	76,000	5,000

Source: Koudra, M.: Industrial and Welfare Catering 1970–1980, HCIMA Review.

Of these, it was estimated that 5,000 units or only 6–7 per cent of the industry total were run by catering contractors. More than 90 per cent of these contractors' units were concentrated in the industrial catering sector, where they represented almost one-fifth of all establishments. Another sector where contractors were relatively well represented was private schools where they probably operated up to 10 per cent of the units. Altogether, catering contractors controlled an estimated one-eighth of the labour force in industrial and welfare catering. The same study also highlights the degree of industrial concentration in contract catering. Of the total of 203 catering contractor organizations it estimates that 9 organizations (4–5 per cent of the total) accounted for 3,600 units, over 70 per cent of the industry total, and that four major firms accounted for over 60 per cent of the units and over half the employees. On the other hand it points out that the great majority of firms remained purely local concerns, restricted geographically to fairly small areas.

[15] Koudra, M., Industrial and Welfare Catering 1970–1980, HCIMA Review, Volume 1, Number 1:
    Koudra, M., Catering Contractors: A Study in Industrial Concentration, HCIMA Review, Volume 1, Number 2.

Table 20

Hotel and Catering Industry in Britain 1975
Principal Component Sectors[16]: Summary

Sector	Unit characteristics	Number of Units — Total	Number of Units — Including	Notes
Hotels	(a) sleeping accommodation supply (some food and service) (b) open to general public	34,000	14,000 licensed, 20,000 unlicensed	Estimated capacity: 500,000 bedrooms (excluding residential clubs)
Restaurants	(a) food consumed on premises (liquor, if any, ancillary) (b) open to general public	35,000	11,000 licensed, 5,000 fish and chip shops with consumption on the premises	Estimated number of restaurants, excluding fish and chip shops, 30,000, of which more than 1 in 3 is licensed
Public houses	(a) alcoholic liquor supply (food if any ancillary) (b) open to general public (c) licensed	62,000		Estimated numbers range from 62,000 to 73,000 according to whether any accommodation units are included; estimate given includes most units with letting accommodation under hotels
Clubs	(a) food and drink supply (sometimes also accommodation) (b) open to members and guests (c) licensed or registered	30,000+	2,800 licensed, 27,300 registered	No licensed clubs in Scotland
Catering Contractors	Normally (a) on other than own premises (b) ancillary service (to main purpose of business) (c) open to restricted groups	5,000	200 organizations	Sectors covered include employee catering, catering in education, hospital catering, other institutional, transport, armed services

[16] As defined by the Standard Industrial Classification (1968).

Part III
The Market

Additional Reading for Part III

British Tourist Authority: *Digest of Tourist Statistics* (annual).

Hotels and Catering EDC: *Hotel Prospects to 1985*, Research Findings, Chapter 3.

Hotels and Catering EDC: *Trends in Catering*, Quarterly and Annual Reports 1974/5, 1975/6, 1976/7.

Howley, M.: The Market for Wine in Hotels and Restaurants, *HCIMA Review*, Volume 1, Number 1.

Pickering, J. F., *et al.*: *The Small Firm in the Hotel and Catering Industry*, Chapter 1.

8. Market and Competition

The economist defines 'market' as a network of dealings in a particular product between buyers and sellers. The product may be a commodity or a service, and there are also markets in productive resources of labour, land and capital.

Some markets are more easily defined than others, and the heterogeneous nature of hotel and catering services presents particular problems of analysis. By many economic tests one activity of the industry often has little in common with another, and in no sense serves the same market: accommodation in a quality hotel and a drink in the 'local' are different products, satisfying different demand, which are supplied by different establishments.

There is thus in the first place a division of markets for hotel and catering services, according to products into three basic categories, corresponding to the three principal products – accommodation, food and drink. There is, within each of these three categories, a further sub-division according to the individual product sold, its standard and price, with corresponding groups of buyers and sellers of each. The infinite variation in individual products arises from the nature of the purchase: the customer is buying not only the room for the night, the food or the drink; his purchase includes the service and the use of the other physical facilities, and the atmosphere of the establishment – the environment. The three elements consitutute together a composite product, which may be accommodation, food or drink.

Individual composite products are not always supplied separately or in standard combinations by individual establishments, let alone by firms. Despite all the economic advantages of specialization, there are good reasons why hotel and catering firms and establishments often engage in more than one activity and why their combinations of activities vary even as between individual units. Similarly, buyers may exercise demand for particular combinations of products rather than an individual one.

Demand for hotel and catering services arises in particular locations, their supply is provided to meet the demand in those locations, and they are consumed at the place of production. Although improvements in means of transport, particularly the more widespread use of individual forms of transport (such as the motor car) widens each market, markets for hotel and catering services are local markets. Demand in a particular location is met by hotel and catering establishments supplying that particular location. This means that the total demand for a particular product or combination of products is split geographically, and so is the supply of that product or combination of products; the hotel and catering industry essentially supplies limited geographical areas, and thus separate spatial markets. Accommodation required for a particular night in a particular district can be only supplied by establishments in that district;

demand for meals and refreshments in a particular town can be met only by establishments in that town or near by.

Markets for hotel and catering services are, therefore, defined by reference to product on the one hand and by reference to buyers and sellers in a particular location on the other. Buyers exercise their demand for one or more products in one location only at a time, although they may exercise demand for the same or different products in other locations at different times. Each establishment is engaged in one or more markets in a particular location at a time; each firm may be engaged in one or more product markets in one or more locations at the same time. The whole industry supplies a multitude of separate markets, which are defined, more or less sharply, by product or products, and by location.

In such circumstances the most useful method of analysis of some aspects of the industry seems to be to consider hotel and catering services without relation to any particular type of firm or establishment; the observations then apply to any particular unit in proportion to the extent to which that particular unit shares the demand characteristics identified generally.

The Market: Entry and Exit

Demand for accommodation and for food and drink is considered separately in Chapters 9 and 10. At a particular time the total demand is made up in each case of a given number of buyers, each of whom has a given level of participation in the market. Demand changes as a result of changes in the number of those exercising demand for accommodation, food or drink, and in their level of purchases. In the former case, growth in the market occurs when those who did not previously exercise any demand for accommodation, food or drink, enter the market for the first time. The level of purchases increases when existing buyers require more accommodation, food or drink than they did before, or when they buy more expensive products than before, or as a combination of the two. Demand is made up of a large number of buyers, each of whom buys a very small proportion of the total output.

Supply changes occur in a similar way, through changes in the number of sellers, or through changes in their individual contributions to the market, or both. However, in any given market the total supply may be in the hands of one firm, several firms or many firms, and it is therefore necessary to consider first how supply may change through the entry and exit of individual firms.

When an entry takes place, a firm which did not operate in one or more of the markets for hotel and catering services before, initiates or extends its activities in the new field. An entry can, therefore, take place in one of two main ways – through the establishment of a completely new unit in the market, or through the extension of the activities of an existing unit. As a market has not only a product but also spatial dimensions, the latter form of entry can mean both product extension – as when an existing firm takes up new activities, or spatial extension – as is the case when an existing firm extends its activities into locations where it did not operate before.

Entry refers to the ease or difficulty with which a newcomer can become a member of a group of competitors by offering a close substitute for what the existing providers offer. In many industries' markets the obstacles encountered by a newcomer consist of combination of those which are inherent in the market in question, and those created by existing firms or by public authorities. An examination of the inherent and 'artificial' influences on entry into hotel and catering markets suggest that legal regulations create more important impediments to new entry than are created by factors inherent in the market structure or by existing firms.

Market Structure and Entry

The costs of building and equipping a new hotel are high, and the larger the unit, the higher are the capital requirements for entry. But new entry may take place through the purchase of an existing smaller hotel or through the conversion of existing private houses. In their study, *'The Holiday Industry of Devon and Cornwall'*, F.M.M. Lewes and his colleagues found that purchase prices of hotels in the two counties corresponded to a constant £3,000 plus £1,100 per bedroom: an hotel of twenty bedrooms would change hands for £25,000.[1] This study, and others, also showed that most new hotels were conversions of private houses, at relatively low capital cost as compared with building a new hotel. Capital requirements imposed, therefore, only a limited barrier to new entry on a small scale.

Restaurants and other catering units allow those with modest capital to establish their own businesses even more easily. The total cost of new entry for a quality restaurant may be in the region of £60–£80,000, but the initial capital outlay may be reduced by renting the premises, rather than acquiring them by outright purchase, equipment may be hired, and, particularly with licensed premises, breweries are often prepared to assist new entrants with loans on favourable terms. New entry is also achieved relatively easily by taking out a franchise of a restaurant, offering a standardized, nationally-known brand product to the newcomer.

A prospective entrepreneur will next consider the performance of existing firms, and will decide to enter the market if his expected achievements compare with the existing firms in general, or with a specific firm such as the representative or the marginal firm. In this respect no universal disadvantages appear to exist to the detriment of the new firm, except those which may result from entrepreneurial skill, unless the market is already saturated with efficient operations. A greater demand for productive resources and the greater supply of services may lead in some markets to an increase in factor prices, for instance of labour, and a reduction in prices to the customer. But it is likely that these price reactions will affect all firms, if they take place. The new firm may be at a disadvantage compared with the situation in which the existing firms found themselves prior to the entry of the new firm, but it is not necessarily going to be affected by these price reactions any more than the existing firms.

[1] Lewes, F. M. M., *et al.*, *The Holiday Industry of Devon and Cornwall*, p. 81.

A discriminatory position may arise in markets in which one or more firms have succeeded in creating for themselves strong goodwill prior to the entry of the new firm. In such circumstances, particularly where the market and the number of competing firms are small, the new firm may be at a disadvantage, and may have to offer high inducements both to the customer and in bidding for labour, actions which may incur extra costs and leave the newcomer with a smaller profit than the established firms. Here we encounter an imperfection in the market, which may be reinforced by customers' inertia and lack of information. The height of the barrier to entry as represented by the price reactions caused by the entry thus depends on the degree of imperfection existing in any one market; the different market situations are discussed later in this chapter.

'Tying' agreements of great intensity exist in alcoholic liquor distribution between brewery firms and retailers, and the question arises whether such arrangements create obstacles to new entry. It must be borne in mind, first, that such arrangements are not collective, i.e. that they are not concluded between two organizations, each representing groups of firms, but individual, which means that the partners to the agreements are individual firms. Secondly, the arrangements vary from complete vertical integration on the basis of ownership, to looser supply agreements with the 'free' trade, as with a minority of licensed houses and with clubs. Whether these contracts imply a real discrimination against new firms or not must depend on the ability of a newcomer to secure supplies on terms not less favourable than those of existing firms. An examination of the supply arrangements suggests that this is, in fact, the case.

The lease or tenancy agreement between the brewery and the tenant, which sometimes provides for a part of his rent to be paid in his supply price, does not appear to constitute a discrimination against a newcomer. Under this arrangement the tenant pays a very low fixed rent for his premises, usually much below the market rate, and is charged a slightly higher price for his beer than is charged to the 'free' trade; this difference in price is termed the 'wet' rent. The combination of a fixed and a fluctuating wet rent, rising or falling with the volume of trade done, has the advantage to the tenant that his outgoings are adjusted to the fluctuations of his turnover. But since supplies are available to those outside these agreements even at a lower price where beer is concerned, and at the same price in the case of other commodities, this aspect of the 'tie' does not constitute an obstacle to entry. Neither do the other arrangements into which a newcomer may usually enter side by side with existing firms, if he wishes to do so.

Market Structure and Exit

Exit refers to the ease, or difficulty, with which an existing firm may discontinue or reduce its activities in a particular market. An exit can, therefore, also take place in one of two main ways – through the closure or sale of an existing unit, or through the reduction of the range of products offered to a particular market. The spatial dimension of a market implies that exit may mean a withdrawal of a firm from a particular market, or a discontinuation of some or all of its activities in more than one market where it operated before.

There is a significant rate of exit from all markets for hotel and catering services, from the sale of premises to be used for the same purpose, from changes of user, and from closures. There is an active market in hotels. A purpose-built hotel is not easy to convert to other uses, but scope does exist for the use of hotels as conference and training centres, hostels, nursing homes, flats, offices, etc. Restaurants experience even more frequent changes of ownership, and restaurant premises are even more easily adapted to other uses, particularly for other retail outlets. Altogether, the catering sector, as distinct from the accommodation sector, displays considerable volatility; not only is it very responsive to demand, but the ease of entry and exit make for a higher degree of change in the market, with probably several thousand new units opening, and a similar number closing down, each year.

There is also a marked difference in business failure between accommodation and catering units, as reflected in the number of bankruptcies recorded annually by the Department of Trade (formerly the Board of Trade): in 1975 there were forty-two receiving orders and three deeds of arrangement for hotels and boarding houses, but 243 receiving orders and three deeds of arrangement for restaurants, cafés, public houses and clubs.[2]

Entry and Existing Firms

When conditions of entry are examined, it is important to decide whether existing firms take any steps in response to entry, or whether they take any measures in order to prevent entry from taking place. There appears to be no evidence that existing firms give much consideration to the threat of new entry, for example, in formulating their price policies, or in advance planning of their activities generally. It is usually accepted that the larger the profit, the greater the likelihood of entry, but there does not seem to be any restraint on the part of hotel and catering firms stemming from the desire not to attract new competitors. Although a restraining influence of this sort would not in itself restrict entry, it could be used at least not to encourage entry, but there is no evidence of attempts in this direction on the part of hotel and catering firms. Neither do firms try to erect barriers to entry by artificially enhancing the capital requirements of a new firm by, for instance, incurring large expenditure on sales promotion, which would have to be matched by the new firm in order to secure a share of the market.

The response of existing firms to a new firm, once the entry has taken place, appears to be equally passive. Trade associations, which are discussed in Chapter 18, accept new firms as members on the same terms as existing firms. Not only are they not parties to price fixing arrangements, but they usually refuse to take any steps which would in any other way restrict their members' freedom in the

---

[2] Department of Trade, *Bankruptcy, General Annual Report for the year 1975*, p. 11.

conduct of their business. Hence there is no discriminatory obstacle placed in the way of new entry by trade association insistence on the acceptance of certain conditions by new firms.

In spite of the absence of steps to prevent new entry, or to retaliate against one on the part of existing firms in the above ways, which are sometimes adopted in other industries, it would be misleading to suppose that existing firms place no obstacles in the way of intending entrants into the British hotel and catering industry. Public regulations affecting entry, which exist in Britain under statutory authority, allow a large measure of influence to be exercised both by private individuals and corporate bodies in any individual case, and it is clear that existing firms take advantage of the facilities provided to oppose a new entry. These steps, taken by existing firms, are discussed next, in conjunction with public regulations affecting entry.

Statutory Regulation Governing Entry

The State influences the entry into industry in numerous ways and with several different motives. It is outside the scope of the present study to provide a comprehensive account of all the relevant laws and regulations; the intention is rather to state the principal ways in which public authorities influence entry into hotel and catering markets. This happens in two principal ways, one being common to all industries, and the other specific to the licensed sector.

Town and Country Planning legislation gives the State the development rights in land and thus, *inter alia*, control over building operations, and over changes in the existing use of land and buildings. The planning provisions of the Acts are administered for their respective areas by district councils, and include a requirement for obtaining planning permission for all development not specifically exempted. This legislation, whilst not discriminating specifically against hotel and catering firms or any other industry, nevertheless frequently creates a barrier against new entry in individual cases and locations when planning permission for building operations or change of user is refused. Since the Acts came into operation, numerous intending entrepreneurs have not only been forced to alter their proposed plans for development, but also to abondon them entirely; in this sense, the State has effectively influenced entry into the industry. The Acts provide for inquiries to take place under the direction of the Secretary of State for the Environment, at which evidence may be given by parties interested in the proposed development. And this is one instance where existing firms, individually or through their trade associations, have on occasions openly voiced their objections to new entry into the industry. The effects of Town and Country Planning legislation are reinforced by Development Area and related legislation, which provide inducements to firms to set up and expand in areas of high unemployment, and which has also from time to time been used to restrain expansion in places where it would lead to excessive pressure on resources.

Effect of Licensing Legislation

By far the most far-reaching legal restriction on entry with regard to the hotel and catering industry exists in alcoholic liquor distribution, where the licensing system described previously creates a barrier against the entry of new firms into the market, and against the extension of existing firms' outlets. The grant of an operating licence as a pre-requisite for entry into the liquor trade has been considered desirable in most countries, with a view to controlling liquor consumption. The system operates by restricting the number of outlets, although no limitation is imposed on the volume of each firm's trade. In Britain the ultimate control is in the hands of local magistrates, whose main considerations are the need for a new outlet, the suitability of the person applying for a licence, and the structural suitability of the premises for which a licence is desired. The first of these criteria, the 'public need' is a nebulous and ill-defined concept. A new licence is often granted only because of the exit of an old firm, or because the growth of the market makes an additional outlet desirable. The magistrates' discretion is absolute, and decentralized administration does not make for uniformity. Thus the height of the barrier to entry as represented by the requirement for a liquor licence is subject to wide local variation.

In England and Wales any member of the local community may oppose the grant of a new licence on public or private grounds; in Scotland the competent objectors to the grant of a new licence are owners or occupiers of property in the neighbourhood or their agents – a community council, an organized church representing a significant body of opinion in the neighbourhood, and the chief constable. Thus the procedure for the hearing of applications provides a greater opportunity for existing firms in England and Wales to create obstacles to new entry than is the case in Scotland. Until recently another form of control existed in Scotland in the local veto system, which allowed the future licensing arrangements in their area to be decided by a poll of electors; however, this was abolished by the Licensing (Scotland) Act 1976.

The Licensing Act 1961 relaxed the law relating to licensed premises in England and Wales by introducing three new forms of licence, which may be refused only on specified grounds, and the 1962 Scottish Licensing Act took a similar step by introducing two new types of licence for hotels and restaurants.

The most thorough restriction on entry, which amounted in practice to an absolute prohibition, existed in the State Management Districts. These districts constituted a local state monopoly in liquor distribution, and no intending entrepreneur could enter the market in liquor in them. However, State Management Districts were abolished in 1971.

There is, however, one potent exception to the above public control of liquor distribution – the registered club, which enables an entry into the market to take place without the necessity for obtaining a magistrates' licence. The only discriminatory element in the case of clubs – the requirement for registration –

cannot be considered as an obstacle to new entry in England and Wales, as a club which submits a return in the prescribed form *must* be registered. But in Scotland registration is discretionary, as objections to registration may be raised.

The Nature of Competition

The economist distinguishes between three main types of market, classified according to the prevailing competitive conditions: perfect competition, imperfect competition and monopoly. The distinction is based on two main criteria – the number of sellers, and the nature of the product.

Perfect competition implies a large number of sellers, each of whom provides only a small fraction of the total supply of the product, and homogeneity of the product – each firm supplies a product, identical with the products of all the other firms for which it is a perfect substitute – so that buyers can have no preference between products of different firms.

In *imperfect competition* one of the two criteria, or both, departs from the requirement of perfect competition. When the number of sellers is large, but product differentiation takes place through, for example, branding and advertising – so that each product is no longer a perfect substitute in the eyes of the buyer – the situation is known as monopolistic competition.

When there are only a few sellers in the market, it is known as oligopoly. If the products are homogeneous – each a perfect substitute for the others – the oligopoly is described as perfect; if the product is differentiated, it is imperfect oligopoly.

Monopoly exists when the whole supply of a single product, for which there is no substitute, is in the hands of one seller.

Few markets in hotel and catering services even approach perfect competition. A few hundred boarding houses in a large seaside resort may offer very similar amenities and services and charge very similar prices. They are far from identical, but for customers who have not been there before, and who make their bookings from a distance well in advance, the market does resemble perfect competition, if a broad enough interpretation is put on the criteria which have to be met; the same does not hold in relation to customers with a knowledge of the products.

The local character of hotel and catering markets makes the other extreme market situation – monopoly – more common than is the case with products which can be transported. An hotel, restaurant or a public house which is the only hotel, restaurant or public house within a wide geographical area, enjoys a monopoly market. Other captive market situations suggest themselves. A monopolistic market is a secure market, not affected by other firms, with a complete control over the supply of a product or a combination of products but not over demand: the firm can either fix the price and let demand decide the volume of sales or, as is more likely for an establishment with a fixed capacity, decide how much is to be sold and let demand determine the price at which it will be sold.

But the great majority of markets for hotel and catering services lie between the two extremes of perfect competition and monopoly – in imperfect competition. One of the three types of imperfect competition, perfect oligopoly, is the least likely to occur. Only with a very broad interpretation of the term could one identify markets for hotel and catering services in which an identical product, or a combination of products, is offered by several firms. But it is clear that there are very many local markets, in which the accommodation or the food or the drink, as composite products, though not identical are yet sufficiently similar to be in competition with each other. This suggests that most hotel and catering firms operate in conditions of imperfect oligopoly, or of monopolistic competition, according to the number of sellers in the particular markets.

The accommodation and catering markets in all but the largest cities fit the description of an imperfect oligopoly. A few hotels control most of the accommodation capacity of the location, and a number of others share the remainder. The anti-trust legislation in the United States was recognized to apply to local hotel markets, and, for example, the Hilton Corporation agreed to divest itself of a number of hotels acquired in the Hilton merger with Statler, under a consent decree in the 1950s. An oligopolistic market is also fairly common in the case of restaurants and public houses. No two restaurants or public houses in the same location offer identical composite products. But their shares of the market often suggest an imperfect oligopoly, as is the case with many accommodation markets in which similar prices are charged for similar products. Moreover, whilst most markets are easy to enter in a small way, the same does not apply to the same degree to large hotels or to public houses.

The second main type of market for hotel and catering services is monopolistic competition, which differs from oligopoly in the number of sellers, and from perfect competition in product differentiation. If it is borne in mind that hotel and catering services constitute composite products, in the last analysis, no two products are identical. Where the markets are large enough, many similar hotels, restaurants and other units are in competition with many others, offering similar services at similar prices, as is the case in large cities and resorts.

In both cases of imperfect competition, covering the great majority of markets in hotel and catering services, competition does not find an expression in price competition alone. In fact, there is much evidence that in many markets price does not rank high in determining the choice of an hotel or restaurant; several other forms of competition may be more important.

A common competitive factor is the actual situation of a unit in a given location; proximity to the city centre, to a given attraction such as a beach or a historical monument, or to an airport terminus may be important. Another is the actual sales mix of a given establishment, the range of amenities and services available, and the second and third components of the composite product – the type and standard of service and the environment. Thirdly, the most successful products are normally easy to buy. The reservation services of hotels constitute a competitive convenience, as do credit arrangements, enabling customers to settle hotel and restaurant bills without the payment of cash.

The competitive nature of the markets in hotel and catering services can be, therefore, seen in the context of each individual market in terms of industry concentration, and in terms of the product. Because of the nature of each market, competition takes the form of both price – and non-price competition. The former may be important in some markets, and in competition with other industries and activities, such as camping, caravanning and holiday flatlets, in which the buyer pays himself for the product; price may limit the market of the industry. But within the industry, particularly when purchases are paid by a third party, pricing may be the less important form of competition in imperfect markets; other factors may assume greater prominence.[3]

[3] Powers, T. F., *The Competitive Structure of the Hotel/Motel Market*, A paper to the Council on Hotel, Restaurant and Institutional Education, 1969.

Table 21
Markets for Hotel and Catering Services

			Sellers	*Product*
Perfect competition			Many	Homogeneous
Imperfect competition	Monopolistic competition		Many	Differentiated
	Oligopoly	Perfect	Few	Homogeneous
		Imperfect	Few	Differentiated
Monopoly			One	No substitute

9. Demand for Accommodation

Demand for accommodation away from home is a function of travel, or more precisely, travel away from home giving rise to overnight stay. In any highly industrialized and complex economic system, both the desire and the necessity for travel, involving overnight stay, are great.

The total demand for accommodation away from home lends itself to a twofold classification. First, there is a broad distinction between holiday and business travel. In most developed countries a substantial proportion of the population exercises demand for overnight accommodation when on holiday, in their own country or abroad. Hotels, guest houses, boarding houses and other accommodation units in large areas of Britain and elsewhere owe their existence to holiday makers, and from them they derive all or most of their income. The second source of demand for accommodation is business travel. Transactions of business, conferences, exhibitions, cultural, political and social meetings, and group and individual travel for a variety of reasons other than holiday, all these create demand for accommodation in locations with few or no holiday attractions, as well as adding to the demand in holiday resorts.

The distinction between holiday and business demand cannot be drawn very sharply. Many visits to destinations away from one's normal place of residence or work may have more than one purpose, and it is sometimes difficult to identify a main one. Business trips and attendances at conferences are sometimes combined with holidays, and increasing numbers participate in active holidays, when the difference between a person's normal occupational and holiday activity is a matter of degree or is blurred altogether. Many surveys of visitor traffic do not differentiate between the two; sometimes because it is technically difficult to do so, sometimes because the distinction has no relevance. But the basic distinction remains and it influences where the demand is exercised, as well as the type of facilities needed to meet it.

The second classification arises from the difference between domestic and international travel. In the former case people travel within their own country; in the latter to a country other than that in which they normally live, and which is a separate national unit with its own political and economic system and often language. To a greater or lesser extent, various obstacles may be put in their way to do so by the authorities. When different currencies are involved, travel and the demand for accommodation have repercussions on the balance of payments. By contrast, domestic travel normally meets neither language, documentation nor currency barriers, and there are no balance of payments implications (except to the extent that it may be a substitute for foreign travel and, therefore, result in a saving of expenditure for the country of residence, and a reduction of income for countries which would have been visited). The distinction between the demand for accommodation generated by the residents of a country and by foreign visitors is one of domestic or home markets, on the one hand, and foreign markets on the other.

In this chapter British residents and overseas visitors to Britain are considered as sources of demand for accommodation, and in both cases the demand is divided into non-business and business demand.

British Holidays

It has been estimated that in 1937 about 15 million people, or about one-third of the British population, took some holidays away from home. In the 1950s the numbers increased from about 23 to about 30 million, i.e. from about 45 per cent to about 60 per cent of the population. In the 1960s, the numbers taking an annual holiday remained at the same level and most of the growth was in second holidays, rather than in the proportion of the population taking any holiday at all, and a growing number of holidays were taken abroad. A sharp rise in holidays in 1970 was also due to an increase in additional holidays while a decrease in holidays in 1974 was, in part, due to a decrease in additional holidays.

Holidays taken by the population of Britain are recorded in two national surveys. The first, the British National Travel Survey, was started in 1951 and covers holidays of four nights or more away from home. It identifies two types of holiday: main holidays and additional holidays. When only one holiday is taken during the year, this is the main holiday. When two or more holidays are taken, the main holiday is the longest or, if there are two or more holidays of equal length, the one in or nearest to the peak summer period. The second survey is the British Home Tourism Survey, which was started in 1972 and covers all holidays of one night or more away from home in addition to travel for other purposes. The volume and value of the British residents' holidays is summarized in Tables 22*a*, *b*, *c* and *d*.

In 1975 40 million holidays of four nights or more and 31 million holidays of between one and three nights were taken in Britain by the British population. Together, these accounted for about 550 million nights spent away from home. During the three years 1973, 1974 and 1975, holidays of four or more nights remained at a fairly constant level. All holidays, on the other hand, declined considerably between 1973 and 1974 which indicates, the fall-off in shorter holidays between these years. Additional holidays declined over the same period, too, and there was also a reduction in the number of holidays taken abroad.

An indication of the type of accommodation used on holidays in Britain was available from the British National Travel Survey until 1971 and is available from the British Home Tourism Survey for 1972 and after. Over the twenty years 1951 to 1971 significant long-term changes took place in accommodation use on main holidays. The proportion of main holidays spent in friends' and relatives' homes declined from over one-third in 1951 to about a quarter;

stay in guest houses and boarding houses declined from almost one-third to less than one-fifth; the popularity of informal and self-catering accommodation increased from less than one-fifth to over one-third. Similar trends were

Table 22a

British Residents' Holidays of Four or More Nights Away from Home
1951, 1955, 1965–1975
(million)

	1951	1955	1965	1966	1967	1968	1969	1970	1971	1972	1973	1974	1975
In Britain	25	25	30	31	30	30	30·5	34·5	34	37·5	40·5	40·5	40
Abroad	1·5	2	5	5·5	5	5	5·75	5·75	7·25	8·5	8·25	6·75	8
Total	26·5	27	35	36·5	35	35	36·25	40·25	41·25	46	48·75	47·75	48

Source: British National Travel Survey.

Table 22b

British Residents' Expenditure[a] on Holidays of Four or More Nights Away
from Home 1951, 1955, 1965–1975
(£ million)

	1951[b]	1955	1965	1966[c]	1967	1968	1969	1970	1971	1972	1973	1974	1975
In Britain	320	365	460	550	560	570	600	790	810	920	n.a.	1,100	1,270
Abroad	60	100	265	320	300	320	390	470	630	830	870	740	1,080
Total	380	465	725	870	860	890	990	1,260	1,440	1,750	n.a.	1,840	2,350

Source: British National Travel Survey.

Table 22c

British Residents' Holidays of One or More Nights Away from Home
1972–1975
(million)

	1972	1973	1974	1975
In Britain	83	85	70	71
Abroad	9	8	8	9
Total	92	93	78	80

Source: British Home Tourism Survey.

[a] Holiday expenditure includes the cost of travel to and from the holiday.
[b] 1951 figures include expenditure on day trips.
[c] Figures from 1966 onwards represent a new series.
n.a. Not available.

Table 22d
British Residents' Expenditure[a] on Holidays of One or More Nights Away from Home 1972–1975
(£ million)

	1972	1973	1974	1975
In Britain	1,000	1,075	1,300	1,550
Abroad	629	611	722	909
Total	1,629	1,686	2,022	2,459

Source: British Home Tourism Survey.

[a] Holiday expenditure includes the cost of travel to and from the holiday.

evident for additional holidays, which were first covered after 1965, except that the largest and growing proportion was spent in friends' and relatives' homes and that self-catering accommodation was less significant. Since 1972, as illustrated in Table 23, the most significant trends in all holidays have been the increase in the proportion of all holidays spent in self-catering accommodation and the decrease in the use of accommodation of friends and relatives. The table

Table 23
Accommodation Used on Holidays in Britain 1972–1975
(percentages)

Type of Accommodation	*Holidays of One or More Nights*			
	1972[a]	1973	1974	1975
Licensed hotel	11	9	11	12
Unlicensed hotel or guest house	10	8	9	9
Holiday camp	3	4	5	5
Total hotel & catering industry	24	21	25	26
Camping	5	5	7	5
Caravan	14	17	20	20
Rented accommodation	6	6	8	6
Paying guest	1	2	2	2
With friend or relative	50	48	44	45
Other	3	4	3	4
Total[b]	103	103	109	108

Source: British Home Tourism Survey.

[a] Adults over 16 only.
[b] Some used more than one type of accommodation.

also shows that the hotel and catering industry is only a minor provider of accommodation for holidays in Britain, although its share has increased in recent years. Estimates of the demand for accommodation in terms of numbers of bednights are provided by the British Home Tourism Survey. These are illustrated in Table 23, which shows that even if holiday camp accommodation is included with the hotel and catering industry, only about one-quarter of the total demand for holiday accommodation is met by the industry.

Domestic Business Demand

The second main component of domestic demand for accommodation is business and conference demand. In contrast to holiday demand, no assessment of business demand was attempted until the end of the 1960s, when the Hotel and Catering Economic Development Committee commissioned a study of the use of British hotels for business and conference purposes,[1] and when Sir George Young made a similar assessment in his study of 'Accommodation Services in Britain 1970–1980'. Since then further studies have been undertaken by the Hotels and Catering Economic Development Committee, which have included an assessment of business and conference demand,[2] and the British Home Tourism Survey has covered business and conference tourism in Britain since 1972.

The business demand is largely made up of a relatively small number of travellers making frequent journeys of short duration. The first study, to which reference has been made above, estimated that the average business traveller made twenty-nine journeys annually of an average duration of three days. According to the British Home Tourism Survey, there were 17 million business and conference trips by British residents in Britain in 1975, which accounted for 45 million nights spent away from home. Of all such trips between 5 and 10 per cent were to conferences or conventions.

Domestic business demand is mostly determined by the level of economic activity, the location of industry and occupational structure. In particular, those employed in executive positions, and in the provision of professional services, generate demand for quality hotel accommodation; in contrast to domestic holiday demand, met by a wide range of accommodation facilities, business and conference demand is largely confined to hotels.

The estimated business and conference demand for accommodation for 1975 is shown in Table 24.

Total Domestic Demand

In 1975, total domestic demand for accommodation was in the region of 550 million bednights. This compares with about 605 million bednights in 1972. Nearly 80 per cent of the bednights in 1975 were accounted for by holiday

[1] Hotel and Catering EDC: *Hotels and the Business Traveller*
[2] Hotels and Catering EDC: *Hotel Prospects to 1980* and *Hotel Prospects to 1985*

demand. Business and conference demand accounted for about eight per cent and about thirteen per cent were accounted for by other demand. Other demand here mainly consists of those visits to friends and relatives, which are not also considered to be a holiday. The decline in demand between 1972 and 1975 was mainly due to a decline in holidays; business and conference demand had remained stable over the period.

The hotel and catering industry meets only about a quarter of this total demand. It is, however, by far the most important provider of business accommodation.

Having regard to the nature of many of the estimates of domestic travel and of the resulting demand for accommodation, the demand pattern for accommodation described above and shown in Table 24 is merely tentative. However, it does provide a broad indication of the order of magnitude of the total domestic market for accommodation, of its composition, and of the share taken by the hotel and catering industry.

Table 24

Demand for Accommodation in Britain by British Residents 1975
(million bednights)

Type of Accommodation	Holiday	Business & Conference	Other	Total[b]
Licensed hotel	44	20	—	62
Unlicensed hotel or guest house	35	9	—	45
Holiday camp	26	—	—	28
Total hotel & catering industry	105	29	—	135
Camping	22	—	—	22
Caravan	88	—	7	95
Rented accommodation	40	—	5	45
Paying guest	9	2	—	11
With friend or relative	153	5	61	219
Other	13	10	2	22
Total[a][b]	430	45	75	550

Source: Based on British Home Tourism Survey.

[a] Some used more than one type of accommodation.
[b] Totals may not agree due to rounding.
Note: These are approximate figures which are intended to give orders of magnitude.

Overseas Visitors to Britain

Almost half-a-million overseas visitors came to Britain in 1937, the peak pre-war year for tourist arrivals. This year is included for comparison with post-war years in Appendix C. In 1948 overseas visitors to Britain exceeded half-a-million, in 1955 one million, in 1963 two million and in 1968 four million. In 1963, US visitors alone reached half-a-million, and exceeded the number of Commonwealth visitors for the first time. The volume of overseas tourist traffic to Britain between 1969 and 1975 based on the International Passenger Survey is shown in Table 25.

Between 1969 and 1975 the total number of overseas visitors increased by more than one-half; there was a particularly rapid growth after 1974 and in 1976 the number of arrivals reached 10 million; the average length of stay fell continuously throughout the period. However, the total number of nights continued to rise, the declining length of stay having been more than offset by the growth in numbers.

This simple outline conceals wide differences between separate elements of the overseas visitor traffic to Britain. United States visitors account for almost one-sixth of it, but Britain is usually only one of a number of European countries visited by Americans on their trip which may last several weeks and cover several countries. After nearly two decades of continuous growth, United States visitors to Britain declined between 1972 and 1974; growth revived in 1975. The average length of stay of United States visitors is less than twelve days, and the demand for accommodation less than one-seventh of the total overseas visitor nights in the country.

If visitors from the Irish Republic are included, Western Europe accounts for over 60 per cent of all arrivals in Britain. Most of the European traffic comes from countries nearest to Britain; the countries of the European Economic Community account for nearly 50 per cent of all arrivals. Unlike visitors from North America, Western European visitors have continued to increase in numbers and have expanded their share of the market. The average length of stay of visitors from EEC countries is 9·5 nights and from the rest of Western Europe 13·5 nights. The demand for accommodation approaches one-half of the total visitor nights in the country.

Commonwealth traffic is fostered by strong links between the various parts and Britain. Australia and New Zealand and Canada alone represent nearly 10 per cent of the total visitors. Family, cultural and other ties are reflected in the length of stay of Commonwealth visitors. Visitors from more distant parts, such as Australia and New Zealand, stay, on average, well over a month; Canadian visitors tend to resemble Americans in some respects, but even their length of stay is over two and a half weeks. Demand for accommodation from Australia, New Zealand and Canada approaches 20 per cent of the total overseas nights in Britain.

The remaining overseas visitors are a heterogeneous group which accounts for less than 15 per cent of total arrivals in Britain. They come largely from distant countries, the average length of stay approaches three weeks and thus generates a residuary demand for accommodation of the order of 15 per cent of the total overseas visitor nights in the country.

Table 25
Overseas Visitors to Britain 1969–1975
Visits, Length of Stay, Tourist Nights

Visits (000)	1969	1970	1971	1972	1973	1974	1975
United States	1,295	1,567	1,637	1,695	1,576	1,342	1,350
Canada	361	408	437	468	483	413	467
North America	1,656	1,975	2,074	2,163	2,059	1,755	1,817
Western Europe–ECC	1,994	2,308	2,423	2,465	2,879	3,141	3,599
Western Europe–Non EEC	594	707	736	785	851	950	1,128
Irish Republic	764	743	721	651	727	729	704
Australia and New Zealand	125	155	179	231	243	319	363
Other	688	804	840	872	965	1,059	1,233
Total	5,821	6,692	6,973	7,167	7,724	7,953	8,844
Average length of stay (nights)	15·5	14·9	14·7	14·6	14·3	13·9	13·6
Total nights (million)	90·3	100·1	102·3	104·8	109·7	110·9	119·9

Source: International Passenger Survey.

Table 26
Demand for Accommodation in Britain by Overseas Visitors[a] 1975
(million bednights)

Type of Accommodation	Non-business	Business	Total[b]
'Hotel' sector [c]	26·2	6·9	33·1
Camping	2·0	—	2·0
Towed/motor caravans	·5	—	·6
Private homes (non-commercial)	54·5	2·4	56·9
Other[d]	18·2	2·5	20·6
Total[b]	101·5	11·8	113·2

Source: International Passenger Survey 1975 Accommodation Analyses.

[a] Excludes residents of the Irish Republic.
[b] Totals may not agree due to rounding.
[c] Includes hotels, guest houses, bed and breakfast and all other kinds of commercial establishment where visitors have to pay (usually fixed rates) for their accommodation.
[d] Includes fixed caravans, boats, leased or rented houses, flats, villas, etc., as well as unknown accommodation used.

Table 27
Demand for Accommodation in Britain 1975[a]
(million bednights)

Type of Accommodation	Domestic Non-business	Domestic Business	Domestic Total[b]	Overseas Non-business	Overseas Business	Overseas Total[b]	Total[b] Non-business	Total[b] Business	Total[b]
Licensed hotel	44	20	62	n.a.	n.a.	n.a.	n.a.	n.a.	n.a.
Unlicensed hotel/guest house	35	9	45	n.a.	n.a.	n.a.	n.a.	n.a.	n.a.
Holiday camp	26	—	28	n.a.	n.a.	n.a.	n.a.	n.a.	n.a.
Total hotel and catering industry	105	29	135	26	7	33	131	36	168
Other	400	17	414	76	5	81	476	22	495
Total[b]	505	45	550	102	12	113	607	57	663

Source: Based on British Home Tourism Survey 1975 and International Passenger Survey 1975, Accommodation Analyses.

[a] Excludes residents of the Irish Republic.
[b] Totals may not agree due to rounding and estimation.
n.a. Not available.

Note: These are approximate figures which are intended to give orders of magnitude.

The total overseas visitor demand for accommodation in Britain is nearly 120 million nights, or about 113 million nights if visitors from the Irish Republic are excluded. This latter figure forms the basis for estimates of the distribution of the demand between non-business and business demand and between different types of accommodation in analyses commissioned by the British Tourist Authority and the National Tourist Boards. These analyses (Table 26) show that demand by non-business visitors accounted for nearly 90 per cent of overseas visitor demand, and that nearly 30 per cent of the demand by overseas visitors was for accommodation in the hotel sector. Approaching 60 per cent of business visitor nights and over 25 per cent of non-business visitor nights were in the hotel sector.

Demand for Accommodation in Britain

The separate estimates of domestic and overseas demand, for travel away from home, whether for holiday or for other purposes, provide an indication of the total pattern of demand for accommodation in 1975. This is summarized in Table 27, which shows that approximately 25 per cent of the total demand of over 650 million nights was for accommodation provided by the hotel and catering industry.

It is difficult to estimate the value of the accommodation market with any degree of precision. Estimates of consumers' expenditure may be obtained from the National Income Blue Book. Unfortunately expenditure on accommodation is not identified here separately but is included with expenditure on meals away from home under the heading 'catering'. Consumers' expenditure on both meals and accommodation is shown in Table 28 and expenditure on food and eating out is discussed further in Chapter 10.

Over the ten years from 1966, consumers' expenditure on meals and accommodation more than doubled at current prices. As a percentage of total consumers' expenditure it declined from over 5 per cent in 1966 to 4·5 per cent in 1975.

Table 28

Consumers' Expenditure on Meals and Accommodation 1966–1975
(£ million at current prices)

	1966	1967	1968	1969	1970	1971	1972	1973	1974	1975
Catering (meals and accommodation)	1,250	1,275	1,346	1,427	1,568	1,700	1,892	2,153	2,452	2,832
+/− % over previous year		2·0	5·6	6·0	9·9	8·4	11·3	13·8	13·9	15·9
Total consumers' expenditure	24,211	25,428	27,338	29,102	31,644	35,165	39,716	45,044	51,832	63,673
Catering as % of consumers' expenditure	5·2	5·0	4·9	4·9	5·0	4·8	4·8	4·8	4·7	4·5

Source: National Income and Expenditure 1975.

10. Demand for Food and Drink

The demand for meals and refreshments outside the home lends itself to a two-fold classification. The first type – the demand exercised in conjunction with overnight stay – has existed since the early days of travel, and has continued in importance into modern times. Only for a limited early period did the traveller have to bring his own food to places where he stayed the night; soon most establishments extended their hospitality to cater for this and other wants. The second type of demand – for meals and refreshments only – developed differently as between food and drink. Ale-houses existed to serve local populations in very early times; but eating-out, separate from overnight stay, did not come into existence on any scale until increasing urbanization took place, and may be viewed on the one hand as the transfer of the eating function outside the home, and as the separation of the eating and accommodation functions on the other hand. As such this demand was met first in taverns, and later in restaurants.

We might expect that the first type of demand would bear a direct relationship to the volume of demand for accommodation, and that increased travel would bring about an increase in demand for the catering services of hotels and other accommodation units. However, this relationship does not necessarily constitute a joint demand in the economic sense in any one establishment. The hotel resident, for instance, may have his meals in the same place where he sleeps, but he may feed elsewhere, as can be seen in many empty hotel dining-rooms, even when the bed occupancy is at a high level. But a high degree of correlation is likely to exist between the total volume of travel, and the total demand for meals and refreshments outside the home. Moreover, many travellers, particularly when on holiday, who may not use the accommodation facilities of the industry, tend to use its catering facilities. They constitute a component of the second type of demand, which is only partly influenced by the volume of travel.

Another two-fold classification may be made when eating-out is considered. First, as a pleasure activity, as part of entertainment, as a particular use of leisure time. Secondly, as a substitute domestic activity when, for example at work, at school or in a hospital. The former is met mainly but not exclusively by hotel and other commercial restaurants, the latter by various forms of welfare catering as well as by commercial establishments.

Growth of Eating-out

The growth of large-scale food consumption outside the home, which the British caterer has experienced since the war, was stimulated by at least three war-time developments: the industrial canteen, school meals and food rationing. The extensive use of catering establishments by the bulk of the population developed markets to an extent not experienced before: *see* Table 29.

Table 29
Catering Establishments and Meals Served 1941–1946

	May 1941	Jan 1942	July 1943	Dec 1944	Aug 1945	Jan/Feb 1946
Catering establishments (000s)	111·0	114·1	137·5	147·2	149·5	143·2
Meals served weekly (millions)	79·0	144·0	170·5	170·5	181·7	157·1

Source: Ministry of Food.

Catering establishments include various canteens, such as school canteens and feeding centres, dining and luncheon clubs, British Restaurants, hotels and restaurants, cafes and other catering establishments open to the general public.

Before the war, eating-out was still for most a relative luxury. The war-time influences established a new, significantly higher level of eating out on the part of the British population, which proved to be not a merely temporary phenomenon. The post-war higher standards of living and the more even distribution of incomes replaced the artificial stimulus of food rationing. According to M. Bryn Jones in his study of *Food Services in Britain 1970–1980* the income elasticity of expenditure on meals away from home changed significantly from 2·25 in 1939 to 1·45 in 1945 when food rationing ended.[1]

Ministry of Food statistics, giving a fairly accurate indication of numbers of catering establishments as well as of meals served in them, were discontinued shortly after the war. Their absence meant that no quantitative assessment of the demand for meals was available in physical volume terms until the Hotels and Catering Economic Development Committee published the results of their study of eating out in Britain in mid-1970s.[2]

M. Bryn Jones showed that between 1954 and 1967 there was only a slight changed in income elasticity from 1·45 to 1·39, and indicated that this was the period in which the position gained during the war had been not much more than consolidated. Eating out, lacking the stimulus of rationing controls, ceded its position as a war-time necessity, but had not yet attained a very prominent place in the consumption pattern of the consumer.

Expenditure on Food

Estimates of consumer expenditure on a wide range of goods and services are published annually in the National Income Blue Book and provide some indication of trends in consumer expenditure on food. Until 1968 the total consumer

[1] Bryn Jones, M., *Food Services in Britain 1970–1980*, Chapter IV.
[2] Hotels and Catering EDC, *Trends in Catering*.

expenditure on food was divided into household and other personal expenditure; the latter consisted of personal expenditure in catering establishments and was, therefore, of some importance in the present context. The figures covered most catering establishments, but represent purchases of food by caterers and not actual expenditure in catering establishments by consumers. They excluded expenditure on food by public authorities.

Table 30

Expenditure on Food by Catering Establishments 1960–1968
(£ million)

	1960	1961	1962	1963	1964	1965	1966	1967	1968
At current prices	495	515	547	567	599	625	650	673	686
At 1963 prices	524	538	551	567	588	589	592	602	603

Source: National Income and Expenditure 1969.

The data in Table 30 illustrate increases in expenditure on food purchases by caterers due to a significant extent to rises in prices. When price increases are removed by the use of constant prices, there has still been an increase in caterers' purchases in real terms but this probably represents only a small increase in volume, with an element of substitution of higher quality for lower quality foods, including a growing use of convenience foods.

In 1969, separate estimates of household and other personal expenditure on food have been replaced in national income and expenditure accounts by estimates of total expenditure on food, covering in addition to household expenditure, all expenditure on food by both commercial and non-commercial establishments. They cover all expenditure on food for civilian consumption, including expenditure on food by public authorities for hospitals, prisons, homes for old people and for school meals, welfare foods and milk. Food issues to HM Forces are excluded. The figures of household expenditure are at prices paid by the consumer, while those of expenditure by catering establishments are generally at wholesale prices.

Table 31

Household and Total Catering Expenditure on Food 1966–1975
(£ million)

	1966	1967	1968	1969	1970	1971	1972	1973	1974	1975
At current prices	6,132	6,312	6,543	6,910	7,381	8,061	8,579	9,781	11,409	14,006
At 1970 prices	7,151	7,218	7,255	7,266	7,381	7,368	7,316	7,395	7,431	7,437

Source: National Income and Expenditure 1965–1975.

Unlike Table 30, Table 31 includes household and public authorities' expenditure on food. In Table 32 expenditure by all caterers and by households is shown separately.

Table 32

Expenditure on Food 1966–1975
(£ million at current prices)

	1966	1967	1968	1969	1970	1971	1972	1973	1974	1975
By caterers	650	673	686	931	1,006	1,085	1,145	1,341	1,540	1,914
By public authorities catering	173	175	188							
By households	5,309	5,464	5,669	5,979	6,375	6,976	7,434	8,440	9,869	12,092
Total	6,132	6,312	6,543	6,910	7,381	8,061	8,579	9,781	11,409	14,006
Caterers and public authorities %	13·4	13·4	13·4	13·5	13·6	13·5	13·3	13·7	13·5	13·7
Households %	86·6	86·6	86·6	86·5	86·4	86·5	86·7	86·3	86·5	86·3

Source: National Income and Expenditure 1965–1975.

The above tables show a rising expenditure on food by caterers throughout the ten years but at a faster rate in the second half of the period – in part due to the effect of inflation. As a proportion of total expenditure on food, caterers' expenditure increased from 12·8 per cent in 1960 to 13·4 per cent in 1966 and to 13·7 per cent in 1975.

A breakdown of expenditure on food by type of establishment, based on estimates by the Hotels and Catering Economic Development Committee, is given in Table 33. This covers broadly the same establishments as those included in Tables 31 and 32 in addition to food purchases by the Armed Services. The

Table 33

Value of Catering Food Purchases by Sector 1968 and 1973
(1973 prices)

		Commercial					Institutional			Industrial Total	Total
		Pubs/clubs	Restaurants	Hotels	Other	Total	Educational	Other	Total		
1968	£ million	110	310	100	140	660	140	155	295	215	1170
	%	9	26	9	12	56	12	13	25	18	100
1973	£ million	140	340	120	150	750	160	170	330	230	1310
	%	11	26	9	11	57	12	13	25	18	100

Source: Hotels and Catering EDC, *The Catering Supply Industry*, p. 2.

breakdown underlines the importance of the commercial sector, which accounted for 57 per cent of the total in 1973. The figures shown also suggest that the average annual growth in food purchases by caterers between 1968 and 1973 was less than 2·5 per cent in real terms.

Expenditure on Eating Out

Between April 1974 and March 1977 the Hotels and Catering Economic Development Committee commissioned a three-year survey of the eating out habits of the residents of Great Britain aged eleven and over.[3] The sample was drawn from households selected at random from the electoral register. The results, which give a detailed breakdown of trends in eating out, were published in a series of quarterly and annual reports.[4]

As shown in Table 34 total expenditure by households on personal meals outside the home between April 1975 and March 1976 was estimated to be of the order of £1,600 million. This represented over 2·5 per cent of total consumer expenditure for 1975. If expenditure in educational establishments, hospitals and penal institutions, local authority and residential homes, and by overseas tourists is included, this gives a figure for total expenditure on food of over £2,500 million or about 4 per cent of total consumer expenditure. Total expenditure on catering in the hotel and catering industry between April 1975 and March 1976 was estimated to be about £7,000 million, if alcoholic drinks and some other services were included.

The findings of the survey suggest that spending on eating out, in current terms, follows consumers' expenditure closely, which in turn follows the level of personal disposable income. This supports the findings of M. Bryn Jones[5] who established that the level of eating out is most closely correlated with income. Table 35 shows changes in personal incomes and consumer expenditure during the ten years to 1975. Spending on eating out increased rapidly during the decade in money terms although in real terms there may have been little growth, after allowing for the effects of inflation. This pattern is broadly supported by the changes in caterers' expenditure on food during the ten year period.

More detailed information on trends in catering is available between April 1974 and March 1977 from the survey by the Hotels and Catering Economic Development Committee. This indicates that between the first year and second year of the survey, expenditure and the number of people eating out rose substantially although the number of meal occasions rose by less than 1 per cent. Between the second and third years, however, expenditure rose by less than the general rate of inflation. These results continue to behave predictably in relation to total consumer expenditure and suggest that the share of eating out in this is being maintained in broad terms.

[3] Hotels and Catering EDC. *Trends in Catering*.
[4] A background to this survey is given in Balsom, E., Trends in catering–the history of a market research project, *HCIMA Review*, Volume 2, Number 2.
[5] Bryn Jones, M., op. cit.

Table 34
Estimate of Annual Expenditure on Catering in the Hotel and Catering Industry,
April 1974 – March 1975 and April 1975 – March 1976
(£ million)

	April 1974–March 1975	April 1975–March 1976
Personal meal (excluding educational establishments, cost of alcoholic drink and other drinks taken without food, but including industrial catering, canteens etc.)[a]	1,223	1,627
Alcoholic drinks (excluding pubs and clubs)[b]	311	375
Alcoholic drinks in pubs and clubs[b]	2,440	3,020
Non-alcoholic drinks without food[c]	38	45
Educational establishments:		
School meals service (including milk)[d]	372	497
Further and higher education (including universities)[e]	62	70
	434	567
Hospitals and penal institutions[f]	150+	170
Local authority and residential homes[f]	80+	90
Overseas tourists[g]	125	150
	4,801	6,044
Other services: cigarettes, tobacco and other goods[b]	774	890
Total	5,575	6,934

Source: Hotels and Catering EDC, *Trends in Catering*.

[a] *Trends in Catering;* cost of all alcoholic drinks whether taken with or without a meal have been excluded.

[b] Department of Trade and Industry, *Catering Trades 1969–Statistical inquiry*, HMSO 1972, Table 1: adjusted for the index for turnover in public houses as given in the *Business Monitor* for the catering trades CSO. (Average index for April 1975–March 1976 = 218; 1969 = 100).

[c] NEDO estimate based on *Trends in Catering* for 1974–1975.

[d] Department of Education and Science. (This includes parental contributions).

[e] A Department of Education and Science estimate based on figures for 1974–1975.

[f] NEDO estimate based on Koudra M: *Industrial and Welfare Catering Services in Britain 1970–1980* (Thesis, University of Surrey, 1974).

[g] British Tourist Authority (an estimated 15% of the total expenditure of £834 million was accounted for by eating out in the period April 1974–March 1975 and an estimated 13% of the total expenditure of £1,151 million in the period April 1975–March 1976).

Expenditure on Drink

Non-alcoholic soft drinks are distributed through numerous channels within and outside the hotel and catering industry and little information can be derived

Table 35

Personal Incomes, Consumers' Expenditure and Caterers' Expenditure on Food 1966–1975
(£ million at current prices)

	1966	1967	1968	1969	1970	1971	1972	1973	1974	1975
Personal disposable income	26,655	27,798	29,701	31,663	34,766	38,454	44,229	50,954	60,295	73,727
% change over previous year		4·3	6·8	6·6	9·8	10·6	15·0	15·2	18·3	22·3
Consumers' expenditure	24,211	25,428	27,338	29,102	31,644	35,165	39,716	45,044	51,832	63,373
% change over previous year		5·1	7·5	6·4	8·7	11·1	12·9	13·4	15·1	22·3
Caterers' expenditure on food	823	848	874	931	1,006	1,085	1,145	1,341	1,540	1,914
% change over previous year		3·0	3·1	6·5	8·1	7·9	5·5	17·1	14·9	24·2

Source: National Income and Expenditure 1965–1975.

from statistics of soft drink consumption for the present purpose. In consumer expenditure estimates in the National Income Blue Book soft drink is included with food. However, *Trends in Catering*[6] suggests a total expenditure on non-alcoholic drink without food in the hotel and catering industry of about £45 million between April 1975 and March 1976. Expenditure on non-alcoholic drink taken with food is included in the survey results with meal expenditure.

Statistical information about total alcoholic liquor consumption is available from two main sources – in terms of quantities from the Reports of the Commissioners of Customs and Excise and in terms of consumers' expenditure from the National Income Blue Book. Data from the two sources are shown for the ten years 1966–1975 in Tables 36 and 37, and illustrate an upward trend in consumption in the 1960s and 1970s.

Beer consumption showed a gradual decline from well over 30 million bulk barrels in the years immediately after the war to less than 25 million bulk barrels in the mid-1950s. However, 1955 marked a reversal of the downward trend and since then, with the exception of a few years with poor summer weather, which influences the consumption of beer more than is the case with other alcoholic drinks, it has continued to rise. The high level of the immediate post-war years was reached again at the end of the 1960s.

Wine consumption reached 20 million gallons for the first time after the war in 1957 and has continued to rise since then, with few interruptions. The total consumption of wines doubled in the ten years from 1966–1975; within this growth, imported wines showed a greater proportionate increase than British ones, but both maintained a rapid growth until 1974 in spite of increases in duty and a general restraint on consumers' expenditure in the late 1960s and early 1970s.

The main increase in the consumption of spirits took place in two periods – in the 1950s when, for example, the level of consumption doubled between 1948 and 1957, and in the early 1970s; the rising trend was interrupted for about five years between 1965 and 1969 when consumption remained relatively static.

The bulk of alcoholic liquor consumption takes place through licensed premises and clubs. Although a substantial proportion is sold through off-licences, which are outside the scope of this study, overall trends in alcoholic liquor consumption are of great importance to the hotel and catering industry, which enjoys a major share of the market. An estimate in *Trends in Catering*[6] gives a total expenditure on alcoholic drink in the industry of £3,395 million between April 1975 and March 1976. This accounts for about 48 per cent of total expenditure on catering in the industry, as identified by the Hotels and Catering EDC, and represents about 5 per cent of total consumer expenditure.

In his study of the market for wine in catering establishments[7] M. Howley estimated that approximately 22 per cent of table wine sales in the fiscal year 1971–1972 went through hotels, restaurants and licensed clubs, and that the growth in table wine sales in the early 1970s was due to off-licences rather than

[6] Hotels and Catering EDC, *Trends in Catering*.
[7] Howley, M., The Market for Wine in Hotels and Restaurants, *HCIMA Review* Number 1.

to on-licensed premises. The same study indicated that, although the market for wine in catering establishments was not expected to expand as rapidly as the market for off-licence sales, at least until 1978, the longer term prospects for the industry were very good.

Table 36
UK Alcoholic Liquor Consumption 1966–1975

		1966	1967	1968	1969	1970	1971	1972	1973	1974	1975
Beer (million bulk barrels)	Brewed in UK	29·5	30·1	30·6	31·9	32·9	34·0	34·8	36·0	37·4	38·4
	Imported	1·3	1·4	1·4	1·4	1·6	1·8	1·9	2·2	1·7	1·7
	Total	30·8	31·4	32·0	33·4	34·4	35·8	36·6	38·3	39·1	40·1
Wines (million gallons)	British	9·4	9·6	11·0	11·2	10·4	11·6	12·2	14·8	17·0	13·4
	Imported	28·3	32·0	35·4	33·7	35·4	42·2	49·7	63·6	65·9	64·1
	Total	37·7	41·6	46·4	44·9	45·8	53·8	61·9	78·4	82·9	77·5
Spirits (million proof gallons)	Made in UK	14·2	14·3	14·6	13·7	15·7	16·2	17·8	22·8	25·6	24·5
	Imported	3·5	3·6	3·8	3·6	4·4	4·9	6·2	7·6	7·9	7·1
	Total	17·8	17·9	18·6	17·5	20·0	21·2	24·2	30·2	33·2	31·7

Source: Based on Monthly Digest of Statistics June 1971, June 1974, June 1976.

Totals may not agree with sums of individual items due to rounding.

Table 37
Consumers' Expenditure on Alcoholic Drink 1966–1975
(£ million)

		1966	1967	1968	1969	1970	1971	1972	1973	1974	1975
Beer	At current prices	961	1,021	1,067	1,201	1,355	1,526	1,662	1,807	2,071	2,679
	At 1970 prices	1,158	1,196	1,235	1,309	1,355	1,419	1,464	1,549	1,551	1,609
Wines, cider and perry	At current prices	222	247	284	308	333	397	471	604	715	831
	At 1970 prices	261	293	325	318	333	385	438	524	543	512
Spirits	At current prices	453	471	519	520	611	670	777	1,004	1,140	1,392
	At 1970 prices	503	512	548	522	611	650	739	916	991	970

Source: National Income and Expenditure 1965–1975.

Part IV
The Firm and the Industry

Additional Reading for Part IV

Hotels and Catering EDC: *Hotel Prospects to 1980,* Volume 1, Chapters 3–5, and Volume 2, Appendix N.

Hotels and Catering EDC: *Hotel Prospects to 1985,* Research Findings, Chapter 4 and Appendix D.

Hotels and Catering EDC: *Hotels and Government Policy.*

Housden, J.: Brewers and Tenants: A Changing Relationship, *HCIMA Review,* Volume 2, Number 1.

Koudra, M.: Industrial and Welfare Catering 1970–1980, *HCIMA Review* Volume 1, Number 1.

Koudra, M.: Catering Contractors: A Study in Industrial Concentration, *HCIMA Review,* Number 2.

11. *Economics of Operation*

Economic activity is organized in establishments, firms and industries. In Chapter 1, an industry was described as a group of firms and establishments having a bond of interest among themselves – which may be one of the type of product, use of materials or process, or a still looser one, such as their general function and place in the total economic activity. The hotel and catering industry has been described so far in this study in terms of establishments, rather than firms, as units of operation. An establishment is a separate place of business at a separate address, in which an activity or activities are carried on. But an establishment does not necessarily also coincide with an ultimate unit of ownership and control. The more or less independent unit in which final decisions are made and ultimate control is exercised is the firm, which raises capital, and employs and organizes productive resources; it is the ultimate unit of accountability and profitability.

A firm may operate more than one establishment, and in more than one industry, which means that in practice the units which make up an industry are establishments rather than firms. This is to a considerable extent the case in the hotel and catering industry, where hotel and catering activities constitute only one branch of the activities of a large number of firms. It occurs, for example, when manufacturing firms (particularly brewery or food firms) enter the hotel and catering industry, in which they find retail outlets for their products. Besides this form of vertical forward growth, a number of firms have expanded laterally and carry on more or less similar activities, such as when property companies operate hotels or when retail grocery and bakery firms operate restaurants.

However, the concept of a firm holds good, even when subject to these qualifications. In this and the two subsequent chapters, the structure of the hotel and catering industry is examined up to and including the level of the firm as an organization of one or more establishments, as a unit of investment and as a unit of ownership, together with a few aspects of the inter-relationship between firms.

Hotel and catering firms display some characteristic features of economic significance, which distinguish them from many others. These features are largely derived from the nature of their activities, and influence both the structure of the industry and the viability of individual operations. Some of these features are examined in this chapter.

Nature of Investment

In most firms it is possible to differentiate clearly between capital invested in fixed assets and the rest of the capital employed. The main characteristic of the former is its use in the business; it includes buildings and equipment, i.e. instruments of production not intended for consumption. Goods which are intended for re-sale in the same or altered form and which are used up continually in the course of business, such as stocks, comprise, together with money capital in its varying degrees of liquidity, the variable assets of firms. According to the intensity of capital investment it is possible to divide firms into those with a high proportion of fixed assets, and those in which variable assets predominate.

Various studies in Britain and elsewhere have revealed that in hotels the proportion of fixed assets is probably higher than in any other business. Investment in accommodation units is primarily an investment in land and buildings, and it is a characteristic feature of the hotel that the bulk of its capital is permanently sunk in fixed assets. Location in relation to transport and other amenities is often of crucial importance and hotels, therefore, frequently compete for sites in town centres and other situations where land values are high. Added to the high cost of the site is the cost of the building, the two comprising between them the greater part of the capital invested in hotels. In addition to the land and building cost, a further substantial proportion of the total investment is represented by interior facilities, equipment and furniture. An examination of most hotel investments discloses that over 90 per cent of the capital is invested in fixed assets alone. Variable assets form only a small part of the total, and have a high rate of turnover. Stocks are usually low, and there is little or no work in progress. In spite of some developments in credit arrangements cash trading still predominates; credit is usually extended to guests only for the length of their stay, and weekly accounts settlement is customary where the length of stay is long.

It is important to appreciate the dual nature of fixed investment in hotels – as an investment in land and building, and as an investment in interior assets. This distinction has been recognized particularly in three principal ways in recent years. A number of hotel buildings are owned by a developer, sometimes as part of some larger project, and leased to an hotel operator. Secondly, many hotel companies have made use of sale and lease-back arrangements as a means of financing, thus reducing the capital requirement. Thirdly, interior assets may be leased by the hotel operator rather than bought.

These characteristics of hotel investment imply that the ratio of capital to turnover is high, and that new hotels have a long pay-back period, at least ten to twelve years and more. They generate demand for long-term finance for the land and building and medium-term finance for three to seven years for interior assets.

Although catering units share some of the investment characteristics of accommodation units, they differ in some important respects, and in particular in the capital intensity of the investment. By comparison the total investment is generally smaller, and the ratio of capital to turnover lower. But the notional fixity of the investment is normally also relatively high. Even when premises are rented and the capital investment is limited to the interior assets, variable assets normally represent a small proportion of the total. The cycle of operation is short, supplies are received at frequent intervals and food preparation takes place in anticipation of demand only a short time ahead. Hence raw materials, work in progress and finished products, all of which may represent a considerable proportion of assets of firms in other industries, are usually negligible in catering. The only exception may be spirits and wines which have a high value and may be held for longer periods. But cash trading predominates in most units, and is the exclusive form in many. Generally the pay-back period in most types of investment in catering is short, often no more than two to three years, and most of the demand for capital is for medium-term finance.

Elements of Cost: Accommodation

Hotels and other accommodation units generally offer three products, and three main activities are, therefore, carried on in an hotel: letting of bedroom accommodation, production and service of meals, service of drink; other amenities and services may be also available, and they may form a significant part of the total activity of a particular hotel.

The letting of bedroom accommodation distinguishes an hotel from a restaurant or a public house. But it may or may not be the primary source of revenue, and the restaurant or bar activities may be the primary sources; the relative proportions of each give the sales mix of a particular hotel. The significance of the sales mix lies in the different gross profit margins derived from these activities. The gross profit margin is the difference between the revenue and the cost of sales incurred in earning that revenue. In broad terms, accommodation generates the highest gross profit margin, meals come next and drink lowest. Thus a change in the sales mix for the same total turnover has an effect on the profit, and ultimately on the rate of return on the capital invested. However, many hotel costs are not easily identified with particular activities. This is the case with a significant proportion of costs of servicing the building, promotion and various other operating costs, which are normally treated as costs of the whole hotel. The total costs may be divided into three main groups: materials, labour and overheads. Materials include mainly food and drink; labour costs includes not only wages and salaries but also the cost of any additional emoluments received by employees from the employer, such as meals, and any other costs incurred by the employer directly for the benefit of his employees; overheads include the remaining operating costs, repairs and maintenance, depreciation of fixed assets and interest on capital employed.

An indication of the relative importance of individual elements of cost in British hotels is given in *Hotel Prospects to 1985*[1], based on information from the University of Strathclyde. They are shown here in Table 38, which outlines the main categories of hotel costs as a percentage of turnover for the three years 1971, 1972 and 1973. The influence of the sales mix on the distribution of costs in hotels for 1973 is shown separately in Table 39. In both tables the percentages are intended to give an order of magnitude rather than an exact figure.

[1] Hotels and Catering EDC, *Hotel Prospects to 1985*.

Table 38

Hotel Costs as a Proportion of Turnover 1971–1973
(Medians[a] percentages)

Element of Cost	1971	1972	1973
Materials[b]: cost of goods sold	34	32	31
Labour	29	29	33
Overheads: operating expenses	23	23	23
Profit	14	16	13

Source: Hotels and Catering EDC, *Hotel Prospects to 1985*.

[a] Median figures represent the figures for the middle hotel of a number of hotels arranged in ascending order of each particular element of cost; they cannot be added.
[b] These figures are approximate orders of magnitude.

Table 39

Hotel Costs as a Proportion of Turnover in 1973 by Sales Bias[c] of Hotels
(Median[a] percentages)

Element of Cost	Accommodation	Food	Liquor	All hotels
Materials[b]: cost of goods sold	18	30	41	31
Labour	32	34	29	33
Overheads: operating expenses	25	24	20	23
Profit	25	12	10	13

Source: Hotels and Catering EDC, *Hotel Prospects to 1985*.

[a,b] See notes to Table 38.
[c] Sales bias denotes main revenue earning activity of hotels.

Most accommodation units have relatively high labour costs in spite of the incidence of gratuities, which enable lower rates of wages to be paid to some categories of employees. This is largely due to the nature of hotels, in which the economic activity takes the form of saleable service rather than, or in addition to, material products; when the service element is reduced, as it is the case with motels, labour costs are reduced significantly. The second factor of some importance, making for high labour costs, is the continuity of activity; the hotel never closes; however, when some hotel activities are carried on only for part of the day, as it is the case with drink-oriented hotels, labour costs are also reduced significantly.

Table 38 shows that in 1973 material costs accounted for under one-third, labour costs for about one-third and overheads for less than one-quarter of the total sales of hotels. The trend of costs in hotels indicates that labour costs have become the most important element of hotel costs in Britain, as has been the case in US hotels for a long time.

Table 39 illustrates clearly the relationship between the sales mix and the profit-to-sales ratio between different types of hotel. Accommodation oriented hotels have the highest gross profit margin, and although their overheads are highest, they produce the highest profit-to-sales ratio. By contrast, hotels in which drink is the main source of revenue show the lowest gross profit margin and, in spite of having the lowest labour cost, the lowest profit-to-sales ratio.

Elements of Cost: Catering

Restaurants generally offer one main product, with one main activity carried on in them, production and service of meals, to which the supply of liquor and the related activities, if any, are ancillary; the reverse obtains in public houses. Licensed clubs approximate more closely to licensed restaurants, and registered clubs to public houses in their sales mix, and the activities carried on in them.

The pattern of costs in catering is similar to hotels, with a somewhat higher ratio of materials cost to sales and a somewhat lower ratio of labour cost to sales, the exact proportions being mainly determined by the sales mix of the individual establishment, its particular product or products and its level of service. In his survey of some ninety restaurants in London in 1967, *Labour Costs in Restaurants,* R. Kotas found a high degree of consistency in the average ratios of labour cost to sales in the region of 25 per cent as between different types of restaurant (Table 40), but he also found wide variations from the average.[2]

Table 40

Labour Costs[a] in Restaurants as a Proportion of Sales
(percentages)

	Highest	Average	Lowest
Restaurants	36·0	24·7	14·6
Speciality restaurants	30·1	23·7	15·6
National restaurants	45·0	26·8	16·0
Wimpy Bars	23·0	22·5	22·0
Other catering establishments	32·0	25·2	16·2

Source: *Labour Costs in Restaurants,* R. Kotas.

[a] Labour cost includes wages, salaries, overtime payments, holiday pay and all other payments by employer to employee.

[2] Kotas, R., *Labour Costs in Restaurants,* pp. 62–63.

Fixed and Variable Costs

Both in accommodation and in catering a high proportion of the costs are fixed or semi-fixed costs, which do not vary in proportion to the volume of business done. Some of them, particularly in hotels, are attributable to the intensity of capital investment and to the high proportion of fixed capital employed; such are, for example, rent, rates, insurances, depreciation, maintenance, interest on capital. Other costs, which must be appropriately described only as semi-fixed, represent also a substantial charge against income and depend only to some extent on the volume of business; such are lighting, heating, repairs, administration, some labour costs. Materials costs vary directly and absolutely, and the costs of food and drink sold are the main variable costs in the industry.

It is admittedly always difficult to separate sharply the fixed from variable costs in practice; the time period has to be brought in and defined in any particular case. When a heterogeneous industry is considered, only a broad generalization can be made. In broad terms, in the hotel and catering industry it is appropriate to consider all costs, except materials, as fixed, on a short-term basis of a few weeks or months. Daily and weekly fluctuations in demand, for instance, can be only partly met by the employment of casual labour. Even if an establishment closes down temporarily for the off-season months, certain costs continue to be incurred. If this measure is not resorted to, most labour and overhead costs are incurred. We have seen earlier in this chapter that wage costs and operating expenses of hotels account together for well over one-half of the revenue of British hotels and that they approach a similar level in restaurants. Therefore, one-half of total costs of normal working and sometimes considerably more must be incurred in order to make the facilities available at all, irrespective of the volume of business.

The cost fixity of accommodation and catering operations has important implications for the profitability of the business, some of which are considered in this chapter.[3]

Hotel Occupancy

The volume of business determines the degree of utilization of available facilities, which is of major significance in firms with high fixed capital investment and high fixed operating costs. Hotels are, therefore, particularly conscious of the importance of a high degree of capacity utilization, which has a major effect on profitability, and measures of utilization are prominent in any examination of operation. As in most service industries, these measures are based on the number of customers; the unit is a guest/night (or bed/night or sleeper/night). The hotel capacity is expressed as bed capacity, and the bed occupancy for any period is calculated as

$$\frac{\text{number of guest/nights achieved}}{\text{bed capacity} \times \text{number of nights}} \times 100.$$

[3] For a fuller discussion see: Kotas, R., *Management Accounting for Hotels and Restaurants*, pp. 26–54.

The bed occupancy tends to be a more accurate measure of capacity utilization than room occupancy, in which the unit of measurement is a room/night and the occupancy for any period is calculated as

$$\frac{\text{number of room/nights achieved}}{\text{room capacity} \times \text{number of nights}} \times 100.$$

When, as often happens, double rooms are let as single, this has a bearing on the revenue and is truly reflected in the bed occupancy, but not in the room occupancy, of the hotel.

Two major indications of the degree of utilization of British hotels in recent years are available from annual surveys of the British Tourist Authority (formerly The British Travel Association) and of the national tourist boards for England, Scotland and Wales, which are reproduced in Appendixes I and J. Both sources show a considerable variation in the occupancy levels achieved by hotels in different locations, as well as by hotels of different sizes and prices. London hotels achieve highest occupancy levels and experience less seasonal fluctuation than hotels in any other area; their peak is in July, and their lowest point in December to February. Town hotels follow a similar but more even annual occupancy pattern; their high level extends from May to October. Country and particularly seaside hotels have the lowest annual occupancy and also the greatest seasonal variations; their peak season is between June and September, but many are closed during the winter months. Overall, the available statistics demonstrate a substantial under-utilization of hotels over the year as a whole; only about a half of the available annual capacity is used.

Costs and Volume: Accommodation

From a closer look at the relationship between costs and volume, the importance of high utilization of capacity emerges very sharply. Total fixed costs remain static irrespective of occupancy, and total variable costs rise more or less proportionately with occupancy. When unit costs are examined, the variable unit cost remains static but the fixed unit cost falls as occupancy increases. As each hotel bed has to bear its share of operating costs, it follows that with a decreased occupancy the income from each occupied bed must meet a higher proportion of fixed costs as unoccupied beds are failing to cover theirs. The unit cost of operation – the bed/night – varies inversely with occupancy; other income, from food or drink sales, should not be allowed to obscure the profitability or otherwise of bedroom accommodation. These effects are illustrated in Table 41.

High fixed costs also provide an explanation of the substantial number of hotels with low occupancies remaining open in many resorts in winter, and of their offering facilities at prices which suggest that they are below cost. There are several considerations involved but, other things being equal, the entrepreneur will consider it worth his while to keep his establishment open as long as his revenue covers his variable costs and makes at least some contribution to his fixed costs; as long as the fixed costs incurred when the establishment is closed

Table 41
Hotel Occupancy and Operating Costs

Bed occupancy	Bed nights	Total Costs			Unit Costs		
		Total	Fixed	Variable	Total	Fixed	Variable
%		£	£	£	£	£	£
20	3,000	18,000	15,000	3,000	6·00	5·00	1·00
40	6,000	21,000	15,000	6,000	3·50	2·50	1·00
60	9,000	24,000	15,000	9,000	2·67	1·67	1·00
80	12,000	27,000	15,000	12,000	2·25	1·25	1·00
100	15,000	30,000	15,000	15,000	2·00	1·00	1·00

exceed the loss incurred by keeping open, it is financially advantageous to keep open. Whilst this simple rule would apply in any business when the question of temporary closure or price reduction arises, it is of vital importance in an industry in which so many units experience severe seasonal fluctuations in the volume of demand for their services. Its application may be illustrated in an example of a small seaside establishment with the following off-season results (Table 42).

Table 42
Off-season Costs and Revenue of a Seaside Establishment

	When open		When closed	
Revenue		£25,000		—
Costs – variable	£24,000		—	
– fixed	£6,000	£30,000	£6,000	£6,000
Loss		£5,000		£6,000

In this case the loss incurred by temporary closing would be greater than the loss incurred by keeping open. Other things being equal, it may be even advisable to reduce prices in order to attain a revenue which covers variable costs completely and at least some fixed costs as above.

However, when demand is inelastic, differential pricing is a doubtful approach. In those circumstances price reductions do not result in a proportionate increase in demand, and the suppliers simply share the same or similar volume of business at reduced prices. The outcome is a loss of potential revenue equal in amount to the extent of price reductions, and possibly representing that marginal proportion of revenue, which might have accrued as profit.

Cost and Volume: Catering

In catering, fixed costs normally form a lower proportion of the total costs than is the case with accommodation units, but it remains true that each meal or drink served must bear its proportion of fixed costs, and that the unit cost of operation varies inversely with the volume of business. If prices and quality are to remain the same, only one of two ways will increase profitability: increased efficiency which will secure a reduction of some fixed or variable costs or both, or an increase in the volume of business, which will lead to the fixed costs being spread over a larger volume of meals or drinks served. The effect of a change in volume may be illustrated by means of a simplified example, in which a meal is sold for £0·50, and in which the volume increases or decreases by a quarter (*see* Table 43).

Table 43
Volume and Operating Costs in Catering

Number of meals	Total costs and revenue				Unit costs and revenue			
	Fixed	Variable	Profit	Sales	Fixed	Variable	Profit	Sales
	£	£	£	£	£	£	£	£
150	60·00	22·50	−7·50	75·00	0·40	0·15	−0·05	0·50
200	60·00	30·00	10·00	100·00	0·30	0·15	0·05	0·50
250	60·00	37·50	27·50	125·00	0·24	0·15	0·11	0·50

In the example total fixed costs, which are independent of the volume of business (in this case the number of meals), remain static with variations in volume; variable costs, which are incurred by a larger volume, rise proportionately with volume. When both types of cost are calculated per unit of performance (in this case a meal sold), variable costs per unit remain the same but fixed costs per unit vary inversely with volume.

Five Hotel Problems

An hotel differs from most other businesses in that it lacks flexibility in supply. The production of its most important product, the hotel bed/night, cannot be adjusted to variations in demand. It is this fixity of supply which causes waste when demand falls, and which imposes an upper limit on the volume of business in a period of peak demand. As the capacity remains constant throughout the year while demand fluctuates, every night on which demand falls short of the maximum which can be accommodated means idle capacity. Conversely, once all beds are occupied, the hotel has reached the limit of its earning capacity.

Moreover, the product is perishable – unoccupied beds on any night represent an irretrievable loss, as the product cannot be stored for future use.

Thirdly, an hotel has a fixed location and cannot follow the customer. The product has to be consumed at the place of production.

These problems are magnified by the bulk of the capital in an hotel being invested in fixed assets, and by a large proportion of costs being fixed.

None of these problems are unique to hotels by themselves but are rarely, if ever, present in the same combination and in the same degree elsewhere. In many other firms, an adjustment of supply to demand is possible by a fuller utilization of plant, by overtime or by shift working (especially in manufacturing) to meet an increase in demand. In others (for example, in retailing) surplus products may be stocked for future sale, and an increase in demand may be met by ordering additional supplies. In most commodity industries, supply may be transported to different locations.

Some of the hotel problems are shared to a significant extent in passenger transport. The total capacity of the carrier is also fixed at any one time, empty seats on a journey are also perishable and unused passenger seat miles cannot be recovered subsequently. Transport calls for a high intensity of investment, and incurs high fixed costs. But even the transport operator has more elbow room: in the way in which he combines scheduled and non-scheduled services, and in his ability to divert his resources within limits to supply increased demand in a particular sphere of his activities.

Several key factors are, therefore, crucial to the viability of an hotel: the right location, correct capacity and a high level of utilization. Although to a greater or lesser extent catering shares some of the economic problems of an accommodation unit and the same key factors influence its viability, it can respond to market changes more readily. This alone is a reason for the lack of a separate discussion of the major catering problems analogous to hotel problems in this chapter.

12. Investment

The strength of an industry, its ability to produce, depends to a great extent on its rate of investment. To ensure future prosperity industry needs new buildings and modern equipment. This is no less important for the hotel and catering industry, which can do much to increase the country's invisible exports, to meet the needs of the business and social life of its population, and to generate employment in areas with low levels of employment. A low rate of investment means that British hotels and restaurants may not have the capacity to meet the demand for their services; that they may compare unfavourably with their competitors in other countries in their range and standard of amenities and facilities; that they may not provide an attraction to labour recruitment.

In the 1960s, the rate of investment was uneven both in the British economy as a whole, and in the hotel and catering industry. It rose fast when personal spending on goods and services was rising and as firms sought to remedy shortages of productive capacity and to exploit market opportunities. It tended to decline when the economy was depressed; when the next boom came, capacity was again insufficient and slowed down the possible rate of growth.

Between 1970 and 1973, there was a massive increase in investment in the hotel industry. This followed the introduction of the temporary Hotel Development Incentives Scheme (HDIS) under the Development of Tourism Act 1969. The Scheme, which was administered by the three statutory tourist boards in England, Wales and Scotland, provided for grants and loans out of public funds for building and fixed equipment for hotels in connection with work started before April 1971 and completed before April 1973 under certain criteria set out under the Act. The grants available were 20 per cent, subject to an upper limit of £1,000 for each letting bedroom created. In Development Areas, the rate was 25 per cent with an upper limit of £1,250. During the period of operation of the Scheme grants totalling over £50 million were made to the industry.

Although no precise figures are available, it is estimated that prior to the HDIS the number of bedrooms added to the nation's stock averaged some 2,000 annually. Investment during the period 1970–1973 showed a six-fold increase in this figure. Changes in the hotel population of Great Britain during the period of operation of the HDIS are shown in Appendix U. Most of the growth was in the larger hotels. During the period there was, in fact, a decline in the total number of hotels while the number of bedrooms increased by 10 per cent. England, and in particular London, gained the lion's share of the new investment. One result of the increase in investment was an initial surplus of hotel capacity in certain key areas, notably London, Birmingham, Manchester, Heathrow and Gatwick.

According to the report commissioned by the Hotels and Catering Economic

Development Committee[1] much of the new investment during the period was encouraged by the HDIS, although the buoyant property market at the time and access to ready finance also played important roles; the HDIS had the effect of bringing forward much new development that was on the stocks.

Since the ending of the HDIS and with the economic recession of the mid-1970s new investment in the industry has shown a considerable decline.

Requirements and Methods of Finance

The nature of capital investment in the industry was described in Chapter 11, as a basis for the examination of the economics of operation. In common with other industries, hotel and catering services require three types of finance. Short-term finance (up to one year), may be called for, particularly by seasonal establishments, to meet operating costs and minor capital expenditure during the off-season, and repaid as income is received during the season. Most medium-term finance (for up to several years), is needed for internal assets, such as equipment, furniture and large-scale modernization. The requirement for long-term finance, for periods longer than a few years, arises mainly in connection with major investments in physical capacity, i.e. for land and buildings.

Short-term finance is largely provided from retained profits, personal savings, other private sources, or by overdrafts or loans from joint stock banks. As it is not normally used to cover permanent investment in fixed assets, it is outside the scope of this chapter, which is concerned with fixed capital expenditure and, therefore, with medium- and long-term investment.

The particular arrangement for external finance varies with the type of borrower and lender and with the period of investment, but the main methods may be summarized as follows.

(*a*) Equity participation by lender provides him with a direct involvement in the business, and acts as a hedge against inflation. It may be arranged from the outset, or as a right to convert a loan into equity at a future date. The lender's participation in company equity may be up to 20 per cent, at which level he would normally require representation on the board of directors.

(*b*) Debentures are normally limited to the larger companies, which can offer group assets as security for the loan, which is only rarely secured on a specific property. The normal duration of the loan is between twenty and twenty-five years.

(*c*) Mortgage loans provide the security of land and buildings to the lender, and are sometimes combined with other forms of finance, such as equity participation. The proportion of the loan is up to 60 per cent and the duration between twenty and thirty years.

(*d*) Sale and leaseback involves the sale of property by the borrower to the

---

[1] Hotels and Catering EDC, *Hotel Prospects to 1985*, p. 16.

lender, who in turn leases it to the original owner. The lessee pays a rent which is normally expressed as a percentage of the sale value.
(e) Bridging finance constitutes a temporary arrangement which can be usually only made when another arrangement has been made to provide the long-term finance.

Sources of Investment Finance

Much investment in the hotel and catering industry derives from personal savings (particularly in the smaller business), sometimes applied from the realization of other assets; some growth takes place from retained profits, i.e. profits ploughed back into the business. Companies obtain finance for investment by issues of shares; in the case of private companies, to a restricted group of people, in the case of public companies to the public at large. Increasingly investment uses external sources of funds and the most important sources are described below.

(a) Joint stock banks commonly provide short-term loans to the hotel and catering industry, but they very rarely provide long-term finance, and the majority of bank loans are granted either as bridging loans, or for extensions and modernizations where the pay-back period is shorter than for new establishments. The main consideration appears to be the cash flow generated by the investment, which has to be sufficient to service the loan and to repay it within a period acceptable to the bank, normally three to five years.

(b) Merchant banks are prepared to undertake long-term financing, but normally only with larger companies, and often only with an equity interest.

(c) Industrial banks provide medium-term finance for equipment as well as for minor building works. Unsecured loans are made available for loans up to several thousand pounds, secured loans for larger amounts.

(d) Building societies are only occasional providers of long-term finance to the industry, in small sums and on similar terms as to private householders, although at higher rates of interest. As such they are of relevance mainly to owner-occupied guest-houses, rather than to larger operators.

(e) Insurance companies are concerned with long-term lending as their normal business, but their practice varies greatly as between one company and another in their approach to the hotel and catering industry. If they are prepared to make funds available, it is normally on a smaller scale.

(f) Company superannuation funds have been a source of long-term finance to the industry from time to time, even for large amounts and there is a tendency for them to participate by taking a share of profits.

(g) Breweries are heavily engaged in providing medium- and long-term finance to tenants of buildings owned by breweries, but they lend also to 'free' houses in return for an undertaking on the part of the borrower to buy exclusively from the brewery.

(h) Equipment suppliers are an important source of medium-term credit to all sectors of the industry through hire purchase, credit sale and rental arrangements, as well as sometimes providing loans.

(i) The Industrial and Commercial Finance Corporation (ICFC) makes loans to the hotel and catering industry; in the 12 months to March 1977 it lent some £400,000 to the industry.[2] It handles loans ranging from £5,000 to £2 million, for periods between ten and twenty years.

(j) The Finance Corporation for Industry (FCI) is mainly engaged in medium-term loans for the larger industrial organizations, and has a very limited involvement in the hotel and catering industry.[3]

(k) The Council for Small Industries in Rural Areas (CoSIRA) in partnership with the Development Commission makes loans out of public funds for certain types of tourist projects in specified rural areas of England and Wales. Loans are limited to £30,000 and may be made up to 80 per cent of the cost of a project; they are for a maximum of twenty years for buildings and for two to five years for equipment; the interest rate is specified by the Treasury. A separate similar scheme operates in Scotland.

(l) The Highlands and Islands Development Board operates a Tourism Development Incentive Scheme in the area covered by the Board. This provides grants and loans for building, furniture and equipment as well as for working capital, in accordance with certain criteria set by the Board.

(m) The Hotel Development Incentives Scheme, already referred to above, made grants and loans out of public funds for hotel investment. The scheme ended in April 1973.

(n) Under Section Four of the Development of Tourism Act 1969, financial assistance is available at the discretion of the National Tourist Boards, normally by way of grant or loan, to developers of selected tourism projects. At present this assistance is available only for projects in the Development Areas and in Intermediate Areas.

(o) Under the Fire Precautions (Loans) Act 1973, local authorities are empowered to make loans, at their discretion, to anyone incurring expenditure in hotels and boarding houses which provide sleeping accommodation for not more than 25 persons, in order to comply with the requirements of the fire authority under the Fire Precautions Act 1971. Such loans are intended only for those who are unable to meet the expenditure in some other way.

There are, therefore, at least fourteen main sources of external finance available to the hotel and catering industry; ten 'private', and four from public funds. Between them they provide a wide spectrum of sources: merchant

---

[2] ICFC *Annual Review* 1977.
[3] In 1974 ICFC and FCI were grouped under a single holding company known as Finance for Industry Limited (FFI).

banks, insurance companies, company superannuation funds, breweries, and ICFC are the main sources of long-term finance; joint stock and industrial banks the main sources of medium-term investment finance for the industry throughout the country. Of these, the merchant banks and company superannuation funds are clearly of main interest to larger businesses, building societies and the Councils for Small Industries only to small ones. The Councils for Small Industries, the Highlands and Islands Development Board and the Tourist Boards provide both long-term and medium-term finance, but their operation is limited geographically. The loans from local authorities are limited to small establishments for specific purposes.

Franchising

In the second half of the nineteenth century breweries began to acquire retail outlets for their beer, and thus began the tied house system, which is described in Chapters 8 and 13. A proportion of public houses owned by the breweries are let to tenants who are under certain obligations to their landlord; in particular to obtain their supplies from them and their nominated suppliers, and to conduct their houses in a way specified by their brewery.

The tied house system preceded in Britain by almost a century a modern version of the tie, the franchise. Whilst primarily a marketing arrangement, franchising may be conveniently considered in the present chapter, as it has important investment implications.

Although franchise agreements vary greatly, their common characteristic is a product supplied to the franchisee to sell, which is designed and controlled for quality by the franchisor. The main advantages to the franchisee are a developed advertised product with a brand image, with assistance often provided by the franchisor in site selection, opening of the outlet and training, and an entry into business with modest capital at a reduced risk.

The main advantage to the franchisor is a reduced capital investment, as part of the required capital is provided by the franchisee. In return for the services provided to franchisees, the franchisor may receive income in form of an initial payment, a share of franchisees' income in form of payment for supplies or percentage of turnover or profit, or a combination of these and other methods.

Major differences between franchise agreements include the range of products and the terms on which they are supplied to franchisees, the range of services provided to them by franchisors and the degree of control exercised by the franchisor over the product.

In contrast to American experience, where franchising has been the main form of growth in several industries (particularly in restaurants, but also in hotels where the largest operator, Holiday Inns, controls some 1,700 hotels), its penetration in the hotel and catering industry in Britain has been slow; by 1977 there were no British hotel franchise systems in operation in Britain, although some franchised hotels were established by overseas companies.

The largest catering franchise in Britain, Wimpy Bars (operated by United

Biscuits), had over 600 Wimpy Bars in 1977, with more than 400 franchisees – an average of 1·5 units per franchisee. The investment costs of most units are between £15–£20,000; many franchisees raise a part of this from banks and finance houses.

The Wimpy illustrates the advantages and scope of a well-conceived franchise, which overcomes many problems, including those of investment finance, facing prospective entrepreneurs, and which may well represent a major direction of growth for the hotel and catering industry in Britain. Although the lack of suitable sites may be an obstacle to further rapid growth of this particular franchise, it is clear that product acceptability in such matters as food varies between different parts of the country. Future growth of the franchise concept may depend as much on new products as on site availability; the concept which has been so successful in beer and later in Wimpy Bars may well be only at the beginning of its modern era in Britain. A research study on franchising in progress at the University of Surrey is expected to establish the pattern and the trends.

The Investment Problem

Investment in the hotel and catering industry has been the subject of several recent studies.[4] The main investment problems identified in these studies emerged in relation to hotel firms. As we have seen earlier, the lower intensity of capital investment in catering means that catering firms are generally only in need of short-to medium-term finance, which can be repaid quickly out of the cash flow if the project is reasonably successful. Investment in catering is speculative but the degree of speculation is reduced substantially by chains, which spread the risk. In view of the low level of investment normally associated with any single unit, investment raises few problems also for entrepreneurs with individually-operated catering units.

However, all the studies drew attention to the particular problems associated with financing investment in hotels. The problems are in part due to the inherent characteristics of hotel operation, discussed in the previous chapter, in part to the availability of capital which stems from these characteristics, and from the view taken of hotel investment by lenders.

The problems no longer constitute an obstacle to growth for the larger hotel companies with a past record of achievement, except that during a period of rapid development they may have utilized all their assets as security. But the problems remain significant for the smaller and newer hotel firms who often have to seek specific mortgage and bridging finance arrangements.

The rate of investment in the economy as well as in particular industries is influenced significantly by fiscal and other government measures. These have

---

[4] Hotel and Catering EDC, *Investment in Hotels and Catering*.
Pickering, J. F. et al., *The Small Firm in the Hotel and Catering Industry*.
Hotels and Catering EDC, *Hotel Prospects to 1980*.
Hotels and Catering EDC, *Hotel Prospects to 1985*.

tended to discriminate in favour of manufacturing and against service industries, particularly in the late 1960s. In view of this it is debatable whether selective assistance to hotel investment by the Government is justified in Britain, as long as hotels are treated differently from other industries. Indeed, informed opinion within the hotel and catering industry has been for a long time in favour of equal treatment rather than of selective assistance. This has been endorsed by the Hotel and Catering Economic Development Committee, in particular in its report on *Investment in Hotels and Catering* published in 1968 which states:[5]

'... the industry will not realize its potential contribution, either to foreign currency earnings or to regional development, unless it is given a greater incentive to invest in hotel development.'

'... it would be immensely difficult to discriminate in favour of hotel development by type of potential business or by location.'

'We examined the effect on the rate of return on investment if the assistance at present given to industrial establishments were extended to hotels. This solution would involve:
  (a) extending industrial building allowances to hotel buildings;
  (b) extending investment grants to hotel equipment and furniture;
  (c) extending the provisions of Development Area legislation in full to hotels.'

'The implementation of these tax changes should go far towards increasing the confidence of individual firms in new investment and would enable them to finance a higher proportion of their capital requirements from cash flow. It would help also to modify the attitude of lenders to financing investment in hotels.'

In spite of this authoritative advice the Government introduced a temporary scheme of selective assistance for hotels in 1969, following an experimental hotel loan scheme created in 1967. The Government's main objective in the Hotel Development Incentives Scheme was to increase rapidly the capacity and quality of the hotel stock at a time when demand for accommodation was exceeding supply in a number of locations, in anticipation of a further major increase in overseas tourism to Britain.

This objective was achieved beyond expectation. The scheme stimulated a massive increase in hotel capacity; more hotels were built in Britain in a few years than in the whole period 1900–1970. Much obsolete hotel stock was replaced and, in conjunction with the new bedroom capacity and separately, a significant hotel modernization took place.

However, this was achieved with a much larger expenditure of public funds than was envisaged at the outset and it is arguable that much of the new investment would have occurred anyway, albeit at a slower rate. The non-discriminatory nature of the HDI Scheme resulted in much indiscriminate expansion and no

[5] Hotel and Catering EDC, *Investment in Hotels and Catering*, pp. 7–9.

special stimulus was provided for particular types of development. The overcapacity created as a result of the concentration of new investment in a small number of centres brought about major problems of viability for many operators, particularly as it was aggravated by the onset of general economic recession.

In 1978 building allowances were introduced for hotels, albeit at a rate of 20 per cent compared with the rate of 50 per cent, for which industrial buildings qualify.

A permanent fiscal framework for hotel investment in Britain still remains to be created, which would not only stimulate desirable expansion in the future, but also bring about a parity of treatment between hotels and other industries in Britain, and between hotels in Britain and elsewhere, particularly in other countries of the European Economic Community.[6]

[6] Hotels and Catering EDC, *Hotels and Government Policy.*

13. Size and Ownership

When the size structure of an industry is examined, there are two dimensions to be considered; the size of the individual establishment, and the size of the firm, which may operate more than one establishment. This distinction is of some importance in the supply of services, through individual outlets essentially serving local markets. Although some factors influence both the size of an individual establishment and the overall size of the firm, it is nevertheless desirable to consider the size structure of establishments and firms separately, and this is the approach adopted in this chapter, in which the discussion of the individual unit precedes the discussion of the firm and of concentration in the hotel and catering industry. In both, the size pattern of the industry is related to the influencing factors on the one hand, and to its implications on the other.

Influences on Unit Size

We have seen in the historial outline that some of the present industry had its origins in the development over the centuries. Many units have developed from the private household and have retained many of its characteristics.

Most parts of the industry offer considerable attractions to men with limited capital resources; they offer economic independence in a business which provides a means of livelihood in an activity full of human interest, and which appears to require little technical skill to conduct it. As with, for example, building and retail distribution, there are good chances of setting up one's own small business in this industry. Since many individuals do enter the industry with modest capital and tend to use their own resources to finance it, they do so on a small scale and their units remain small.

If technical economies of scale offer an inducement to large-scale operation in industries where they are present, especially in heavy industries where small-scale operation may be often impossible, it appears that such advantages are not so substantial in the hotel and catering industry, and that they are not a requirement of a viable operation. But it also seems that such technical economies as do exist have not yet been fully exploited in the industry.

Two fundamental inherent factors favour the small unit in the industry. The first is the nature of hotel and catering services; the small unit enjoys an advantage in satisfying the individual wants of the customer, in being able to pay attention to detail and in facilitating the co-ordination of inter-connected activities. Hotel and catering services demand close and flexible day-to-day management, in which the personality of the proprietor or manager can have an important effect on customer and employee satisfaction.

The strongest influencing factor, exercising a decisive influence on the size of many units, is the size of the market and the extent of competition. If there is a need for an hotel of a particular type in a particular location with fifty beds, one can hardly hope to attract sufficient custom to fill one twice that size, and much the same goes for other types of establishment. It is significant in this connection that for some licensees and other proprietors, their catering business does not necessarily provide their only employment, or even their chief livelihood.

Not only does the market limitation impose a limit on size; it also determines the degree of specialization as between different establishments in a particular location. Only where the market is sufficiently large, units of a specific type and standard emerge; only then does one find a more or less sharp differentiation between, for instance, transit and long-stay hotels, between a variety of speciality restaurants and between quality and utility establishments.

Inadequate data exist on the size structure of the industry to allow establishments to be analysed, using the same unit of measurement in all sectors of the industry; what follows, therefore, provides only an indication of the size of establishments in different sectors, in terms of capacity and turnover.

The Size Pattern of Units

The scale of hotels and other accommodation units has been traditionally expressed in terms of bed or bedroom capacity. The former is more satisfactory, as it takes account of the proportion of single and double bedrooms and, therefore, of the capacity to accommodate a given number of guests. Whichever of these methods is used, no regard is paid to the other activities of the hotel, which may account for a substantial proportion of revenue and of the numbers employed. An hotel with, say, fifty beds with substantial sales to non-residents, may in fact, achieve a higher revenue and employ larger numbers than one with twice the bed capacity which restricts its services to residents. Size measured in terms of turnover may, therefore, provide a better indication.

The most up-to-date analysis of the size structure of British hotels in terms of bedrooms was made in the *Hotel Prospects* study of the Hotels and Catering Economic Development Committee for 1974, which adopted a wide definition of the term 'hotel'. It included some 14,000 licensed and 20,000 unlicensed units with a total capacity approaching 500,000 bedrooms, over 300,000 of them in licensed and close on 200,000 in unlicensed hotels.

Table 44 and Appendixes K and L show that the average British hotel is small – if licensed, over twenty bedrooms and unlicensed, less than ten. Just over 1 per cent of all hotels have more than 100 bedrooms and just over 2·5 per cent between 50–100 bedrooms; the bulk of these are licensed. By far the largest hotels are in London; London hotels account for less than 4 per cent of British hotels, but for about 13·5 per cent of the total bedrooms. About one-half of all British hotels and of their total bedroom capacity are in coastal areas; well over a third of licensed hotels and of their bedroom capacity are in these areas, but the share of coastal areas of unlicensed hotels is over two-thirds of the total and

Table 44
British Hotels and Bedroom Capacity by Size of Hotel in 1974

	4–10	11–15	16–25	26–50	51–100	Over 100	Total
Bedrooms							
Establishments							
Licensed	6,199	2,474	2,029	1,762	836	368	13,668
Unlicensed	14,508	4,224	921	278	44	16	19,991
Total	20,707	6,698	2,950	2,040	880	384	33,659
Total Bedrooms							
Licensed	44,367	31,609	40,751	61,823	57,952	74,351	310,853
Unlicensed	101,172	52,668	18,337	9,214	2,947	2,311	186,649
Total	145,539	84,277	59,088	71,037	60,899	76,662	497,502

Source: Hotels and Catering EDC, *Hotel Prospects to 1985.*

The distribution of British hotels and of their bedroom capacity by size and location are shown in Appendixes K and L.

they account for two-thirds of the total unlicensed bedroom accommodation in the country.

Turnover as an indication of size takes into account the total activity of an establishment and its sales mix. The 1969 Catering Trades Inquiry, which covered 8,000 hotels and holiday camps with a total turnover of over £400 million, confirmed the predominance of the small hotel with an average turnover of £53,000, but also illustrated the significantly higher turnover of group hotels and, in particular, of the average holiday camp, as shown in Table 45.

After all that has been said about the factors, which tend to affect the present size structure, and after an examination of the distribution of British hotels by size, the question arises as to the optimum scale of hotel. In other words, is there an economically most efficient size, below and beyond which little advantage or even positive disadvantages exist? This is an extremely difficult question to answer simply in terms of a particular bedroom capacity, particularly as most hotels combine the letting of bedroom accommodation to a greater or lesser extent with the supply of food and drink. However, in broad terms, when the letting of bedrooms constitutes the main activity, there appears to be a critical size, which presents most problems in operation and which may be least viable. This is in the middle, probably between some 25 to 50 or 60 bedrooms or some 40 to 80 or 100 beds. Small units below this size can operate with family labour, have to rely only to a limited extent on outside staff, and can be supervised directly without intervening levels. Larger units call for larger staffing and a supervisory structure, which is rarely financially viable until the unit reaches a larger size, when it can also reap certain other economies of scale. This is con-

Table 45
Turnover of Accommodation Units in 1969

Type of establishment		Turnover[a] (£000)	Establishments (Number)	Average (£000)
Hotels	multiple[b]	157,600	1,194	132
	other licensed	256,900	6,659	39
	total	414,500	7,853	53
Holiday camps		30,000	148	203

Source: Department of Trade and Industry, Catering Trades 1969, Statistical Inquiry.

[a] The turnover figures in this table differ slightly from those in Appendix A, which relate to organizations rather than establishments.

[b] Organizations with ten or more establishments.

firmed by the approach of the most successful hotel companies, which have been disposing of their smaller units, and rarely building new hotels with less than eighty bedrooms in recent years. There would also appear to be economies of scale for hotels with several hundred bedrooms, which tend to be the most profitable ones.

Little statistical information is available about the unit size of catering establishments. The Attwood Survey of 1965 from which certain information is quoted by R. Kotas in his study of labour costs in restaurants,[1] provides an indication of the size of more than 28,000 restaurants in terms of their seating capacity. According to this source, over 60 per cent had a seating capacity of no more than forty and over 80 per cent no more than sixty (Table 46).

Table 46
Seating Capacity of Catering Establishments in 1965

Seating capacity	Establishments	% of total
10 or less	1,400	4·9
11–40	16,000	56·3
41–60	5,500	19·4
61–80	2,400	8·4
81–130	1,900	6·7
131–150	300	1·1
151 or more	900	3·2
Total	28,400	100·0

Source: Quoted in *Labour Costs in Restaurants*.

[1] Kotas, R., op. cit., p. 33.

Size and Ownership

According to the 1969 Catering Inquiry, 131,000 establishments recorded a turnover of £2,368 million, an average of £18,000 per unit. The highest average was for multiple restaurants, the lowest for fish and chip shops and registered clubs. See Table 47.

Table 47
Turnover of Catering Establishments in 1969

Type of Establishment		Turnover[a] (£000)	Establishments (Number)	Average (£000)
Restaurants	multiple[b]	97,600	1,777	55
	independent	402,200	27,978	14
	fish and chip shops	123,900	14,282	9
	total	623,700	44,037	14
Public houses	managed	490,400	13,340	37
	run by tenants	719,200	43,641	17
	free	98,800	4,343	23
	total	1,308,400	61,324	21
Clubs	licensed	64,200	2,488	26
	registered	371,800	23,367	16
	total	436,000	25,855	17
Total		2,368,100	131,216	18

Source: Department of Trade and Industry, Catering Trades 1969, Statistical Inquiry.

[a] The turnover figures in this table differ slightly from those in Appendix A, which relate to organizations rather than establishments.

[b] Organizations with ten or more establishments.

Similar observations would seem to apply to catering as to hotels: there may be a critical size for a restaurant as there is for an hotel, below and above which there is a viable operation, but the heterogeneous nature of the establishments does not make it possible to generalize.

Growth of Chains

In the hotel and catering industry most of the increase in scale has taken place by a process of diffusion, whereby the market obstacle has been met by firms setting up or acquiring units in different locations, and placing them under central management. These establishments may be grouped within a restricted geographical area or distributed widely over large parts of the country. When a firm comprises more than one establishment in this industry, considerable latitude is often allowed within a broad policy framework to individual managers.

This is the case particularly with hotels, and particularly when the units are scattered; distance sets a limit on the amount of contact with the head office and increases problems of effective central direction and supervision. Generally, the central management sets operational guide lines, advises and controls financially. There is a growing tendency to group marketing and centralized purchasing. But there is also a growing tendency to standardization of operation. Whilst unit managers are encouraged to take full advantage of local conditions and to attain results by their own initiative, in order to obtain the advantages of size, firms increasingly co-ordinate their separate units. In the larger companies, regional and area management structure becomes necessary to achieve this.

A high degree of centralization and standardization is particularly apparent in the operation of restaurants and public houses. The growing application of marketing in catering has found an expression in the increasing use of market research, product formulation and in the creation of chains of restaurants with a standard product in different locations, and in the fostering of a brand image through advertising and other promotion media. Central food production and quality control of individual units completes the translation of the total marketing concept to catering, in which close monitoring of operations leads to the adjustment of the product, and to the design of new facilities.

Hotel Groups

In 1969 the Catering Trades Inquiry covered some 8,000 licensed hotels and holiday camps. Of the 8,000 units 1,200 were multiples operated by organizations with ten or more establishments.

If unlicensed hotels are included, following a series of mergers and takeovers and an increase in new hotel building in the early 1970s, there were in 1976 some thirty hotel groups with 700 or more rooms each. Their list is shown in Appendix M.

The first ten operated together 600 hotels with a total capacity of over 60,000 rooms, or over two-thirds of the capacity of the thirty organizations included in the table. Over one-quarter of the units and one-third of the room capacity belonged to the two largest, Trust Houses Forte and Grand Metropolitan Hotels; the five largest, including J. Lyons, Bass Charrington and Centre Hotels accounted for over one-half of the room capacity of the thirty leading hotel operators. Following the acquisition of most of J. Lyons' hotel interests at the beginning of 1977 by Trust Houses Forte, the latter has more than one-quarter of the room capacity of the thirty organizations.

Only one of the thirty organizations in Appendix M operated exclusively unlicensed hotels (North Hotels); the bulk of the hotels of the remaining groups were licensed. Twelve of the thirty organizations were predominantly or entirely hotel operators, seven were brewery companies with significant hotel interests in addition to their public house involvement in the industry, four were mainly hotel and catering companies, and seven were subsidiaries of other diversified companies.

In terms of ownership British Transport Hotels are State-owned, Travco Hotels are in co-operative ownership, Imperial London Hotels are a private company; the remaining twenty-seven are public companies or subsidiaries.

There are altogether several dozen companies owning more than one hotel in Britain. The independently-owned unit is still the typical firm in the industry, but its share of the total accommodation capacity continues to decrease.

The holiday camp sector is dominated by the 'Big Four' – Butlin (Rank Organization), Pontin, Ladbroke and Warner – who accounted in 1976 for fifty-eight camps and close on 150,000 beds in Britain, the bulk of holiday camp capacity. The numbers of units and bed capacities of the four leading operators are shown in Appendix O.

Restaurant Chains and Contractors

The 1969 Catering Trades Inquiry covered close on 30,000 restaurants, cafes, and snack bars, excluding establishments of organizations mainly engaged in retailing and certain other fields. Of the establishments covered by the Inquiry, 1,770 were operated by multiple organizations with ten or more establishments. The largest operators of commercial restaurants in Britain with more than ten establishments at the end of 1976 are listed in Appendix N. They include between them over 2,700 establishments. Independent restaurants, therefore, predominate in Britain, and this is likely to be the case even if firms with fewer than ten establishments are included. But the bulk of the restaurant chains are licensed and their market penetration is far more prominent in the licensed restaurant sector: it is likely that as many as a third of all licensed restaurants are operated by multiples.

The 'Big Four' restaurant operators in Britain are Trust Houses Forte with 500 units, Allied Bakeries and British Transport with some 400 each, the latter consisting of restaurants and refreshment rooms at railway stations, and Grand Metropolitan with some 300 establishments outside their hotels.

The great majority of catering contractors operate more than one contract and these vary greatly in size. The sector is dominated by five leading companies with a total of about 3,750 contracts between them. Of these by far the biggest is Gardner Merchant Food Services, owned by Trust Houses Forte, with some 1,800 contracts. The second biggest is the Sutcliffe Catering Group, followed by Bateman and Midland Catering, both owned by Grand Metropolitan with about 500 contracts each; Taylorplan Catering claims nearly 200 contracts. Details of the five contractors are shown in Appendix O.

In 1972 there were an estimated 200 catering contractors' organizations operating a total of 5,000 units and employing up to 70,000 staff. The five biggest may, therefore, operate between them three-quarters of all units under contract and they are likely to account for about one-half of the contractors' labour force.

The Tied House System

Organizations consisting of large numbers of establishments are most prominent in the licensed sectors of the industry, owing to what has come to be known as the 'tied house system'. Although it was mentioned in earlier parts of this book and in particular in Chapters 4, 7, 8 and 12, the distinction between the 'free' and 'tied' house is of such importance in the organization of the industry that it calls for further explanation.

The free house is owned by a proprietor who is under no obligation to obtain any of his supplies from any particular source. Under the 'tied house system', on the other hand, the owner or lessor of the licensed premises is usually a firm of brewers, for whom the premises represent a retail outlet. The firm may then run the establishments in one of two ways, i.e. under direct management or under tenancy. In the former case, the manager is a salaried employee with no financial stake in the business. In the latter, the tenant takes the premises on lease or under a tenancy agreement from the brewery, and undertakes to purchase from his landlord, the brewer-owner, and from no one else, either all his beers or all his beers and also some other commodities (such as wines, spirits, and tobacco), at agreed prices. The tie for beer is fundamental to the system, its extension to other goods is not.

The system represents vertical forward integration, as its origin lies in the desire of the brewer to secure an outlet for his beers; it was given a stimulus in the second half of the last century by legislation, which led to a reduction in the number of licences, thereby increasing their value. The Peel Commission estimated that in 1898 the proportion of on-licensed houses owned by the brewers was about 75 per cent. The Amulree Commission expressed the view that in 1930 the bulk of them in England and Wales were owned by brewers, and estimated the proportion at 95 per cent.[2] The houses under direct management represented a small proportion of the whole number owned by brewers, and the 'tied house' system through tenancy must be regarded, therefore, as by far the most common method of public house operation. The Amulree Commission also thought that there was a tendency for the system of tying to increase in scope and intensity. The Monopolies Commission found that in 1967 over 80 per cent of all on-licensed premises in Britain, including hotels and restaurants, were owned by breweries, but a significantly higher proportion of public houses.[3] Over three-quarters of all on-licences were tenanted and less than one-quarter managed but the trend to management was on the increase. However, a recent study suggests that this trend may have been halted or even reversed.[4]

[2] Amulree Report, pp. 65–7.
[3] Monopolies Commission, op. cit., Chapter 3, *passim*.
[4] Housden, J., Brewers and Tenants, *HCIMA Review*, Volume 2, Number 1.

Whilst among public houses the tied house is almost universal in England and Wales, it is far less common in Scotland where fewer licensed premises are owned by breweries, and where the public house has been much more associated with its owner who has conducted a free house. No doubt the system of local veto which applied in Scotland until 1976, and which periodically put the existence of licensed premises in any district at the mercy of the local electorate, was an important factor in reducing direct ownership by the breweries. Loans are sometimes made by brewers to public house owners in exchange for agreements to take draught beer; when the loan is paid off the publican is, however, free to change his source of supply.

In 1976 five brewery groups owned between them nearly 40,000, more than one-half of all on-licences (mainly public houses); the remaining brewery-owned on-licences were in the hands of several dozen brewery companies. A number of mergers and take-overs since contributed to an increase in the dominance of the large firm in this field in which by 1976 there were five brewery companies with 6,000 or more public houses each. The leading public house operators at the end of 1976 are listed in Appendix O.

Growth and Concentration

The emergence of large organizations in the hotel and catering industry was first stimulated by three almost concurrent developments over a century ago. First by increased travel in general and by the railways, in particular. The railways increased the scale to which business could profitably grow in industry generally; it is significant for our purpose that they created the conditions in which a large hotel and a large hotel company became a business proposition and that they, in fact, built the first large hotels. The limited liability company removed a further obstacle to the growth of firms by granting protection to shareholders of joint stock companies and thus providing a stimulus to investment in industry and commerce. At about the same time licensing legislation created an inducement for brewers to acquire licensed houses, and to enter the hotel and catering industry on a large scale as owners and operators.

Until the middle of the nineteenth century large units and organizations were almost unknown in the provision of hotel and catering services. The second half of that century brought into existence the first large hotel, restaurant and public house organizations in Britain whose number grew further in the first half of the twentieth century, largely as a result of the three original stimuli. However, the representative establishment and firm in the hotel and catering industry remained small. The mode of entry into the industry and the method of financing have continued to influence both. As the individual proprietor is still a typical entrepreneur in the provision of hotel and catering services, his working life often determines the length of life of the firm. Not all capital is re-financed in each generation; not only is some handed down from father to son, but the many corporate firms have an existence separate from the lives of their owners. However, since so many individuals enter the industry with modest capital and tend to use their own resources to finance it, there is bound to be a limit imposed not only on the size of an individual unit, but also on the growth of firms by the size of their resources.

Expanding market opportunities in the thirty years after the war have largely influenced further growth of firms, and also further concentration in the hotel and catering industry. Three major themes run through the chronicle of major events in the 1960s and 1970s in Appendix E: new developments in facilities, increasing concentration, and increasing moves towards co-operation in the industry.

It is clear that many factors favour the large firm. There may be limited economies of scale in a single establishment, after a certain point is reached, but economies accompany groups and chains of hotel and catering establishments for a long time, before strong managerial obstacles set in. These economies are in the first place *financial,* enabling large firms to marshal capital resources from their own cash flow, and from external sources, beyond the reach of small firms. Secondly, there are *marketing* economies, allowing business promotion on an adequate scale, including catering for groups and referral business. Thirdly, a large firm enjoys economies of *buying* through its weight in the market. Fourthly, there are substantial *managerial* advantages. Management costs do not keep pace with increased volume of business at all levels, and the larger firms have the capacity to secure good quality management and to employ specialists. *Technical* economies arise with size, particularly in firms concentrated geographically, in the provision of central production facilities. Last but not least, there are economies of *risk-spreading* which enable large firms to reduce risk by product and geographical diversification.

Only on two of the above counts can the smaller firm compete successfully – in marketing and in the management of an operation, because it is normally owner-managed. This enables the entrepreneur to market his services with a personal touch and individuality, and to generate a substantial volume of repeat business; he is also able to direct the firm as an individual and generate a personal loyalty in his employees. He may enjoy non-monetary advantages in the provision of free accommodation for himself and his family, which represent a significant part of the revenue of the firm. But as we noted in connection with an individual establishment, there may be a critical size also for a firm; when it has lost the advantages of being small and when it is not large enough to have the strengths of the large firm.

Co-operative Groups

We have seen that franchising offers some of the advantages of large firms to small independent operators, particularly in marketing, by centralizing certain functions which are provided by the franchisor whilst individual franchisees retain a large measure of independence.

In recent years major strides have been made with similar objectives by co-operative groups of hotels. These have been of two main types. Local groups of independent competing hotels have formed consortia, such as Torquay Leisure Hotels, in which mutual trust and confidence have led to group marketing, buying and other forms of co-operation, securing significant economies of scale for the participants.

The other main development has been the formation of marketing consortia of independent non-competing hotels widely distributed geographically. Prestige Hotels, Interchange Hotels and Inter Hotels have been outstanding examples with varying degrees of integration and common strategy amongst members.

The development of co-operation, its forms and characteristics, and the approach adopted by the leading groups have been well described by Dr Pickering and his colleagues in their study of The Small Firm in the Hotel and Catering Industry, which shows the advantages and the problems associated with co-operative action, as well the opportunities this development offers to the smaller firm in the future.[5]

[5] Pickering, J. F., *et al.*, op. cit., Chapter VII.

Part V
Human Resources

Additional Reading for Part V

Commission on Industrial Relations: *Report No. 23, The Hotel and Catering Industry, Part 1, Hotels and Restaurants,* Chapters 5, 6, and 7.

Commission on Industrial Relations: *Report No. 27, The Hotel and Catering Industry, Part 2, Industrial Catering,* Chapters 3 and 4.

Commission on Industrial Relations: *Report No. 36, The Hotel and Catering Industry, Part 3, Public Houses, Clubs and Other Sectors.*

Department of Employment: *Manpower Studies No. 10, Hotels.*

Department of Employment: *Manpower Studies No. 11, Catering.*

Hotels and Catering EDC: *Manpower Policy in the Hotels and Restaurant Industry.*

Hotels and Catering EDC: *Employment Policy and Industrial Relations in the Hotels and Catering Industry.*

14. Manpower and Employment

Between Census days in April 1966 and April 1971 the total working population of Britain increased by some 200,000; from 24·8 million to 25 million. The numbers of economically active females increased by over 250,000 in the five years; the male working population declined by over 100,000.

In the same period numbers engaged in the hotel and catering industry showed a small decline. There was an increase in the numbers of men in the industry of 11,000, while the numbers of women decreased by 13,000.

In the early 1970s the hotel and catering industry accounted for almost 3 per cent of the total working population of Britain and nearly 5 per cent of the women at work were engaged in hotel and catering activities.

These data extracted from the Census Reports for 1966 and 1971 cover the hotel and catering industry as defined by the Standard Industrial Classifications of 1958 and 1968 respectively; the broad scope of the industry remained the same under both editions of the classification. The data, which include self-employed as well as employees, and which represent the numbers of those who declared themselves as being engaged in the industry on Census days in the two years, are shown in Table 48.

Table 48

Numbers Engaged in Hotel and Catering Industry 1966 and 1971

1961 000s	*1971 000s*	*Change %*		*1966 %*	*1971 %*
253	264	+4·3	Men	1·6	1·7
438	425	−3·0	Women	5·0	4·7
691	689	−0·2	Total	2·9	2·8

Source: Census of Population 1966 and 1971.

Statistics of the working population for the period after 1971 produced by the Department of Employment suggest that the working population has increased only slowly in recent years. The expansion of full-time education and the decrease in the demand for labour help to explain the slow growth in the working population both in the period 1966 to 1971 and after 1971; these influences were to some extent offset by an increase in the numbers of working women.

Data comparable to those generated by the 1966 and 1971 Census will not be available again until reports are produced from the next Census scheduled to take place in 1981. In the meantime the main indications are provided by the Department of Employment statistics, which showed an increase of 800,000 or about 3 per cent in the working population between 1972 and 1976; no breakdown between males and females was provided. However, an indication of trends is suggested by statistics of employees in employment, which show over the period a decrease in male employment of 200,000, or 1·5 per cent, while female employees increased by 600,000, or 7 per cent.

Self-employed and Employees

The Census Reports provide an indication of the numbers of self-employed as compared with employees in the industry. The former include employers who employ others as well as those working on their own account without employees; employees include all who work for someone else under a contract of service, whether written or not. Table 49 shows the position in the industry in 1966 and 1971.

Table 49

Self-employed and Employees in Hotel and Catering Industry 1966 and 1971

	Self-employed		Employees		Total	
	1966 000s	1971 000s	1966 000s	1971 000s	1966 000s	1971 000s
Men	75	81	178	183	253	264
Women	55	54	383	371	438	425
Total	130	135	561	554	691	689

Source: Census of Population 1966 and 1971.

It appears that in 1966 almost 19 per cent of all persons engaged in the industry were self-employed and that their total numbers increased between 1966 and 1971, largely as a result of an increase in self-employed men, while numbers of self-employed women remained relatively static between the two years. As a proportion of total numbers engaged in the industry, self-employed men and women taken together rose to close on 20 per cent, or one in five of the total.

The hotel and catering industry comprises a large number of small independently-owned and operated units. It is, therefore, not surprising to find a high proportion of self-employed manpower in the industry. However, the trends to greater concentration of ownership and to an increase in size of an individual unit in some sectors are likely to result in a decrease in the proportion of self-employed in the industry.

There are conflicting views on the stability of an industry in the light of this pattern and trends. A high proportion of self-employed tends to point to a volatile industry, but it also suggests a greater stability of employment in a depressed economy – at least in terms of visible unemployment – than would be the case otherwise.

Employment between 1966 and 1975

The main indications of annual changes in industrial employment are provided by the Department of Employment. Until 1971 the estimates were based on mid-year counts of National Insurance cards. Since 1971 they have been based on a postal enquiry to employers relating to a particular date in June of each year. The two methods are not directly comparable with each other and the data derived from them are not directly comparable with those derived from the Census of Population for the years 1966 and 1971. However, the estimates from the three different sources are considered to be reasonably compatible. Statistics of employment in the hotel and catering industry based on the Department of Employment estimates are shown in Table 50.

Table 50
Hotel and Catering Industry
Employment 1966–1975
(000s)

June	1966	1967	1968	1969	1970	1971	1972	1973	1974	1975
Men	256	243	243	265	264	255	266	286	288	293
Women	453	438	425	431	423	426	457	498	507	523
Total	709	681	668	696	687	681	723	784	795	816

The bases of calculation of these figures and of classification of establishments were not consistent throughout the period, but the above estimates can be regarded as reasonably consistent, as the effects of the changes in compilation were relatively small for the hotel and catering industry.

The employment series reveals a decrease in hotel and catering employment in the late 1960s and a substantial increase from 1971 onwards; by 1975 employment in the industry exceeded the 1966 level by 15 per cent. Male and female employment followed a similar pattern, but the decline in the employment of women in the first few years of the decade was much sharper and more prolonged than of men. Since 1971 growth in part-time employment[1] both among men and women has been significantly greater than the growth in full-time employment, and the growth in female employment has been greater than the growth in male employment.

As far as the component sectors are concerned, employment in public houses

[1] Part-time workers are defined by the Department of Employment as those normally employed for not more than 30 hours per week (excluding main meal breaks and overtime).

and by catering contractors increased fastest between 1971 and 1975, and a major part of this growth was accounted for by part-time female employees. By contrast, the lowest growth occurred over the period in restaurants, cafes and snack bars, where full-time female employment actually declined.

Table 51

Hotel and Catering Industry
Full-time and Part-time[a] Employees in Employment by Sector 1975
(000s)

	Men			Women			Total		
	Full-time	Part-time	Total	Full-time	Part-time	Total	Full-time	Part-time	Total
Hotels and other residential	86·5	16·2	102·7	87·3	65·5	152·8	173·8	81·7	255·5
Restaurants, cafes, snack bars	46·6	11·0	57·4	39·2	66·2	105·4	85·6	77·2	162·8
Public houses	36·9	40·7	77·6	35·0	117·2	152·2	71·9	157·9	229·8
Clubs	17·0	21·7	38·7	13·7	46·6	60·3	30·7	68·3	99·0
Catering contractors	14·4	1·8	16·2	32·8	19·8	52·6	47·2	21·6	68·8
Total	201·2	91·4	292·6	208·0	315·3	523·3	409·2	406·7	815·9

Source: Department of Employment Gazette, 1976.

[a] Part-time employees are defined by the Department of Employment as those normally employed for not more than 30 hours per week (excluding main meal breaks and overtime).

Table 52

Hotel and Catering Industry
Employees in Employment by Region 1975
(000s)

	South East	East Anglia	South West	West Midlands	East Midlands	Yorks and Humberside	North West	North	Wales	Scotland	Great Britain
Hotels etc.	81·6	9·6	39·5	10·7	9·6	14·4	18·6	11·4	15·5	44·5	255·5
Restaurants etc.	62·3	5·1	16·1	9·7	8·4	13·9	15·5	7·1	7·4	17·2	162·8
Public houses	66·8	4·3	14·0	28·9	13·2	22·0	34·1	16·8	7·9	21·7	229·8
Clubs	16·8	1·4	5·1	9·8	6·7	12·5	15·1	14·2	7·7	9·7	99·0
Contractors	32·0	1·0	4·8	7·4	2·7	5·0	6·6	2·0	2·1	5·0	68·8

Source: Department of Employment Gazette, August 1976.
Totals may not agree with the sum of individual items due to rounding.

Employment in Sectors and Regions

On the basis of the Standard Industrial Classification (1968), in which the hotel and catering industry is divided into five main component sectors, the Department of Employment statistics of full-time and part-time employees in employment in individual sectors were in June 1975 as shown in Table 51.

Table 51 indicates that almost 50 per cent of employment in the industry is part-time. Over 60 per cent of all women and about 30 per cent of all men are employed in the industry on a part-time basis. Public houses and clubs have the highest proportions, with over two-thirds of their employees being part-time.

Sectoral analysis indicates that almost one-third of the industry employees are to be found in hotels and other residential establishments and over one-quarter in public houses. The highest proportion of women is employed by catering contractors, the lowest in hotels and clubs, although even there women outnumber men.

The regional distribution of hotel and catering employees in the five main sectors is shown in Table 52. It demonstrates clearly the dominance of the South East Region, which accounts for well over one-third of all employees in the industry in Great Britain.

Unemployment

Numbers of registered unemployed represent persons who are registered as unemployed at four- or five-weekly intervals falling on dates approximately in the middle of each month, and whose last employment was in the hotel and catering industry.

In the period 1966-1975 unemployment in the hotel and catering industry followed closely unemployment in the whole economy as shown by the monthly averages for each year during the period in Table 53.

Table 53
Unemployment in Great Britain 1966-1975[a]
(000s)

	1966	1967	1968	1969	1970	1971	1972	1973	1974	1975
All industries	323	510	538	531	568	737	816	581	572[b]	890
Hotel and catering industry	19	26	25	25	25	30	34	26	25[b]	44[b]

Source: *Department of Employment Gazette*, January 1976.

[a] Wholly unemployed excluding school leavers and adult students.
[b] Figures based on averages for 11 months.

The annual pattern of unemployment for all industries and for the hotel and catering industry is shown in Table 54 for the year 1975. Unemployment in all industries increased steadily throughout the year, giving an annual rise in unemployment in the country of over 50 per cent. In hotels and catering unemployment declined during the first half of the year, rose slowly during the third quarter, including the peak season, and very rapidly during the last quarter; between June and December unemployment in the industry doubled. Table 54 illustrates to some extent also the seasonal pattern of unemployment in the industry, particularly if this is shown as a percentage of unemployment in all industries.

Table 54

Monthly Unemployment in Great Britain 1975[a]

	Jan.	Feb.	Mar.	Apr.	May	June	July	Aug.	Sept.	Oct.	Nov.	Dec.
(1) All industries (000s)	731	749	763	788	799	810	889	944	979	1,033	1,080	1,120
(2) Hotel and catering industry (000s)	n.a.	37	36	35	34	32	37	41	43	55	65	65
(3) 2 as % of 1		4·9	4·7	4·4	4·3	4·0	4·2	4·3	4·4	5·3	6·0	5·8

Source: Department of Employment Gazette January 1976.

[a] Wholly unemployed excluding school leavers and adult students.
n.a. Not available due to industrial action.

Separate unemployment statistics for the five sectors of the hotel and catering industry are shown on a monthly basis for 1975 in Table 55. They show again an increase in unemployment for all sectors over the year as a whole. Most sectors were to some extent influenced by seasonality, but it is clear that the main seasonal effects are to be found in the hotel sector, which accounted in most months for some two-thirds of the unemployment in the whole hotel and catering industry.

Demand for Labour

Monthly statistics of unfilled vacancies represent the number of vacancies notified to employment offices and careers offices by employers, and remaining unfilled on the first or second Wednesday each month. The figures do not purport to represent the total number of vacancies which need to be filled, as some employers do not notify their vacancies but prefer to rely on other methods of recruitment. Nevertheless, comparison of the figures for various dates provides some indication of the changes in the demand for labour as a result of seasonal variations in activity.

The annual pattern for 1975 given in table 56 shows that notified unfilled vacancies in the hotel and catering industry more than double as between June when the outstanding vacancies are at their peak and late autumn and the winter months when they are at their lowest.

Table 55
Hotel and Catering Industry
Registered Unemployed by Sector in 1975
(000s)

	Jan.	Feb.	Mar.	Apr.	May	June	July	Aug.	Sept.	Oct.	Nov.	Dec.
MEN
Hotels	n.a.	15·9	15·3	14·7	13·7	13·3	15·0	16·5	17·2	22·2	25·6	25·5
Restaurants	n.a.	3·4	3·5	3·3	3·4	3·2	3·5	3·9	4·3	5·3	5·9	6·2
Public houses	n.a.	2·7	2·8	2·8	2·9	2·9	3·2	3·4	3·6	4·0	4·4	4·7
Clubs	n.a.	1·6	1·7	1·7	1·7	1·8	1·9	2·0	2·1	2·3	2·4	2·4
Contractors	n.a.	0·7	0·7	0·8	0·9	0·9	0·9	1·0	1·1	1·2	1·2	1·3
Total	n.a.	24·3	24·0	23·3	22·6	22·1	24·5	26·8	28·3	35·0	39·5	40·1
WOMEN
Hotels	n.a.	8·1	7·6	6·8	6·2	5·9	7·1	8·1	8·8	12·9	16·7	16·6
Restaurants	n.a.	2·5	2·6	2·5	2·6	2·4	2·8	3·2	3·4	4·3	4·9	4·9
Public houses	n.a.	1·0	1·0	1·0	1·0	1·1	1·2	1·3	1·4	1·6	1·8	1·9
Clubs	n.a.	0·4	0·4	0·5	0·5	0·5	0·6	0·6	0·7	0·8	0·8	0·9
Contractors	n.a.	0·5	0·5	0·5	0·6	0·6	0·7	0·7	0·8	0·9	0·9	1·0
Total	n.a.	12·5	12·1	11·3	10·9	10·5	12·4	13·9	15·1	20·5	25·1	25·3
TOTAL
Hotels	n.a.	24·0	22·9	21·5	19·9	19·2	22·1	24·6	26·0	35·1	42·3	42·1
Restaurants	n.a.	5·9	6·1	5·8	6·0	5·6	6·3	7·1	7·7	9·6	10·8	11·1
Public houses	n.a.	3·7	3·8	3·8	3·9	4·0	4·4	4·7	5·0	5·6	6·2	6·6
Clubs	n.a.	2·0	2·1	2·2	2·2	2·3	2·5	2·6	2·8	3·1	3·2	3·3
Contractors	n.a.	1·2	1·2	1·3	1·5	1·5	1·6	1·7	1·9	2·1	2·1	2·3
Total	n.a.	36·8	36·1	34·6	33·5	32·6	36·9	40·7	43·4	55·5	64·6	65·4

Source: Department of Employment Gazette, February 1975–January 1976.

n.a. Not available due to industrial action.

Table 56
Hotel and Catering Industry
Unfilled Vacancies 1975
(000s)

	Jan.	Feb.	Mar.	Apr.	May	June	July	Aug.	Sept.	Oct.	Nov.	Dec.
Men	n.a.	n.a.	6·9	7·6	7·3	7·2	5·8	5·4	6·1	5·3	3·7	3·3
Women	n.a.	n.a.	12·1	14·0	13·8	14·2	10·2	10·0	11·6	9·0	6·2	5·1
Total	n.a.	n.a.	19·0	21·6	21·1	21·3	16·0	15·5	17·7	14·3	9·9	8·4

Source: Department of Employment Gazette, April 1975–January 1976.

Totals may not agree with the sum of individual items due to rounding.
n.a. Not available due to industrial action.

The Industry and Local Employment

We noted earlier that the main sectors of the hotel and catering industry account for almost 3 per cent of the total working population, and almost 5 per cent of working women in Britain. However, the significance of hotel and catering services from the point of view of employment emerges sharply in particular areas of high concentration; these regional and area variations are concealed when only national figures are examined.

If a variation of plus or minus one-third from the national ratio is accepted as within normal limits, between 2 and 4 per cent of the working population engaged in the hotel and catering industry would suggest a normal concentration in a particular area or locality. However, in a number of areas and in many individual localities the proportion of hotel and catering employment rises sharply; in a number of resorts between 6 to 15 per cent of the working population is engaged in the industry, i.e. between two and five times the national ratio, and in a few it rises above that.

A concentration of more than 4 or 5 per cent almost invariably reveals a high degree of dependence of the locality on hotel and catering services and related trades, which tend to accompany them, for much of the inhabitants' income. Particularly where the areas are deficient in natural resources and have limited suitability for other forms of economic development, their development as holiday areas has often brought to them prosperity, which they could not have enjoyed otherwise. Hotels and restaurants thus often became the backbone of a local economy, in which other holiday trades participate, and in which a higher standard of amenities was brought about than the local community itself could support. But this also often led to the development of a one-dimensional economy with its resultant drawbacks.

In many of these areas of high concentration of hotel and catering services, a low degree of diversification of economic activity creates unemployment problems resulting from a concurrent and sometimes quite short season of the activities, which account for a high proportion of the working population. The problem of out-of-season employment then presents itself with great acuteness, as it does whenever a number of industries and trades subject to the same seasonal fluctuations concentrate in one area and form the main means of livelihood of the community. This problem still remains to be solved successfully, as ill-conceived industrial development may well destroy the amenities of a locality as a resort, and deprive it of benefits which had hitherto accrued to it.

It is significant that a number of areas with a high proportion of the population engaged in the hotel and catering industry were included in the Development Area legislation designed to promote a high and stable level of employment in these areas in the 1950s and 1960s. But the most promising developments have occurred where activities complementary to the traditional ones have been identified and developed, whilst preserving the amenities of the area. Thus a winter sports season provided a solution for parts of Scotland, and conferences have been attracted in growing numbers to several coastal resorts. Institutions of higher education have created a growing demand for accommodation facilities in several resorts from October to June in each year. Some communities have decreased their dependence on visitor traffic, and have developed more as places of residence generating their own demand for all-year-round entertainment and eating-out facilities.

15. Occupations, Recruitment, and Training

Men and women in their working capacity may be classified either according to industry or according to occupation. The industry in which an individual is engaged is determined (whatever may be his particular occupation) by reference to the business or economic activity for the purposes of which his occupation is followed.

The occupation of any person is the kind of work he or she performs, due regard being paid to the conditions under which it is performed; this alone determines the particular group in an occupational classification to which the person is assigned. The nature of the factory, business, or service in which the person is employed, has no bearing upon the classification of his occupation, except to the extent that it enables the nature of his duties to be more clearly defined.

A single business may employ a number of individuals belonging to widely varying occupations in order to provide a particular product or service. The industrial classification differs essentially from the occupational, in that the former has regard only to the nature of the product or service to which an individual's work contributes; the latter takes account only of the nature of the work performed by the individual. The man who is, by virtue of his occupation, a clerk, for example, is classified industrially to building if employed by a builder, but to brewing if employed by a brewer.

When all those engaged in a particular industry are grouped into occupations, the pattern of occupational distribution within the industry emerges, which is of particular importance to recruitment and training.

The official Classification of Occupations 1970[1] classifies occupations into more than 200 groups and a large number of them occur in the hotel and catering industry. However, the great majority of those engaged in the industry belong to a limited number of what may be termed typical hotel and catering occupations; only a minority are classified to a large number of occupations, which provide, in most cases, a service to the main activities of the firms in the industry.

In practice, the large units with a high degree of labour specialization provide the best ground for a general occupational analysis. However, the distribution of occupations varies from one sector of the industry to another, and in any particular unit it is also influenced by the particular range and standard of services provided, as well as by the size of unit.

When viewing the industry as a whole, there emerge eight principal categories of occupations, some or all of which may be observed in any particular unit:

1. Managerial.
2. Food preparation and cookery.

[1] Office of Population Censuses and Surveys, *Classification of Occupations*, pp. xviii–xxii.

3. Food service.
4. Bar service.
5. Domestic.
6. Uniformed staff.
7. Clerical and commercial.
8. Miscellaneous.

Managerial Occupations

According to the Reports of the 1966 and 1971 Census of Population, close on 200,000 or almost 30 per cent of the men and women enumerated as being engaged in the industry, were in management positions. Of these, between 130–135,000 or some 20 per cent of the total work force were self-employed or employers. The remaining 60–70,000 or about 10 per cent of the total were, therefore, employees in management positions.

These statistics point to three manpower characteristics of the hotel and catering industry. First, in common with other small-unit industries, to the high proportion of proprietors, many of whom manage their own businesses. Secondly, to the high proportion of men and women in management positions. The industry provides much scope for economic independence and for reaching a management position. Thirdly, with increasing concentration in the industry, there are many management posts at various levels in addition to individual proprietorship. For some time, salaried management has been more widespread in the British hotel and catering industry than has been the case in some other countries, such as France and Switzerland, and significant salaried management is likely to continue. However, the owner/manager is still the dominant phenomenon even in Britain. For these reasons proprietors and managers have been grouped together and no sharp distinction is drawn between the two groups in this chapter.

Several traditional approaches to recruitment and training for management predominated in the industry until recently. Many 'learnt the trade' from their fathers, as had been the practice from the early days of innkeeping. Most recruitment to management positions took place from 'the ranks', with insistence on a long and thorough practical experience in all or most aspects of operation, and working experience on the Continent was regarded favourably by many hotels, restaurants and clubs. Numerous individuals with some capital entered the industry and learnt by trial and error how to run their businesses. Little formal training was available for management in the industry, and it was rare for firms to recruit management trainees with a view to developing them systematically for positions of responsibility. Until about 1950 those who had any formal training for the industry at all, largely technical rather than managerial, had been through courses at Westminster Technical College, the only hotel school in Britain, at the Swiss Hotel School at Lausanne or in one of the Services.

The recommendations of the Catering Wages Commission in the 1940s contributed much to the development of hotel and catering education in postwar Britain. Three major influences may be identified in the late 1940s and in the 1950s. First, this period saw the emergence of professionalism in the industry, manifested in the foundation of the Hotel and Catering Institute, which became the main spearhead in the advancement of technical education generally and of management education in particular, and in the activities of the Institutional Management Association. The courses and professional examinations of these two bodies marked the beginning of recognized standards of education and training for management in the industry.

The second major influence has been the pioneering work of a number of colleges, which developed courses of diploma standard, specifically designed for the 'cadetship' stream of entrants to the industry, as well as courses for those already in management positions in the industry. By 1960 Britain had a network or more than twenty diploma level colleges, in addition to numerous others.

Thirdly, in the same period, recruitment for training with a view to management was also developing in the industry itself. There was a slow growth in the number of firms which realized the importance of management training, and which were recruiting men and women with and without previous college training with a view to management.

Between 1960 and 1970 the traditional modes of entry to management positions gave way to the new thinking, and formal courses became the principal path for potential managers for the industry. Three happenings stand out amongst many in this period. In mid-1960s hotel and catering studies came to be established in two new British Universities. Degree courses were introduced at the University of Surrey, which evolved from Battersea College of Technology, in 1964 and at the University of Strathclyde, which included the former Scottish College of Commerce, in 1965; the first students graduated from these Universities with Bachelor degrees in this field in 1968.

In 1969, twelve courses leading to the Higher National Diploma in Hotel and Catering Administration and eight leading to the Higher National Diploma in Institutional Management were introduced in proposed polytechnics and colleges of further education in England and Wales, in addition to Higher National Diploma courses, which began earlier in Scotland. At the same time Ordinary National Diploma courses preparing students for supervisory positions in the industry were introduced in Hotel and Catering Operations, and in Institutional Housekeeping and Catering, at numerous educational establishments.

Last but not least, from 1966 onwards the Hotel and Catering Industry Training Board provided a powerful stimulus to management training in industry through its levy-and-grant system.

Since 1970 a number of further developments have taken place in higher education for the British hotel and catering industry, of which three deserve particular mention.

In 1970 the Council for National Academic Awards (CNAA) was established as a degree-awarding body for approved courses outside universities; by 1977 six courses in hotel and catering subjects leading to the award of CNAA degrees were offered at four centres in England.

In 1971 the Hotel and Catering Institute and the Institutional Management Association merged to form the Hotel, Catering and Institutional Management Association as a unified professional body for the industry. Following its formation the HCIMA completed a series of investigations into professional education[2] and, based on research undertaken at the University of Surrey[3], developed a corpus of knowledge for professional management in the industry[4]. With this information a major review of the HCIMA professional qualification has been completed, with a view to the implementation of the new course structure in 1978.

Thirdly, the Technician Education Council (TEC) and its Scottish counterpart (SCOTEC) were set up with the aim of developing a unified system of technical education. It is proposed that their qualifications will replace the Ordinary and Higher National Diplomas and Certificates, including those in hotel and catering subjects by the early 1980s, thus providing the industry with a unified system of courses and qualifications below degree level.

Therefore, in the late 1970s the British hotel and catering industry not only has a statutory organization with a strong interest in management training and a professional body concerned with management education, but also a wide range of degrees and diploma courses at colleges and universities, providing various levels of education and training for management.

Food Preparation and Cookery

According to the Reports of the 1967 and 1971 Census of Population, over 60,000 (or about 9 per cent) of those engaged in the hotel and catering industry were cooks and other food workers, such as butchers and bakers. In addition close on 30,000 (or about 4 per cent) were kitchen hands.

This wide occupational group ranges from the chefs of large hotels, restaurants and clubs, and various grades of cooks in these and other establishments, to ancillary kitchen employees. The former are skilled occupations representing the craft of the industry, the latter unskilled or semi-skilled. They all have certain characteristic working conditions in common. However, the different degrees of skill required have conditioned the mode of entry into these occupations, which is radically different between the two categories.

The recruitment to the semi-skilled and unskilled occupations has always been haphazard, as it has been to occupations requiring little skill in other industries. They offer little attraction and have been usually filled by men and women with no ambition who have tended to look upon them as 'just another job'.

The craft occupations of cooks have, on the other hand, tended to attract a

---

[2] HCIMA, *Tomorrow's Managers*.
[3] Johnson, P. W. R., *Professional Development and the Corpus of Knowledge in Hotel, Catering and Institutional Services* (PhD Thesis).
[4] HCIMA, *The Corpus of Professional Knowledge in Hotel, Catering and Institutional Services*, HCIMA Research Fellowship Final Report.

better type of entrant. To women they offer the opportunity of practising on a large scale the skills which they have probably learnt in their own homes and it is not surprising that women cooks predominate in some sectors of the industry. But few of them have contributed to the concept of cookery as a trade craft, as it was evolved in hotels, restaurants and clubs, by men. From the time these establishments emerged, men assumed the dominant and frequently exclusive position in their kitchens. Skilled chefs were partly recruited from the Continent, partly through numerous 'house apprenticeships' to which individual establishments attracted school leavers desirous to learn the craft. This 'on the job' training was the only mode of entry available almost up to the First World War when the employment of foreign labour was considerably reduced. The first Hotel and Restaurant School was opened at the Westminster Technical Institute in 1910, which retained its exclusive position in chef training until after the Second World War.

A national approach to training in trade cookery was evolved during and after the Second World War with intensive courses of training for canteen cooks, with training provided by the Services and particularly through the introduction of syllabuses and examinations in trade cookery by the City and Guilds of London Institute. Full-time and part-time City and Guilds courses were conducted soon after the war at numerous technical colleges, training both young entrants and those already in the industry.

There is no doubt that the industry has continued to benefit from the training schemes run by many firms, and also from the many courses of training in domestic cookery and housecraft which, although not specifically designed for the needs of the industry, have not been without their use for those who have subsequently entered the industry.

In 1952 the National Joint Apprenticeship Council for the Hotel and Catering Industry was established, and it is significant that the first apprenticeship in the industry on the lines of apprenticeships in other crafts was introduced for cooks, first of five years and subsequently reduced to four years; this was followed in 1957 by the introduction by a national committee set up for the purpose of a three-year trainee scheme for cooks. In both cases, day release to technical colleges was an integral part of the schemes of training, and City and Guilds Certificates represented formal courses and examinations taken by the apprentices and trainees. In the twenty years after the war, training in trade cookery made, in terms of numbers, greater strides than other forms of training for the industry, as national schemes added considerably to private arrangements of firms.

Soon after the setting up of the Industrial Training Board the schemes came to be administered by the Board. A review of the training arrangements began in consultation with the industry, catering teachers and the City and Guilds of London Institute, with a view to ensuring that the individual City and Guilds courses were not regarded in isolation but as continuing steps in the development of the craftsman, whilst recognizing the need to distinguish between career training on the one hand, and job training on the other. The latter is seen as training in a limited number of specified related tasks appropriate for popular catering establishments, carried out in the form of short basic induction courses common to all entrants, followed by further training courses in the various tasks appropriate to their particular jobs.

Career training in food preparation and cookery is based on three courses leading to nationally recognized qualifications awarded by the City and Guilds of London Institute.

The first two courses are the City and Guilds of London Institute 706/1 Basic Cookery for the Catering Industry and the City and Guilds of London Institute 706/2 Cookery for the Catering Industry. These programmes are offered on a two-year part-time basis or on a one-year full-time basis. The 706/1 is the basic craft course, the 706/2 course is normally available for those who have completed the 706/1 course or an equivalent.

Students are normally required to hold the 706/2 Certificate before they can proceed to the City and Guilds of London Institute 706/3 Certificate in Advanced Cookery for the Catering Industry. This is in three parts – kitchen and larder, taken over two years part-time, and pastry 1 and 2, each of which is taken over one year part-time. The 706/3 course is designed to meet the needs of those who have already had a high level of training and is intended for chefs and skilled cooks.

The three courses provide a clear continuity in career development, intregrating technical college training with industrial training and experience. Each phase constitutes one to two years of training and the whole programme also enables further career developments of students entering industry from full-time college courses, such as the City and Guilds 705 General Catering Course.

Food Service

According to the Reports of the 1966 and 1971 Census of Population about 125–140,000 of the men and women, some 20 per cent of the total enumerated as being engaged in the hotel and catering industry, were waiters and counter hands. They constitute the largest occupational group in the industry other than management.

Food service is common to all sectors of the industry, but its form varies not only between sectors, but also between different establishments and even between different parts of the same establishment. Accordingly this group covers a range of occupations from waiters and waitresses serving meals and refreshments at tables to counter hands whose work is more closely linked to food production. They all have in common their close contact with the customer. Although the customer may initially enter the premises without any influence on their part, their role is frequently not limited to the passive receipt of the customer's orders and serving him; they are often in a position to influence both his choice and satisfaction. In that sense food service employees are salesmen. A good waiter is a skilled man who has acquired his skill and technical knowledge over a number of years and who represents the skilled element of this occupational group in quality hotels, restaurants and clubs; the majority of food service employees represent a semi-skilled occupation.

Traditionally waiting has been learnt by successful generations 'on the job' and their standard has been, therefore, largely conditioned by the standard of the establishment in which they learnt. Even the courses conducted between the wars by the Westminster Technical Institute were often considered more as preliminary training for higher positions in hotels and restaurants, than as training for potential waiters. The majority of the candidates for the examinations of the Hotel and Catering Institute in waiting, introduced in the 1950s, were full-time students at technical colleges, taking the examinations merely as part of a wider course and not with a view to waiting as a career. The courses and examinations failed to attract both potential waiters and waiters in the industry, as the qualifications gained would have made little or no difference to their earnings or prospects.

In 1959 the National Joint Apprenticeship Council for the Hotel and Catering Industry introduced a three-year apprenticeship scheme for waiters and waitresses, similar in concept to that already in existence for cooks. Training took place in approved catering establishments and apprentices attended a technical college on a day-release basis. But the scheme was designed for the minority of establishments with high standards of service, and relatively few took part. It also failed to attract entrants in sufficient numbers who would see waiting as a craft, for which it would be worthwhile to undergo training of several years' duration; less than a hundred completed their apprenticeship in its eight years of existence. When responsibility for the National Joint Apprenticeship Council was assumed by the Hotel and Catering Industry Training Board in 1967, the apprenticeship was discontinued.

The new approach to food service training, introduced by the Training Board, distinguishes between job training and career training. The former is intended for food service employees requiring a limited range of skills and knowledge, and is carried out through short intensive courses based on groups of related tasks to suit the requirements of particular establishments.

Those who require training for a progressive career in food service in establishments offering more complex forms of service have available to them three career courses, sponsored jointly by the Training Board and the City and Guilds of London Institute and leading to national certificates. They are a combination of further education and industrial training on a block release basis; periods in a training centre, normally in a technical college, alternate with training periods with an employer in a catering establishment. The trainees are registered with the Board.

The City and Guilds 707/1 Food Service Certificate is intended for new entrants and is offered on an eight to twelve weeks' full-time basis or the part-time equivalent. It provides trainees with an introduction to the industry and to food service in particular, and deals with basic technical skills and knowledge as well as social skills.

The City and Guilds 707/2 Advanced Serving Techniques Certificate is intended for those who have completed the 707/1 Certificate. The four to six weeks' programme or its part-time equivalent provides trainees with the skills and knowledge required for a range of advanced serving techniques, including cooking in the restaurant and an introduction to supervision.

The City and Guilds 707/3 Alcoholic Beverage Service Certificate is intended for those who have completed the 707/1 Certificate. It is a four to six weeks' full-time programme or the part-time equivalent, provides trainees with the skills and knowledge required to sell and serve wines and other alcoholic drinks and includes an introduction to supervision.

The three courses provide a clear career development path integrating further education and training with industrial training and experience.

Bar Service

According to the 1966 Census of Population over 80,000 (about 12 per cent) of the men and women enumerated as being engaged in the hotel and catering industry were barmen and barmaids. By 1971 their number increased to over 90,000 (about 13 per cent), which was the largest proportionate increase for any occupational group in the industry in the five years. A further large number of the manpower of the industry was identified as publicans and innkeepers who were included with managerial occupations in this chapter, although their recruitment and training is often related to bar service.

Bar service occupations are occupations common to the licensed sector of the industry, and are to be found mainly in hotels, public houses and clubs. They range from skilled work in cocktail bars of quality hotels to semi-skilled work in the bars of most public houses. They all have in common their close contact with the customer, and certain common tasks; however, beyond this the type of clientele and the range of drinks served in particular bars determine the skills required in particular situations.

Training for bar service has taken place customarily on the job. In view of the small size of the typical public house it has been common for the publican and his family to undertake much bar work, and a substantial proportion of staff have learnt their skills in those circumstances; others have received their instruction, if any, from the more experienced staff. The licensing laws, which preclude anyone under the age of eighteen from serving in the bar of licensed premises, have prevented any recruitment of school-leavers, and in this respect the licensed trade has been, no doubt, at a disadvantage. On the other hand, the limited number of permitted hours make bar work particularly suitable for part-time employment; a high proportion of bar service employees are part-time employees, and the majority are women.

National schemes of training consisting of short courses and leading to examinations for licensed house staff have been organized since 1949 by the National Trade Development (formerly Defence) Association, in co-operation with establishments of further education, whilst individual companies have organized their own bar training. More recently group training schemes have developed. Other associations such as The United Kingdom Bartenders' Guild and the Wine and Spirit Association of Great Britain have been organizing training courses for many years too. Residential training centres on an industry basis have been also in operation.

Following the establishment of the Hotel and Catering Industry Training Board the task approach to training has been applied to bar and cellar training, in which a need for flexibility was recognized in order to provide a variety of training programmes, according to the requirements of particular business units and their employees. Five main training programmes have been established as follows:

1. bar staff – introductory programme of commonly accepted tasks;
2. cocktail bar – for those who have completed the bar staff training programme to acquire further knowledge and skills in dispensing cocktails and other associated tasks;
3. cellar – beer, spirits, minerals – covering the handling of these beverages;
4. cellar – wines – to equip the cellarman who has completed course 3 to handle and bottle wines and carry out related tasks;
5. house management – a programme for staff who wish to attain a managerial position and who have completed programmes 1 and 3; it covers mainly supervisory and managerial tasks.

The five programmes offer nationally recognized qualifications, and are jointly sponsored by the National Trade Development Association and the Training Board.

Domestic Occupations

The domestic character of many accommodation units is particularly reflected in the employment in the hotel and catering industry of substantial numbers in domestic work which differs from similar work in a private house mainly by its magnitude and multiplication. According to the 1966 and 1971 Census Reports over 80,000 persons (12 per cent of those enumerated as being engaged in the hotel and catering industry) were maids, or cleaners or in similar housekeeping occupations.

Most of them are semi-skilled or unskilled; their work calls for no particular standards of education but high standards of physical fitness and an agreeable personality, as much contact with the guest may be involved in the performance of duties.

It is perhaps not surprising that little attempt has been made to introduce national schemes of training for these employees. Many women have been recruited to the work from essentially the same sources as domestic servants for private households. The hotel and catering industry may have the advantage of greater human interest to the potential entrant to domestic work over private domestic service; however, it offers little incentive in the form of pay or promotion prospects in these occupations, and it has had difficulties in recruitment in spite of the diminished extent of private domestic service for some years now.

The increased training consciousness in the industry has been reflected recently in the emergence of organized training in housekeeping. In many establishments the learning period, consisting of informal introduction to work and learning on the job, has been augmented with short formal induction courses for new employees.

Staff for supervisory positions in housekeeping departments of hotels and other accommodation units have been often recruited from courses leading to qualifications of the former Institutional Management Association and more recently of the Hotel, Catering and Institutional Management Association, as well as from other courses in hotel and catering subjects.

The City and Guilds of London Institute 708 Housekeeping Certificate course is normally offered as an industry-based course lasting eight to twelve weeks full-time or the part-time equivalent. The course is specifically intended for those who wish to make a career in housekeeping, and covers the technical knowledge and skills required for housekeeping services in accommodation units, as well as providing an introduction to supervisory skills.

Uniformed Staff

To a greater extent in accommodation units, and to a lesser extent in non-residential establishments, there are found several other occupations, which are mainly or wholly concerned with personal service and attendance on the customer. In hotels they are mostly grouped together as 'uniformed staff' and include hall porters, luggage porters, doormen, pages, cloakroom attendants and similar occupations. They are far less common in other sectors of the industry, although some work in large restaurants and clubs. The only comparable group in the occupational analysis of the 1966 Census of Population, listed as 'lift operators, commissionaires, etc', accounted for between 13–14,000 employees, about 2 per cent of those engaged in the industry. There was no comparable group identified in the 1971 Census.

Uniformed staff provide ancillary services to customers, such as handling luggage, dealing with inquiries and messages, porterage and the like; in smaller hotels they also relieve reception staff and some service staff. The extent of personal contact with the customer is reflected in their earnings, which consist of gratuities probably to a greater extent than most other employees'. As such they offer a prospect of quick reward for those engaged in them. With the exception of the hall porter's position, most require little formal education, but a high degree of physical fitness and an agreeable personality. No formal training was considered necessary for this group of employees until recently. It is not unknown for a promising boy to begin as a page and to work his way up to the coveted and lucrative post of head hall porter over twenty or thirty years.

The first attempt at systematic training for uniformed staff was made by the Hotel and Catering Industry Training Board, after consultation with the industry, through its task approach to training. In distinguishing between two distinct categories – those to be trained to meet the specific needs of particular establishments and those to be trained for a career, the Board identified groups of tasks to be developed into training programmes. The City and Guilds of London Institute 710 Hotel Uniformed Staff Certificate provides a systematic scheme of training on a part-time basis for those who wish to make a career in uniformed staff leading to the position of hall porter. The Certificate course includes salesmanship and social skills, as well as organizational, operational and legal aspects.

Clerical and Commercial Occupations

In the hotel and catering industry, clerical and commercial occupations include accountants, book-keepers, cashiers, receptionists, clerks and typists. However, to say that one is a book-keeper, clerk or typist in an hotel or restaurant, tells little about the duties, hours, or conditions under which the work is performed. Some of the occupations are comparable to similar ones elsewhere, in that they involve little or no contact with the customer, that they offer regular hours and that aptitude for clerical work is their main requirement. But others call for much direct contact with customers and place high demands on personal qualities and social skills, particularly front office and reception occupations in hotels.

According to the Reports of the 1966 and 1971 Census of Population, more than 30,000 men and women or some 5 per cent of those enumerated to the hotel and catering industry, were clerical and office workers.

Until relatively recently this occupational group had little or no systematic training; most learnt their work 'on the job' within the industry or in similar occupations elsewhere. Many positions were filled at any one time by those who did not intend to remain in them for more than a limited period of time, and who viewed them merely as stages in their training for higher positions.

However, commercial education and training has been changing the above pattern in recent years. In higher positions, as accountants or company secretaries, men and women with professional qualifications are increasingly found. In other clerical occupations growing numbers of employees have had full- or part-time training, mainly of a secretarial nature, to prepare them for a variety of office occupations. The other two groups are the products of the industry's own efforts in formal training. Two and three-year courses at technical colleges in hotel and catering studies including commercial subjects, have been supplying the industry with entrants possessing qualifications designed for the needs of the industry for more than twenty years. Over a similar period full-time and part-time courses specifically designed to prepare students for careers in hotel book-keeping and reception were conducted at many centres for the Hotel Book-keeping and Reception examination of the Hotel and Catering Institute.

The City and Guilds of London Institute 709 Hotel Reception Certificate, which replaced the Hotel and Catering Institute examination, has become the nationally-recognized qualification in this field. It is offered as a one-year full-time course at technical colleges or as an industry-based block release course, including formal instruction in a college and planned experience in industry.

Miscellaneous Occupations

Having considered seven particular groups of occupations separately in turn, there remains a residuary wide range, which cannot be regarded as typical hotel and catering occupations. According to the Reports of the 1966 and 1971 Census of Population they accounted for some 50,000 and represented in the region of 7 to 8 per cent of those engaged in the industry.

They are mostly engaged in activities ancillary to the main purpose of the business. The skills of most of them are not peculiar to the industry and differ little from those required in comparable occupations elsewhere. However, often they assume a distinctive character owing to the place where the work is performed or because of the nature of commodities handled, as happens, for example, with storekeepers.

The largest group is that of the maintenance workers, concerned with the upkeep and maintenance of buildings and equipment in larger establishments, and with heating, lighting, power and water supply. A high degree of specialization may occur between these occupations in the large undertakings, where an

Table 57

Hotel and Catering Industry
Estimated Occupational Breakdown in 1966 and 1971[a]

Occupational Category	1966 000s	1966 %	1971 000s	1971 %
1 Managerial – self-employed	130	19	135	20
– employed	68	10	63	9
2 Food preparation and cookery	88	13	91	13
3 Food service	141	20	124	18
4 Bar staff	84	12	92	13
5 Domestic	86	12	82	12
6 Uniformed staff	14	2	14[b]	2[b]
7 Clerical and commercial	33	5	35	5
8 Miscellaneous	47	7	53	8
Total	691	100	689	100

Source: Census of Population 1966 and 1971.

[a] For various reasons the estimates for the two years are not strictly comparable.
[b] Based on the 1966 Census of Population.

Table 58
Principal Courses for the Hotel and Catering Industry 1975

Title	Nature and duration
CITY AND GUILDS OF LONDON INSTITUTE	
CGLI 705 General catering	One year full-time
CGLI 706/1 Basic cookery for the catering industry	One year full-time
	Two years part-time
CGLI 706/2 Cookery for the catering industry	One year full-time
	Two years part-time
CGLI 706/3 Advanced cookery for the catering industry	
Kitchen and larder	Two years part-time
Pastry 1 and 2	One year part-time each
CGLI 707/1 Food service	8/12 weeks full-time[a]
	Part-time equivalent
CGLI 707/2 Advanced serving techniques	4/6 weeks full-time[a]
	Part-time equivalent
CGLI 707/3 Alcoholic beverage service	4/6 weeks full-time[a]
	Part-time equivalent
CGLI 708 Housekeeping	8/12 weeks full-time
	Part-time equivalent
CGLI 709 Hotel reception	One year full-time
	30 weeks block release
CGLI 710 Hotel uniformed staff	Four terms part-time
NATIONAL EXAMINING BOARD FOR SUPERVISORY STUDIES	
Certificate in supervisory studies	One year part-time
JOINT COMMITTEE FOR NATIONAL DIPLOMAS IN HOTEL CATERING AND INSTITUTIONAL MANAGEMENT	
OND in hotel and catering operations	Two years full-time
OND in institutional houskeeping and catering	Two years full-time
OND in hotel, catering and institutional operations	Two years full-time
HND in hotel and catering administration	Three years sandwich
HND in institutional management	Three years sandwich
HND in hotel, catering and institutional management	Three years sandwich
HOTEL CATERING AND INSTITUTIONAL MANAGEMENT ASSOCIATION	
HCIMA Intermediate	Two to three years part-time
HCIMA Final	One year full-time
	Two years sandwich/part-time
HCIMA Abridged	One year full-time
DEGREES	
BA in hotel and catering management	
University of Strathclyde	Three years full-time
BSc in hotel and catering administration	
University of Surrey	Four years sandwich
BSc in catering studies (Huddersfield Polytechnic, CNAA)	Four years sandwich
BSc in catering systems (Sheffield Polytechnic, CNAA)	Four years sandwich

Source: Nightingale, M. A., Catering Education in the Seventies, *HCIMA Review*, Number 2, Volume 1.

[a] Often included in other full-time courses.

effort is often made to provide an almost complete service without recourse to outside firms. In those circumstances the employees are often qualified craftsmen, such as electricians, plumbers, fitters, joiners, carpenters, painters and decorators, who have in the main received their initial training elsewhere. In smaller establishments this category of staff is less common, as more frequent use is made of outside specialist services, and more versatile maintenance staff combining several skills may be employed. As compared with similar occupations elsewhere the remuneration of maintenance workers may fall below that obtainable in comparable employment outside the industry, but in hotels and other catering establishments they often enjoy a greater stability of employment. For this reason, men are often attracted to the industry who prefer steady employment in one place to the frequent changes and the unsettled conditions of a contractor's labour force.

16. Conditions of Employment

When studying employment conditions in an industry we are mainly concerned with hours of work, pay, and holidays. In service industries, hours of work are influenced more than elsewhere by the nature of the product and by the pattern of demand, which give rise to many operating characteristics of the establishments in the industry. It is, therefore, appropriate to begin this chapter by considering those characteristics of the hotel and catering industry which affect the times of work of those employed in it.

Influencing Factors on Times of Work

The first important feature of many establishments in the hotel and catering industry is the *continuity of activity*. Hotels and other accommodation units, but also many catering units without sleeping accommodation, are open daily, including Sundays and public holidays. They have no closing days. In some, especially hotels, the continuity of activity is absolute; in others, morning, afternoon and evening are included in the day's business, and only a few hours elapse between the end of one day's and the beginning of next day's activities.

Within the above pattern, *alternating periods of high and low demand* occur *during the day*, which are determined by the meal times of customers, by their hours of leisure and by their mode of life when travelling and when on holiday.

Licensing laws influence within narrow limits the actual daily hours of business of whole establishments, particularly public houses, and parts of other premises and also the availability of services on different days of the week in different parts of the country.

A *weekly pattern* of activity is discernible in many establishments in the industry quite apart from the influence of licensing laws, which in their application often merely reflect the pattern of daily and weekly demand. Many hotels, restaurants, pubs and clubs derive all or most of their revenue from mid-week business and little or none at weekends; the reverse is true of others. Only when two or more complementary sources of demand are met in the same establishment, can anything approaching a steady level of activity through the week be achieved.

Last but not least, many establishments in the industry are subject to *seasonal fluctuations* of activity, arising from high and low demand for their services at different times of the year. This is not only the case in resorts, but also, for example, in industrial and commercial centres, where demand for hotel and catering services decreases significantly at holiday times.

Effect on Times of Working

Some or all of the five influencing factors identified above apply to a varying extent to most establishments in the hotel and catering industry, depending on their product, location and market. They have in turn created some characteristic features of employment in the industry, rarely found to the same extent in other industries.

An indication of the average *weekly hours worked* by full-time manual workers of twenty-one and over in the hotel and catering industry in April 1975 emerges from the *New Earnings Survey 1975*, a sample survey of earnings of employees in employment in Great Britain. The survey results do not suggest that the actual hours worked by men in the hotel and catering industry as a whole are unduly long. The average for men was 45·5 hours, the same as the average for all industries and services in Britain; but women in the industry worked 40·3 hours as compared with the average of 39·4 hours for women in all industries and services (including overtime in all cases).[1]

These findings are also supported in an examination of the manpower situation in the industry by the Hotels and Catering Economic Development Committee. As a part of this examination a postal survey showed that the occupational group working the longest average weekly hours of those sampled, i.e. male kitchen hands, worked a shorter week than the average for all industries.[2]

However, in order to meet the demand for the industry's services, full-time employees often work *irregular hours*. Shift work is a frequent feature of employment, and not uncommon is the practice of split duties within the compass of a day's work, designed to secure a high labour utilization at peak times of the day and avoidance of slack capacity between the peaks. The same objective is often in view in employing versatile workers who perform several different duties at different times of day, thus reducing the extent of split-duty working. While considerable numbers are employed in the evenings, in many cases beyond midnight, the proportion of those on all-night duty is small.

Based on their examination the Hotels and Catering Economic Development Committee suggest that the spread of hours in the industry is wide and although, in comparison with all industries, a small proportion of catering staff work overtime, those concerned work more such hours on average than overtime workers in all industries. They also indicate that less than one-third of the sample worked conventional day shifts (i.e. between 7.30 a.m. and 7.30 p.m.) and over half the waiters and chefs were on split shifts (defined as those with at least one break of two hours or more).[3]

Daily and weekly fluctuations in activity make the industry eminently suitable

---

[1] *Department of Employment Gazette*, 1975.
[2] Hotels and Catering EDC, *Manpower Policy in the Hotels and Restaurant Industry, Summary and Recommendations*, p. 8.
[3] Hotels and Catering EDC, *Manpower Policy in the Hotels and Restaurant Industry, Summary and Recommendations*, p. 8.

for *part-time employment*, which arises when workers are engaged on a regular basis (normally weekly) but for shorter hours than constitutes a full working week in a particular employment. Between 1971 and 1975, the number of men working part-time in the industry increased from 29 to 31 per cent, and the number of women increased from 52 to 60 per cent.

The industry is also a large employer of *casual labour*, i.e. of workers engaged for irregular employment for particular occasions by the hour or on a day-to-day basis. This arises particularly in hotels and restaurants for functions and other *ad hoc* occasions.

Seasonal fluctuations in activity during the year give rise to substantial *seasonal employment* for temporary periods of a few weeks or months at times of seasonal pressure. This demand for labour is partially met by seasonal movements of the permanent labour force, but in the main the industry relies on married women, students, the retired and similar sources of temporary labour, who make themselves available for work only at particular times of the year. Although monthly statistics of hotel and catering employment are no longer available, those relating to the early 1960s indicated a difference in the region of 100,000 employees in the industry between February and August each year.

Elements of Pay

Only a small proportion of workers in the industry are paid their remuneration wholly in cash by their employer. For many the amount received in gratuities from customers forms a substantial part of their total remuneration. Probably to a greater extent than in any other industry, hotel and catering employees are provided with all or some of their meals at their places of work, and many employees live on the employer's premises, being provided by him with board and lodging. In some cases workers may enjoy other additional benefits, such as provision of free uniform, free laundering, an allowance of beer, and various commissions. Any information as to cash wages only does not, therefore, provide a reliable indication of the remuneration of hotel and catering employees, as their real wages may consist of some or all of the above elements in addition to cash.

The proportion of employees receiving gratuities varies between different sectors of the industry; it is highest in those sectors where the incidence of personal service occupations is high; the numbers are, therefore, large in hotels and other residential establishments and in restaurants; they are less significant in public houses and clubs, and almost non-existent in contract catering. The occupations deriving varying amounts of their income in the form of gratuities are those of food and drink service, such as waiters (especially head waiters), some barmen, uniformed staff, and also domestic staff, such as chambermaids. Besides the direct system of gratuities, in which the employee keeps those received by him, many employers and workers have adopted various methods of pooling and sharing gratuities on a pre-arranged basis, principally by means of a 'tronc' or a service charge. Whilst probably in most instances these methods only secure a re-distribution of gratuities to the same categories of worker who would have received them anyway (except that the individual shares may vary), attempts have been made to secure a share of gratuities also for non-service workers under the latter two methods, and particularly under the service charge method. Although customers might have been aware of the introduction of the statutory wage-regulating machinery, which had provided minimum rates of pay for hotel and catering workers, it did not appear to bring about any lessening of the incidence of tipping, either in degree or in amount.

No reliable information is available as to the extent of payment in kind in the form of meals and lodging. Undoubtedly those who do not receive either are in the minority. The incidence of full board and lodging is most common among women in the hotel sector of the industry, although living-in employees are also to be found among men and in other sectors.

The incidence of the other elements of hotel and catering workers' remuneration is even more difficult to assess generally. Pecuniary and other emoluments have been known to accrue to holders of certain positions in some establishments, so to speak by virtue of their office, in the form of commissions, sometimes agreed between the employer and employee, and invariably in circumstances rarely found in other employment. Such may be a part of a chef's income from the suppliers with whom he places orders for food and where, as is not uncommon, he is also responsible for purchasing his own raw materials. The head porter's income may be still more varied, as he may be sharing in income from taxi, car hire and other firms in consideration of custom placed with them. At all levels, workers' nominal wages may be enhanced by provision of uniform or protective clothing, free laundering of these items and, in the case of living-in workers, also of their personal laundry. An allowance of beer is still to be found in some firms.

Results of the *New Earnings Survey 1975* include an analysis of the make-up of earnings in terms of basic, overtime and other pay in April 1975. Payments in kind and gratuities are excluded. It emerges that on this basis, manual workers in the hotel and catering industry receive a significantly higher proportion of their weekly cash pay from the employer in form of basic pay than workers in most other industries (Table 59).

Statutory Regulation of Wages

Statutory minimum wages for most employees in the hotel and catering industry are provided by the Wages Orders of three separate Wages Councils, covering licensed hotels and restaurants, unlicensed restaurants, and public houses and clubs. A fourth Wages Council covering industrial and staff canteens was abolished in June 1976. The origin and development, composition and procedures of these statutory bodies are described in Chapter 19; their composition, coverage of the industry, and the principal features of their Orders are shown in Appendixes R, S, and T.

Even in licensed hotels and restaurants, where Wages Orders were the latest

Table 59

New Earnings Survey 1975
Make-up of Pay

		Overtime Pay	Payment by Results	Shift and other Premium Pay	Basic and other Pay	Average Gross Weekly Earnings
Full-time manual men 21 and over	All industries and services	14	8	3	75	100
	Hotel and catering industry	10	5	1	84	100
Full-time manual women 18 and over	All industries and services	3	10	2	85	100
	Hotel and catering industry	5	2	—	93	100

Source: New Earnings Survey 1975, Part C Analyses by Industry.

to be introduced of all parts of the industry, statutory wage regulation has been in operation for a number of years; in canteens, where it was brought in first, since 1945. This appears to be sufficient time for a general assessment of its effect in the hotel and catering industry. There is no doubt that the Wages Boards pursued a very moderate policy with regard to minimum wages, and that most employers had enough time to adjust themselves to the new standards of remuneration. The post-war period of full employment and rising prices stimulated an upward trend of wages, and it seems that rates at least equivalent to the statutory minima would have had to be paid in most districts, and to most grades of workers, even in the absence of statutory regulation. In fact, many employers pay wages far in excess of the prescribed minima when, as is often the case, the forces of supply and demand in the labour market determine the wages the employer has to offer if he wishes to attract and retain labour. This is the case particularly with highly skilled and experienced workers; those paid only the minimum rates are, mainly, service workers in receipt of gratuities, workers in remote parts of the country where alternative sources of employment are scarce, trainees, and women in unskilled occupations.

Changes in the basic working week (that is, in the normal hours beyond which overtime rates become payable), since statutory regulation in this industry began, are shown in Table 60. The four catering Wages Councils were completely unaffected by the first major movement towards shorter hours, which took place in British industry after the war. Between 1946 and 1949 most manual workers in a variety of industries had an average reduction in their working week from 47 or 48 to 44 or 45 hours; the only and rather belated change to affect catering workers was a reduction in the basic hours of canteen employees in mid-1950s.

The second movement towards greater leisure, more overtime, or both, took place in this country between 1959 and 1962, when most manual workers secured a reduction of their basic week to between forty-two and forty-four hours. At this time three of the four catering Wages Councils reduced their basic working week to between forty-four and forty-six hours; further changes by all four catering Wages Councils took place in 1965 when even licensed hotels and restaurants reduced their basic hours for the first time since 1948.

By the end of the 1960s most manual workers in the country covered by collective agreements or statutory orders brought their basic working week to forty hours or less but the basic working week of all four catering Wages Councils remained above forty hours. Only in June 1970 the Industrial and Staff Canteen Wages Council reduced weekly hours from forty-one to forty, thus becoming the first of the four to achieve a basic week of forty hours. By the mid-1970s the basic working week of the other three Wages Councils had been also reduced to forty hours.

Until 1963, relative movements of wages in the British economy were recorded in the Guardian Wage Index produced by Professor Ely Devons and Mr J. R. Crossley at the London School of Economics. The Wage Index gave separate figures for some two hundred industries and trades, and included the parts of the hotel and catering industry covered by the four Wages Councils, which are compared with all industries in Table 61.

Table 60
Catering Wages Councils Changes in Basic Hours of Work 1945–1975

	Late 1940s	Mid- 1950s	Early 1960s	Mid- 1960s	Late 1960s Early 1970s	Mid- 1970s
Canteens					June 1969 41	
	Nov 1945 47	May 1955 45	Jan 1962 44	July 1965 42	June 1970 40	
Unlicensed restaurants	Aug 1947 47	—	Apr 1962 45	Oct 1965 44	Apr 1973 42	June 1975 40
					Oct 1973 41	
Licensed hotels & restaurants	March 1948 48	—	—	Aug 1965 46	July 1969 44	March 1974 40
					Nov 1970 42	
					Dec 1972 41	
Public houses & clubs	Feb 1947 48	—	Aug 1961 46	Aug 1965 44	Aug 1972 42	Jan 1974 40

Table 61
Guardian Index of Weekly Wage Rates
(1948 = 100)

		March 1958	March 1959	March 1960	March 1961	March 1962	March 1963
All industries	Men	167·0	173·4	175·4	185·0	190·7	198·5
	Women	166·4	172·0	176·0	182·9	189·2	198·0
Industrial and staff canteens	Men	155·4	161·6	161·6	168·3	172·2	172·2
	Women	157·1	165·0	165·0	170·9	185·6	185·6
Unlicensed places of refreshment	Men	149·3	149·3	158·4	165·2	165·2	178·9
	Women	145·5	145·5	153·6	159·6	159·6	172·4
Licensed residential and licensed restaurant	Men	137·4	143·9	143·9	147·0	165·3	165·3
	Women	140·0	146·8	146·8	150·9	167·3	167·3
Licensed non-residential	Men	157·2	163·6	165·3	172·1	188·9	189·3
	Women	156·0	162·2	162·2	167·5	181·4	181·7

Two important points should be borne in mind in interpreting the Index. First, the figures were based on rates agreed in collective bargaining between employers' associations and trade unions or, as was the case with most of the hotel and catering industry, on rates fixed by statutory or other wage-fixing authorities; in general they were minimum rates and not earnings, and took little or no account of local agreements, of firms paying above the minimum, of overtime earnings, bonuses, payments in kind, etc. Secondly, the index numbers showed comparative movements in rates, and gave no indication of the absolute level of rates in different industries.

Nevertheless, it would seem that up to 1963, at any rate, the statutory minimum rates did not keep pace with the general rate of increase in wages over the fifteen years between 1948 and 1963 and that the statutory wage regulation in this industry acted to some extent as a brake on increases in minimum rates, even if not in actual earnings. The index for all industries showed a greater upward tendency.

New Earnings Survey 1975

Comparisons of earnings between hotel and catering employees and others are fraught with difficulties, because of substantial numbers receiving payments in kind, and because of the incidence of gratuities for many employees. Both of these elements of employees' income may enhance significantly individual earnings of hotel and catering workers in comparison with others, but are not included in surveys of earnings.

The *New Earnings Survey 1975* disclosed[4] that hotel and catering workers ranked among the lowest paid. In 1975 the median gross weekly earnings for full-time manual men workers in the industry aged twenty-one and over were £38·80 and for non-manual men workers £40·80, compared with £53·20 and £61·80 respectively in all industries and services.

The gap between the hotel and catering industry and others was less pronounced as far as women were concerned. The median gross weekly earnings of full-time manual women aged eighteen and over were £22·80 and of non-manual women £29·80; the corresponding figure for all industries and services were £31·00 and £35·90 respectively. Less than one-quarter of manual women were earning more than £30 a week and only a few more than one-half of the non-manual women were earning more than £30 a week.

Gross hourly earnings revealed by the 1975 survey show a similar pattern. The hourly earnings of more than three-quarters of manual men workers were less than £1·20, whilst among those in all industries and services only a little over one-half came into this category; nearly three-quarters of manual women in the industry earned less than £0·75 per hour, whilst less than one-third came into this category in all industries and services.

The above data do not include the values of payments in kind or gratuities; the former are, moreover, often not subject to tax. According to research findings made available by the Hotels and Catering Economic Development Committee[5], even with the addition of an allowance for meals and after eliminating the effect of free accommodation, earnings in most occupations in the industry still compare unfavourably with average earnings for all industries. If gratuities are included, where these are received, the situation is more favourable. Many staff, however, do not receive tips, and those who do would in many cases (notably male employees) need a substantial amount to bring them up to the general average for all industries.

Annual Holidays

The results of the *New Earnings Survey 1974* included an indication of actual paid annual holiday entitlements (other than bank or public holidays) of manual and non-manual employees in April 1974. The results for all industries and services and for the hotel and catering sector are shown in Table 62. More than 90 per cent of employees in all industries and services had annual holiday entitlements of three weeks and above. In the hotel and catering industry, only in the case of non-manual male employees did more than 90 per cent have holiday entitlements of three weeks and over, although in most cases more than 80 per cent had three weeks and over.

Throughout the 1960s, the statutory minumum holiday entitlement of workers

---

[4] *New Earnings Survey 1975, Part C Analyses by Industry*, and *Department of Employment Gazette*, November 1975.
[5] Hotels and Catering EDC, *Manpower Policy in the Hotels and Restaurant Industry, Summary and Recommendations*, pp. 6–7.

Table 62
Hotel and Catering Industry
Annual Holidays with Pay in 1974

	Percentages of employees with annual holiday entitlements of					
	Under 2 weeks	2 weeks and over Under 3 weeks	3 weeks and over Under 4 weeks	4 weeks and over Under 5 weeks	5 weeks and over
FULL-TIME MANUAL MEN AGED 21 AND OVER						
All industries and services	1·5	4·4	71·0	21·7	1·6
Hotel and catering industry	5·0	13·5	74·7	6·2	0·8
Hotels	5·5	11·8	75·7	7·0	—
Restaurants	4·0	20·0	73·0	3·0	—
FULL-TIME NON-MANUAL MEN AGED 21 AND OVER						
All industries and services	1·0	2·0	36·6	42·9	17·5
Hotel and catering industry	1·2	6·4	62·7	27·6	2·3
FULL-TIME MANUAL WOMEN AGED 18 AND OVER						
All industries and services	2·6	6·6	78·7	10·9	1·3
Hotel and catering industry	5·3	12·8	78·2	3·1	0·9
Hotels	5·8	13·6	76·5	3·7	0·4
Restaurants	4·8	15·0	76·4	3·2	0·8
Contractors	5·6	4·8	86·3	1·6	1·6
FULL-TIME NON-MANUAL WOMEN AGED 18 AND OVER						
All industries and services	2·1	4·0	51·9	26·8	15·3
Hotel and catering industry	2·2	9·7	78·9	8·4	0·9
Hotels	2·6	12·3	76·3	7·0	1·8

Source: *New Earnings Survey 1974.*

in the hotel and catering industry provided for by the four catering Wages Councils remained firmly fixed at two weeks' holiday with pay. The Hotels and Catering Economic Development Committee's manpower survey[6] indicated that three-quarters of the staff interviewed expected at least fourteen days' paid leave in the year beginning 15 April 1973 and that many of the staff enjoyed paid holidays in excess of the statutory minimum.

[6] Hotels and Catering EDC, *Manpower Policy in the Hotels and Restaurant Industry, Summary and Recommendations*, p. 9.

Wages Orders in 1975 for Licensed Non-Residential Establishments, Licensed Residential Establishments and Licensed Restaurants, and Unlicensed Places of Refreshment, increased the statutory minimum holiday entitlement for full-time employees in these sectors to twenty days, which represents over three weeks' paid holiday.

Statutory Regulation in Retrospect

We have seen that the conditions of employment of many hotel and catering workers have tended to lag behind other industries and services. Has statutory wage regulation achieved the general purpose for which it was established?

Where the main object was to eliminate 'sweating', this was largely achieved where it had existed. In the hotel and catering industry, in common with some others, it may be argued that it raised the status and morale of the worker, and that it compelled less efficient employers to improve their use of labour. It virtually abolished competitive under-cutting of wages, and there are few indications that it imposed a strain on firms in the industry. It brought about a somewhat greater degree of equality in wages within the industry.

But one of the principal motives for extending the statutory wage regulation outside the original 'sweated trades' was to provide machinery transitional to voluntary collective bargaining. In this respect little progress has been made; indeed, statutory intervention is regarded by many as having retarded such development. Representative organization on both sides of the industry has made some little progress over the past twenty years, and the number of voluntary collective agreements has increased, particularly in the canteen sector of the industry, where in many cases the high degree of union organization and established bargaining procedures in the firms served by the canteens stimulated the same development in relation to catering workers. But the basic difficulties of an industry consisting of a large number of predominantly small firms spread over the whole country hinder the establishment and maintenance of a voluntary machinery. There are several trade associations, which, although far from being fully representative, could assume a prominent part as employers' organizations. The trade unions are, however, far from representative of the workers in the industry. Moreover, the existence of statutory machinery has probably hindered trade union recruitment, as the inducement to join on the part of the worker might have been lessened by the awareness that there is statutory machinery designed to protect his interests.[7] Even employers have sometimes used the statutory machinery as a reason for their unwillingness to negotiate individual or local agreements, or for their readiness to negotiate only on matters other than wages. Yet, it is probably in this direction, in the development of firm or area agreements, that any progress towards voluntary negotiation, which would in time replace the Wages Councils, could be made. But there does not appear at present sufficient dissatisfaction either on the part of workers or

[7] However, a number of sources suggest that many workers are not aware of the existence of the statutory machinery.

employers with the Wages Councils, which would provide an inducement for any development in that direction. As long as this situation persists, the hope expressed by the Catering Wages Commission that in time voluntary machinery may develop in the industry is unlikely to be realized, and the power possessed by the Minister to abolish any Wages Council which becomes unnecessary is unlikely to be exercised, although a move has been made in the case of canteens.

In November 1969 the First Secretary and Secretary of State for Employment and Productivity referred the hotel and catering industry to the Commission on Industrial Relations with the following terms of reference:

'Having regard to the desirability of strengthening the machinery of voluntary collective bargaining in industries in which employers and employees are not well organized, the First Secretary and Secretary of State for Employment and Productivity refers to the Commission on Industrial Relations for examination and report the functioning and development of voluntary collective bargaining in the hotel and catering industry, with particular reference to the securing of any improvements in industrial relations that appear necessary and desirable.'

After a preliminary survey of the industry the Commission decided to concentrate first on two major sectors, licensed hotels and restaurants, and industrial and staff canteens, with a view to examining institutional catering, public houses and clubs subsequently. The first Report, on the hotels and restaurants sector,[8] recommended various means of strengthening the role of employers' and employees' organizations in industrial relations, an extension of voluntary collective bargaining through area and company agreements, with a number of other specific recommendations; the Commission saw a continuing role for the Wages Council.

A largely forgotten national agreement between the British Hotels and Restaurants Association[9], the National Union of General and Municipal Workers[10] and the Union of Shop Distributive and Allied Workers was in existence from 1947, until replaced by a revised agreement signed in September 1970, following an industrial dispute in Torquay hotels. The agreement provided for the establishment of a National Council, District Councils and House Committees, appointment of staff representatives, and a procedure for settling differences. In view of the greatly diminished interest of USDAW in hotels, the NUGMW was the only signatory union to the 1970 agreement. The most significant change was that the 1970 agreement provided for the discussion of pay, which was excluded previously. The basic framework for negotiation had been, therefore, agreed by the parties before the publication of the first Report by the Commission. Early in 1978 the agreement was abandoned by mutual consent of the parties, following extensive legislation on employment and industrial relations.

[8] Commission on Industrial Relations, *Report No. 23, The Hotel and Catering Industry, Part 1, Hotels and Restaurants*.
[9] Now the British Hotels, Restaurants and Caterers Association.
[10] Also referred to as the General and Municipal Workers' Union (GMWU).

The second inquiry of the Commission focused on industrial catering and, in particular, on the extent and functioning of collective bargaining, and on the relevance of the Industrial and Staff Canteen Wages Council in this sector. The Report[11] provided a wealth of statistical information on industrial catering, and confirmed the high degree of voluntary collective bargaining which covered the majority of employees. It made recommendations on how it could be extended and its functioning improved. It recommended the termination of an agreement on union recognition negotiated between the Caterers Association and two of the principal unions in the industry in 1947, as far as it applied to industrial catering, which had been a dead letter. Having found that the Wages Council had little relevance to conditions of employment in industrial catering, and that the criteria for the abolition of a Wages Council had been met, the Commission saw no justification for its continuance.

In 1974, following this Report, the Secretary of State for Employment published his intention to make an Order abolishing the Wages Council. Following objections, it was decided to refer the draft Order to a Commission of Inquiry. The Commission reported[12] in December 1975 and recommended that, in view of the fact that it was no longer necessary for the purpose of maintaining a reasonable standard of remuneration for the workers, the Wages Council should be abolished. The Industrial and Staff Canteen Wages Council was accordingly abolished in June 1976.

The Commission on Industrial Relations' third and final Report[13] on the hotel and catering industry, which was published in 1973, dealt with public houses, clubs and other sectors. It again focused on the extent and functioning of collective bargaining and, in particular, it drew attention to the absence of voluntary collective bargaining among club employees and bar staff. It also drew attention to the fact that a substantial number of employees in clubs and pubs were employed at rates of pay which were close to the statutory minimum, although it pointed out that salaries paid to public house managers were substantially greater than the statutory minimum. Against this background, it considered that the continued existence of the Licensed Non-Residential Establishment Wages Council was essential, although it recommended the removal of public house managers from its scope. The Report also made suggestions for improving the employment situation in pubs and clubs.

---

[11] Commission on Industrial Relations, *Report No. 27, The Hotel and Catering Industry, Part 2, Industrial Catering*.

[12] Department of Employment, *Report of the Commission of Inquiry on the draft Order to abolish the Industrial and Staff Canteen Undertakings Wages Council*.

[13] Commission on Industrial Relations, *Report No. 36, Part 3, Public Houses, Clubs and Other Sectors*.

Manpower Policy in the Industry

In 1972 the Hotels and Catering Economic Development Committee set up a Manpower Working Group to gain a fuller understanding of the manpower situation in the industry. Following a comprehensive programme of research, the Group presented a report to the EDC, which was later published as a consultative document for discussion by the industry.[14]

In addition to presenting a substantial amount of statistical information on employment conditions, the report also identified a number of underlying problems in relation to employment policies and practices in the industry. In particular, the report drew attention to the unsophisticated selection methods employed by many organizations, the high labour turnover in the establishments studied, which varied from a few per cent to 282 per cent, the average being 83 per cent, the lack of provision for formal training in many establishments and the frequent absence of any formal grievance procedures. The report indicated that the slackening in demand in the economy and a consequent easing of the labour market would ease some of the industry's manpower problems. Most developments would, however, make manpower problems more acute. For instance, the report drew attention to the increase in Government involvement in employment matters; the trend to more democratic social control, including that of work; the growing desire for higher living standards; the increase in trade union membership; rising labour costs which as a percentage of sales in the industry rose from 31 per cent in 1969 to 35 per cent in 1973; and the changing structure of the industry as a result of successive waves of takeovers and mergers. All these, it suggested, would increase rather than decrease the need for effective use of manpower in the industry, which in turn would require a more sophisticated approach to planning for manpower.

[14] Hotels and Catering EDC, *Manpower Policy in the Hotels and Restaurant Industry, Summary and Recommendations.*

Hotels and Catering EDC, *Manpower Policy in the Hotels and Restaurant Industry, Research Findings.*

Part VI
Organizations

Additional Reading for Part VI

Commission on Industrial Relations: *Report No. 23, The Hotel and Catering Industry, Part 1, Hotels and Restaurants,* Chapters 4, 6, and 9.

Commission on Industrial Relations: *Report No. 27, The Hotel and Catering Industry, Part 2, Industrial Catering,* Chapters 2, 3, and 4.

Commission on Industrial Relations: *Report No. 36, The Hotel and Catering Industry, Part 3, Public Houses, Clubs and Other Sectors,* Chapters 3 and 5.

Annual Reports of individual organizations.

17. Voluntary Organizations of Individuals

The men and women providing hotel and catering services, as well as hotel and catering firms, have tended to be highly individualistic and strongly competitive. Many of them show no desire for co-operation with others engaged in similar activities, have little sense of a common purpose and no feeling of belonging to an industry. In part these attitudes probably stem from the structure of the industry, with its predominance of small, individually-owned units, and many diverse occupations. However, as in other industries, common issues and problems have also encouraged an increasing degree of joint discussion, co-operation and association among hotelmen and caterers on the one hand, and among the firms which they operate and in which they earn their livelihood on the other. Growing Government interest and intervention in the industry created further links and platforms within the industry.

The outcome is a large number and variety of organizations in the hotel and catering industry. There are in the region of fifty national bodies, in addition to many local associations and several 'outside' organizations with an interest in the industry. There are several main explanations for this pattern.

First, the size of the industry; both by numbers engaged and by numbers of units it is a large industry. Secondly, it is a heterogeneous industry, consisting of many sectors, each with its own specific type of unit and function. Thirdly, the industry contains a wide range of occupations, each with interests of its own. Last but not least, organizations tend to serve different purposes, irrespective of considerations of industry structure. The individualistic character of those engaged in the industry has tended to re-inforce the trend to separate organizations, many of them quite small, and the wide geographical spread of the industry with numerous concentrations has been conducive to the formation of local associations.

It is possible to divide the organizations of interest in the present context into two main groups; voluntary and Government-sponsored bodies.

According to their functions and membership, the voluntary organizations lend themselves to a two-fold classification into organizations of individuals (including professional bodies, personnel associations and trade unions), and trade associations. In the following pages each type is considered in terms of its functions and membership; an attempt is made to evaluate its relative importance and to set out possible lines of its future development. This is followed by a discussion of the Government-sponsored bodies in similar terms. As regards all types of organization, the scope is confined to national bodies.

In the widest sense individuals engaged in a particular industry or occupation come together in an organization in order to further their common interests. According to their particular background, disposition and ambitions, they may more specifically seek professional status, contact with others with similar interests, protection in their employment, or a combination of these. Corresponding to these three main reasons there have developed three types of organization: professional bodies, personnel associations, trade unions. Although they share an important characteristic in that their membership is made up of individuals, unlike that of trade associations whose membership consists of firms, their functions are different and it is the principal purpose of this particular chapter to outline their respective characteristics.

Professional bodies

Professional bodies are organizations of individuals engaged in a particular occupation, normally a vocation or calling, requiring a long period of training or learning, which seek to provide standing and prestige for their members, and which control admission, usually by examination. Therefore, professional bodies adopt certain defined standards and members qualify for admission by formally meeting these standards, and by agreeing to observe them once they are admitted into membership. The standards are normally based on standards of competence shown in knowledge and experience, and on standards of conduct in the exercise of their occupation. The professional body tests the competence of candidates on admission, and insists on the acceptance by them of its standards of conduct, which may be formally defined in a code of conduct.

Hotel, Catering and Institutional Management Association

The professional body of those engaged in the hotel and catering industry is the Hotel, Catering and Institutional Management Association (HCIMA), which was formed in November 1971 when the Hotel and Catering Institute (HCI) and the Institutional Management Association (IMA) merged to form one professional body for management in the industry. Membership of the former two and of the new body between 1966 and 1975 is shown in Table 63.

The former Hotel and Catering Institute was incorporated as a company limited by guarantee in 1949. During the period to 1971 the Institute established itself as the principal educational body for the industry and acted as the main examining body, not only for its own professional examinations, but also for other hotel and catering occupations. It provided numerous membership services to assist members in their professional work and developments, organized conferences, courses and seminars, and undertook a wide range of other activities. Entry to corporate membership was normally by means of a qualifying examination of the Institute, or an examination giving exemption from it, and while membership did not constitute a restriction on entry into practice, there is no doubt that it was increasingly recognized as a qualification for managerial appointments in the industry.

The Institutional Management Association was formed in 1938 and granted its certificate of incorporation in 1960. Admission to the Association was

Table 63
Hotel and Catering Industry
Membership of Professional Bodies 1966–1975

1966	1967	1968	1969	1970	1971	Grade	1972	1973	1974	1975
\multicolumn{11}{c}{HOTEL AND CATERING INSTITUTE (HCI)[a]}
854	975	1,033	1,031	1,091	1,105	Fellows FHCI				
3,521	3,659	4,036	4,456	5,312	6,272	Members MHCI				
289	146					Associates[b] AMHCI				
4,664	4,780	5,039	5,487	6,403	7,377	Corporate members				
		6	9	29	47	Associates[c] AHCI				
636	599	671	778	744	839	Graduates GradHCI				
1,760	1,771	2,616	4,698	5,858	5,699	Students				
2,396	2,370	3,293	5,485	6,631	6,585	Non-corporate				
7,060	7,150	8,332	10,972	13,034	13,962	Total				
\multicolumn{11}{c}{INSTITUTIONAL MANAGEMENT ASSOCIATION (IMA)[d]}
198	216	211	267	286	286	Fellows FIMA				
2,185	2,312	2,581	2,572	2,889	2,940	Members MIMA				
1,317	1,579	1,714	2,068	2,286	2,558	Associate Members AMIMA				
13	11	10	9	15	16	Affiliates				
3,713	4,118	4,516	4,916	5,476	5,800	Corporate				
1,481	1,710	1,708	1,622	1,551	1,301	Students				
5,194	5,828	6,224	6,538	7,027	7,101	Total				
\multicolumn{6}{c}{HCI and IMA[e]}		\multicolumn{4}{c}{HCIMA[f]}
						Fellows FHCIMA	1,365	1,342	1,284	1,241
						Members MHCIMA	8,582	8,395	9,612	9,041
						Associate Members[g] AMHCIMA	2,195	1,761		
8,377	8,898	9,555	10,403	11,879	13,177	Corporate members	12,142	11,498	10,896	10,282
						Associates AMHCIMA	51	58	60	60
						Licentiates[h] LHCIMA		49	189	296
						Graduates	1,018	1,219	1,453	1,723
						Students	8,338	8,289	8,387	7,954
3,877	4,080	5,001	7,107	8,182	7,886	Non-corporate	9,407	9,615	10,089	10,033
12,254	12,978	14,556	17,510	20,061	21,063	Total	21,549	21,113	20,985	20,315

Source: Annual Reports.

[a] At November 30.
[b] Corporate grade discontinued.
[c] New grade introduced for specialists.
[d] At April 30.
[e] HCI at November 30, IMA at April 30.
[f] At November 30.
[g] Corporate grade discontinued.
[h] New grade introduced for managers without formal qualifications who will eventually proceed to corporate membership.

based on the attainment of one of its educational awards and subsequent experience and, as with the Institute, membership was recognized as a qualification for appointments to posts of responsibility in the industry. Like the Institute, the Association also provided various services to members. Unlike the Institute, it had a more specialized orientation and influence in the industry, covering in the main institutional management, which was interpreted to include education, hospitals and employee feeding services, i.e. non-profit-making welfare catering and residential units. Its membership was much smaller than the Institute's and the bulk of its members were women. In 1965 the National Association of School Meal Organizers (NASMO) was formed under the aegis of the IMA to further the particular interests of school meal organizers.

Since its formation the new Association has continued and built on the work of its predecessors in the fields of professionalism, education, training and services to members. Membership of the HCIMA is now widely recognized as a qualification for managerial appointments in the industry. Its corporate membership examination, or an examination giving exemption from it, is normally the only means of entry to corporate membership, although a new Licentiate grade of membership was introduced in 1972 as a means of qualifying for corporate membership for the experienced manager without formal qualifications. In education the HCIMA is now recognized as the principal organization for the industry; in this role it has developed an important coordinating function and become a focal point for the student, teacher and industry, in education and training. Since its formation the HCIMA has been involved in a major review of its professional qualification and, following the publication of two major reports in 1974[1] and in 1977[2] based on investigations into management occupations, knowledge, and skills, the Association has revised and updated its membership qualification; courses leading to the new qualification are scheduled to begin in 1978.

Other activities covered by the HCIMA for its members include information and advisory services, meetings, publications and increasingly the representation of professional management in the industry to employers and other bodies. Recently the Association adopted a Code of Conduct for its members as a further step towards earning greater status and recognition for its members within and outside their own industry.

Personnel Associations

This category of organizations is more difficult to define than is the case with professional bodies or trade unions. It includes associations of employees in particular occupations. Although they are sometimes described as professional bodies, they are differentiated from professional bodies on the one hand in that admission to membership is usually not restricted by examination, and from

---

[1] Hotel, Catering and Institutional Management Association, *Tomorrow's Managers*.
[2] Hotel, Catering and Institutional Management Association, *The Corpus of Knowledge*.

trade unions on the other hand in that their aims do not extend to the negotiation of wages and conditions of employment. Their principal functions are to provide an opportunity for exchange of information and contact between those engaged in the same occupation, and to promote their interests. The most common criterion for admission is employment in a particular occupation, although this is sometimes accompanied by a requirement of attaining a minimum grade in that occupation, a minimum length of experience or a similar condition. Personnel associations may be divided into those which are primarily for management in a particular sector or sectors of the industry, and those for other than managerial occupations.

The old-established management personnel associations are the Catering Managers' Association and the Industrial Catering Association, both of which have in membership catering managers in welfare forms of catering, and the Hospital Caterers' Association, with members of hospital catering officer status. The newer associations in this category include specialist bodies, such as the Catering Teachers' Association and the Hotel Industry Marketing Group[3]. Within a short space of time, specialist organizations of accountants, personnel and training officers, and food and beverage managers, in the hotel and catering industry have also been established.

A second group includes the Guild of Sommeliers, an association of wine butlers, the Society of Golden Keys, an association of hotel hall porters, and the United Kingdom Bartenders Guild. These and other individual bodies have the character of craft guilds, and a strong pride and tradition of association.

In the late 1960s personnel associations at management level followed the initiative of the Hotel and Catering Institute in bringing together a number of personnel associations in a working party, to explore the possibilities of a single professional body for the industry.

The following nine organizations, including the two professional bodies described earlier, came together in the working party: Association of Marine Catering Superintendents, Catering Managers' Association, Catering Teachers' Association, Hospital Caterers' Association, Hotel and Catering Institute, Hotel Sales Managers' Association, Industrial Catering Association, Institutional Management Association, Society of Catering and Hotel Management Consultants Limited. Their interim report, produced late in 1969, summarized the reasons for establishing this new body as follows:

1. The aims and objectives of each organization are practically the same and a combined effort would achieve better results.
2. A nationally represented professional body setting standards to which members subscribe would gain greater national recognition.
3. The views of one organization with a significant membership could be expressed with more effect to international, national and regional authorities. Further, the weight of all the membership could support a minority with a specific interest or activity.

[3] Formerly Hotel Sales Managers' Association, now a Group within the Institute of Marketing.

4. There is a belief that there are too many organizations striving with limited resources to achieve similar objectives.
5. The establishment of one strong professional body would encourage non-members engaged in professional activities to participate.
6. Implicit in the existence of a professional body is that all members should have certain knowledge and skill. A wider membership would encourage more people to acquire this knowledge and skill, through study.
7. A significant part of the knowledge and skill both technical and managerial required in the profession is common to all sectors of the industry. The career patterns of individuals engaged in the profession often extend over several sectors.
8. The present confused picture of education and career opportunities which discourages school leavers from entering the industry could be rationalized.
9. There would be more opportunity for members with different backgrounds and experience to pool their knowledge.
10. The current activities of each organization would become a part of a much wider public relations activity and this in turn could attract a higher calibre of speakers and contributors.
11. A rationalization of administration would release more resources to be devoted to achieving broader objectives and extending activities, information and service to members.
12. A large permanent secretariat would be able to service both the general and specialized requirements of the membership.

The interim report[4] of the working party also set out the proposed aims and objectives of the new body, the grades of membership, how members of the existing organizations as well as new members might qualify for them, the proposed organization framework of the national organization, and an estimate of its corporate membership.

In 1970 the discussions of the working party led to the decision to concentrate, in the first instance, on the possibility of a merger between the two professional bodies, the HCI and the IMA, before extending them again to the other associations. This led to the formation of the HCIMA, described earlier in this chapter. Soon afterwards a number of the personnel associations represented in the working party came together with others in a loose National Catering Federation.

There are no moves to extend the HCIMA to implement the working party concept as this book is going to print. However, this should not be ruled out for the future. It is also conceivable that some of the personnel associations may in time assume a negotiating role on behalf of their members, and acquire the character of a trade union, either by themselves or as part of a wider body.

---

[4] Interim report of the professional associations' working party set up to explore the possibility of establishing a wider professional body.

Trade Unions

Trade unions represent a clearly-defined type of association of employees in a particular trade or industry, or of particular employees in more than one industry, whose principal function is the negotiation of wages and conditions of employment. It is possible to identify three types of union. The industrial union, such as the National Union of Railwaymen (NUR), covers one industry with little or no distinction as to occupation within the industry; the craft union, such as the Electrical Trades Union (ETU), organizes mainly skilled employees in a particular occupation, in whatever industry they may be found; the general union, such as the Transport and General Workers' Union (TGWU) includes in its membership mostly unskilled and semi-skilled employees in more than one industry and occupation.

Some twelve million people in Britain (well over 40 per cent of the working population of the country), belong to several hundred trade unions. However, in contrast to many industries where trade unions have exercised a powerful influence, the hotel and catering industry is one of the least organized economic groupings in the country. Various estimates put the trade union membership of hotel and catering employees at no more than 5 per cent of the total, with a significantly higher degree of concentration in the public than in the private sector of the industry, and in the welfare forms of catering than in the commercial sectors. For example, in health service and local authority catering activities the majority of employees are estimated to belong to trade unions.

There is no hotel and catering workers' union as such; the organized employees belong to various unions, which sometimes have catering sections. The only industrial union with a substantial membership of hotel and catering workers is the National Union of Railwaymen (NUR), which has since 1948 organized workers in the British Transport hotels and other catering activities, and prior to that in the former railway companies' employment. The three principal general unions with hotel and catering membership are the General and Municipal Workers' Union (GMWU), the Transport and General Workers' Union (TGWU), and the Union of Shop, Distributive and Allied Workers (USDAW). A demarcation agreement between them and other unions provides a broad basis according to which each union has an exclusive right to organize hotel and catering employees in certain areas, in particular sections of the industry and in particular firms. The GMWU is mainly active in licensed hotels and restaurants, and in industrial catering. The TGWU membership is mainly in industrial catering but some is also in hotels and public houses. The USDAW organizes workers in unlicensed restaurants, public houses, clubs and in industrial catering. Employees in institutional and welfare catering in the public sectors belong to the National Union of Public Employees (NUPE).

Eight unions with members in the hotel and catering industry come together in the TUC Hotel and the Catering Industry Committee, to which each sends one or two representatives. The objects of the Committee are to give assistance and advice to the affiliated unions in all matters concerned with the industry, to act as a co-ordinating body on manpower policy and other matters of union concern in the industry, and to promote goodwill and understanding between the affiliated unions. The following unions are also represented on the Committee, in addition to those mentioned above: Transport Salaried Staffs' Association, National Association of Theatrical and Kine Employees, and the Bakers Union.

The low degree of trade union organization among hotel and catering workers may be explained by a number of complementary factors. As in some other industries which consist of a large number of employers spread over the whole country, of whom many employ only a few workers each, unions have had to face considerable organizing difficulties. The industry has a variety of jobs with a corresponding variety of occupations, many of which have little affinity of interest with each other. Much of the work is seasonal, which contributes to a high labour turnover and thus accentuates the organizing problem. The industry employs a large proportion of women, traditionally less interested in trade unions than men, and substantial numbers of foreign workers, whose stay in the country is for many only temporary. The incidence of gratuities in several occupations may give rise to divided loyalty on the part of employees; the existence of statutory wage regulation in the industry may have in itself reduced the inducement to join a union. In a situation where trade unionism is not commonly accepted, there is often a fear of management attitude to union membership on the part of employees. There are also signs that the absence of an industrial union has affected interest in trade unions, as the general unions may have little appeal to those committed to the industry.

But the influence of trade unions in the industry is greater than their membership would suggest. In addition to full voluntary negotiation in some parts of the industry and in some firms, unions are recognized in others as the consultative and negotiating bodies for conditions of employment other than those covered by the statutory machinery. They participate fully through their own representatives in the Government-sponsored bodies of the industry and are parties to both the statutory negotiation in Wages Councils and to the development of training. In official circles more so than otherwise they are recognized as the representative organizations of employees in the hotel and catering industry. Moreover, recent reports of the Commission on Industrial Relations on the hotel and catering industry provided a strong stimulus to their development in the industry. There is much evidence to suggest that trade unions have been gaining ground in the industry in recent years.

18. Trade Associations

Trade associations, whose incidence and activities in the hotel and catering industry are described in the present chapter, have been largely formed for what can be described as 'defensive' purposes – to protect the interests of entrepreneurs in one or more sectors of the industry. As time passed, many have added to their activities, and the original motive for the association's existence need not have retained the same prominence or, indeed, continued to exist. But an examination of the factors influencing both the increase in the number of trade associations and the growth in their numbers of members suggests that both have taken place at times when the firms in the industry were faced with a situation affecting their businesses. This has been the case in industry generally; although some associations were in existence at the beginning of the last century, they became more numerous, stronger, and more active in the second half of the century when legislative changes of importance were made and proposed.

The first major problem facing the London Coffee, Restaurant and Dining Room Keepers' Trade Protection Society, founded in 1900, was the threatened competition of the London County Council's lodging houses, for which the Council sought powers 'to provide, cook, prepare and sell' to the occupants 'food of every description, whether solid or liquid' through a clause in the General Powers Bill passing through Parliament.[1] In 1906–7 a trade journal, *The Caterer*, provided the rallying point to counteract Government attempts to introduce far-reaching licensing reforms. These reforms aimed at large-scale reduction in public and other licensed houses, and proposed that the remaining licensed houses, including hotels, should provide compensation for abolished licences; in 1907 the efforts of the trade journal led to the formation of the National Hotel Keepers' Association.[2] It is hardly a coincidence that the Caterers' Association was formed in 1917 when war-time shortages and controls adversely affected catering firms.

The earliest associations in this industry were formed at the end of the nineteenth and beginning of the twentieth century and most present-day bodies trace their origin to one of these first attempts to provide for the representation of a group of firms with common interests. Greater specialization within the industry and the development of new forms of catering led to the emergence of a few new bodies; such was the origin, for instance, of the Milk Bars Association (now dissolved), which came into existence in the late 1930s, and the British Motel Federation formed in the late 1960s.

[1] National Caterers Federation, *The Golden Jubilee of the Caterers Federation 1900–50*, pp. 5–6.
[2] British Hotels and Restaurants Association, The Story of the Association, *BHRA Journal*, November, 1957, pp. 329, *et seq.*

Little statistical information has been published about changes in trade association membership in this industry, but there is no doubt that the external forces which give rise to them also exercise influence on membership. The motives which persuade autonomous units to act together have been particularly strong during the world wars, and at the time of the introduction of statutory wage regulation in the industry after 1945. The increasing complexity of economic life generally must be also regarded as an influencing factor on trade association membership, which may be even more important in an industry comprising a large number of small firms. It brings in turn the need for a wider range of services to be provided by an association to its members; in the hotel and catering industry most trade associations have greatly extended their activities in this direction, and can thus provide a greater inducement to outsiders to join, and to existing members to remain.

What is a Trade Association?

Some interests of hoteliers and caterers are served by bodies, sometimes loosely described as trade associations, which are principally concerned either with providing an opportunity for exchanges of views and social contact between those engaged in various hotel and catering occupations, usually at managerial level, or with advancement of culinary or other knowledge. As their membership consists, however, of individuals and not firms, and as their objects do not include the usual objects of trade associations, they are not dealt with in this chapter.

A trade association is commonly understood to be a voluntary non-profit-making body formed by independent firms to protect and advance their common interests. This basic definition is adopted here, and in common with other associations, those in the hotel and catering industry, therefore, share three main features. In the first place, their members are individual firms, which have a common interest, in that they operate the same or a similar type of establishment and supply a common product or service. Secondly, their membership is voluntary, in that firms in the industry are free to join or not as they wish. Thirdly, the identity of member firms is fully preserved.

Some interests of hotel and catering firms are better cared for by local associations, sometimes by chambers of commerce. As in other industries, this is usually the case where there is a sufficiently high concentration of the industry in a region or locality, or where the market is limited geographically. We have seen previously that both conditions prevail in the hotel and catering industry; the incidence of local associations of hotel and catering firms is correspondingly high, and many of them are affiliated either to the British Federation of Hotel, Guest House and Self Catering Association with its headquarters in Blackpool, or to a national trade association or to both. These geographically-based local or regional associations are also left out of further consideration in the present context, and the remainder of this chapter is devoted to national bodies.

Principal Associations

The principal trade association for the hotel and catering industry is the British Hotels, Restaurants and Caterers' Association (BHRCA), which was formed in 1972 when the British Hotels and Restaurants Association (BHRA) merged with the Caterers' Association of Great Britain.

The BHRA was formed in 1948 by the amalgamation of two associations of long standing, the Hotels and Restaurants Association of Great Britain and the Residential Hotels Association. At the end of the 1960s the BHRA had over 4,000 hotels and restaurants in direct membership, and with others affiliated to it through local associations, represented over 10,000 establishments.

The Caterers' Association of Great Britain was formed in 1917. Its membership consisted of a variety of catering businesses, most of them non-residential, and in the late 1960s it represented more than 4,000 businesses, which operated some 15,000 establishments. Its Industrial and Staff Canteen Division included most of the firms, which were until 1948 members of the association of catering contractors, the National Society of Contractors to Industry. The Association also had affiliated to it two local associations with some 500 establishments.

In 1969 the BHRA set up a high-level working party under the chairmanship of Lord Shawcross to review the future role and work of the Association. The working party report was accepted by the Association in 1971 and led to a reorganization of the BHRA. In order to enable the reorganized Association to represent fully all hotels, restaurants and caterers, the Caterers Association resolved at the same time to seek approval for voluntary winding-up of that Association and to recommend all its existing members to become members of the new trade association. As a result the BHRCA was formed in 1972. In the mid-1970s membership of the Association was estimated to be in the region of 7,500, with about 2,000 indirect members through affiliated associations.

The National Association of Holiday Centres (formerly the National Federation of Permanent Holiday Camps) is the trade association of holiday camp operators, which represents about eighty camps with catering and entertainment facilities and also a small number of self-catering centres. The British Motel Federation has in its membership about a third of the motels in Britain.

Some influence is exercised in the licensed sector of the industry by the Brewers' Society, formed in 1904 by the amalgamation of the Country Brewers' Society, the London Brewers' Association, and the Burton Brewers' Association. The Society is first and foremost a trade association of brewing firms and it has now for all practical purposes 100 per cent membership in the brewing industry; through the ownership of licensed houses by breweries, the Society also plays an important part in the hotel and catering industry, although trade association functions of brewery firms with hotel interests are exercised by the BHRCA. According to The Monopolies Commission Report on Beer all but sixteen of the 111 separate brewery companies or groups of companies at the end of 1967 were full members of the Society; however, together the sixteen accounted for only 2 per cent of total UK production of beer and owned only about 500 of the 68,000 licensed premises owned by brewers.

Three trade associations, which represent various sectors and geographical areas in the licensed trade, are joined in the National Brewer/Retailer Liaison Committee: the National Union of Licensed Victuallers, the Scottish Licensed Trade Association and the Brewers' Society.

Functions and Activities

The activities of the principal trade associations enumerated above are of two main kinds: *representation*, in which they act as channels of communication with the Government and other organized groups, and *services to members,* in which associations provide information, advice and assistance to their members in the conduct of their businesses. These two categories are not absolutely clear-cut, but it is useful to consider the predominantly representational functions separately from others when the activities of trade associations are examined.

The need for voluntary organizations, as fully representative as possible of the industrial interests covered by them, is generally recognized by the Government as it is always a matter of great convenience to have one or at most a few consultative bodies to deal with rather than a large number of individual firms; trade associations are also a source of expert knowledge and advice on matters relating to the industry or a section of it, and can provide up-to-date information required by the Government. Hotel and catering trade associations contacts are mainly with the Departments of Trade and Industry, the Ministry of Agriculture, Fisheries and Food, and the Department of Employment, but with others also from time to time. Their representations and negotiations deal with such subjects as proposed legislation and draft orders, taxation, rating of premises, recruitment and training of staff, etc.

In addition to making representations through administrative channels, hotel and catering associations sometimes press their case through parliamentary activity. Some Members of Parliament are themselves either directly connected with firms in the industry, and these firms are association members, or indirectly in their constituencies, in which the industry may be highly concentrated. Although these contacts with members, who are prepared to express the views of the industry in the House, may not be as frequent as direct approach to Government departments, they are of growing importance.

Some associations are in contact with public corporations and other public bodies; these include primarily electricity, gas and water undertakings, *ad hoc* bodies such as the Milk Marketing Board, and local authorities. In all these cases the representation is mainly 'protectionist', and is concerned with such matters as prices of supplies, competition with commercial catering firms, etc. Associations with strong hotel interests are in frequent consultation with the motoring organizations over such matters as the appointment and classification of hotels, and with other organizations on matters of common interest. The setting up of statutory Tourist Boards under the Development of Tourism Act, 1969, has led to a further major liaison activity of trade associations in the field of tourism.

Hotel and catering firms have been brought together as trade association members more in their capacity as hoteliers and caterers than as employers of labour. Lack of trade union organization has limited their representative activities in the field of negotiation with workers' organizations, which takes principally the form of representation on the statutory Wages Councils, discussed at a later stage. The voluntary agreements which are in existence are, as a rule, concluded between workers' and employers' representatives at a local or company level.

It appears that the concern of trade associations with the promotion of helpful legislative and other developments and resistance to what was unfavourable, established their reputation, and that their appeal to individual firms has been strong on these grounds. Other trade association activities have usually been of later origin. Services to members do not primarily involve representation to other groups but arise out of the recognition that some things can only be done, and other things more effectively done, by a collective body. Sometimes these services form part of the external economies of the firms. In an industry in which the typical firm is small, and as such unable to have some services provided by specialists within its own organization, this aspect of association activities assumes even greater importance. Most bodies within the industry publish their own journals or bulletins, which provide a link with members and serve as a means of disseminating information. In addition they engage to a considerable extent in providing specialist advice on legal and other problems to individual members on request. At least one association has provided a collective buying service, which enables member firms to purchase a wide range of supplies on more advantageous terms than they would be able to do on their own. Some maintain an employment bureau, on the services of which members may draw for staff. The BHRCA has organized schemes for bringing foreign workers to this country to alleviate the labour shortage.

A number of trade association services are of a distinctly promotional character, with the object of securing publicity for their members or for the industry as a whole, and of contributing to the development of the industry. Most consider it as one of their objects to take steps to maintain and improve the prestige of the industry or of the sector which they represent. Thus replies to adverse criticisms in the press, and contributions to press discussions of the industry are made by association secretaries or other officers. The BHRCA publishes an Hotel Guide featuring its members, which is sold to the public, and has undertaken collective advertising campaigns for members. Under this heading also comes the organization of and participation in exhibitions. The rapid post-war development of training facilities for the industry has received active encouragement and support of most associations.

Apart from their lack of involvement so far in industrial relations, in another important respect hotel and catering trade associations differ from some others, namely in their lack of concern with regulation of competition. Whilst this aspect is by no means common even to other associations, activities normally described as restrictive practices often do constitute an important aspect of a number of trade associations in other industries, and have occupied considerable public and official attention in this as in other industrial countries.

In Switzerland, for instance, price fixing has been even applied in hotels.[3] No similar instance has been known in this country, except for the temporary wartime control of meal prices, which was, however, instituted by the Government. Trade association pronouncements recommending to members that there was a justification for an increase in prices in the region of so many per cent, which have been quite common in post-war years, cannot be considered in the same light. The intention was to speed the rise in prices, which was gradually occurring as a result of the increased pressure of costs; prices did remain at much the same level for a number of years despite increased costs of materials, wages, rates, light and power, etc., or only increased a little. But the associations' pronouncements carry no sanctions and do not amount to price fixing by any stretch of the imagination. Undoubtedly, the wide variations in product and service preclude such action even if it were desired by trade associations; the difficulties experienced in this respect in overseas countries where it has been attempted have been considerable. Any control of competition, whether by price agreements or otherwise, also requires an adequate coverage of the industry in question by the trade association, which is, at present, far from being the case in the hotel and catering industry. The only case of persistent concern with competition on the part of trade associations can be discerned in the case of local authorities and some other bodies operating catering establishments for the public. Here the trade associations' attitude has always been that they represent unfair competition to the commercial caterer as they operate on advantageous terms, and that their entry into the industry is undesirable. In a number of cases, as a result of trade associations' objections, these bodies have refrained from opening new establishments and have discontinued some of the existing ones.

Future Development

It now remains to consider future avenues of trade association development in the hotel and catering industry. There is little justification for any new organizations being formed, as the interests of all sections of the industry are provided for by existing bodies. Indeed, there may well be a case for further amalgamation between trade associations serving similar interests to facilitate better co-ordination in cases of representation, and to avoid duplication of some other activities. There is, next, scope for more effective coverage of the industry through larger membership. Although few membership statistics have been published, the proportion of firms belonging to no association is certainly considerable. A higher income resulting from increased membership would enable existing

---

[3] Muench, T., *Das Hotelunternehmen in Lichte Betriebswirtschaftlicher Lehre und Praxis*, pp. 128, et seq.

associations to extend and improve the range and quality of their services to members.

It is probably in this direction, the extension of member services, that the main progress may be expected in the trade association field in the future. If the developments in other industries and in other countries can be taken as a guide, some lines of activity suggest themselves. American and Canadian hotel and restaurant associations have been very active in public relations activities for a number of years, and have made considerable efforts to influence customer goodwill through the press, radio, television and films designed for the general public. Testing of products and equipment and technical research has so far received attention only from a few very large firms in the industry in this country; statistical and market information has not been collected to any extent by any British association in this industry. There is no doubt that problems specific to hotel and catering firms call for investigation, and that the results of such investigations could be of benefit to the majority of firms. Trade associations are the natural agencies to undertake such projects, and it would be a pity if they were prevented from such activities by fragmentation and the lack of resources.

Currently none of the trade associations in the hotel and catering industry are involved in industrial relations as employer organizations. The Reports of the Commission on Industrial Relations on the hotel and catering industry in the early 1970s drew attention to the significance of such organizations for the industry and it is possible that in time one or more of the trade associations may become increasingly involved in this field.

19. Governmental and Statutory Bodies

In a study of the institutional framework of an industry it is essential to examine not only voluntary associations of individuals and of firms, but also 'official' bodies created by the Government for the particular industry. In a study of the hotel and catering industry three main types of organization emerge which deserve more than a passing reference; they are the Economic Development Committees, Industrial Training Boards and Wages Councils. Wages Councils have been in existence much longer than the other two, first as Wages Boards, before they became Wages Councils. Training Boards and Wages Councils are statutory bodies, whilst Economic Development Committees are not. Their respective functions are different. However, all three types of organization represent some of the principal directions of state intervention in the industry in modern times, and also of Government recognition of hotel and catering services as an industry. It is, therefore, convenient and desirable to view these bodies together. None of them are unique to the hotel and catering industry, as their counterparts are to be found in other industries, but their existence in respect of this industry also provides some recognition of the importance of the hotel and catering industry.

Economic Development Committees

In 1962 the National Economic Development Council was created to achieve more effective ways of co-ordination and co-operation in the formulation of economic policy in Britain. Under the chairmanship first of the Prime Minister and now of the Chancellor of the Exchequer it brings together Ministers of the Crown and leaders from both management and trade unions, together with a few independent members.

In 1964 the National Economic Development Council began to create a series of Economic Development Committees for particular industries, to pursue similar objectives and as a new experiment in methods of consultation within industry, as well as between Government and industry.[1] The NEDC provides through the network of EDCs a major channel of communication with indivi-

---

[1] Most information on Economic Development Committees was provided by the National Economic Development Office and derived from the following four addresses:

Fraser, T. C., *Economic Development Committee – A New Dimension in the Relations between Government and Industry*, Special University Lecture, London School of Economics and Political Science, February 10, 1966, pp. 1–22;

Swallow, Sir W., *The Hotel Industry's Contribution to the Economy*, Scottish Tourist Board Conference, Aviemore, November 9, 1967, pp. 1–20;

Swallow, Sir W., *Summer Meeting of the British Resorts Association*, Worthing, June 12, 1968, pp. 1–6;

dual industries to ensure that the implications of national policies are understood in each industry, and that the circumstances of each industry are taken into account in the preparation of policy. Thus the need for Economic Development Committees for individual industries grew empirically from the work of the Council. Indeed, the terms of reference of all the committees begin 'Within the context of the work of the NEDC'.

The EDCs are sometimes called 'Little Neddies', after their parent body, the NEDC, which has been nicknamed 'Neddy'. There are now eighteen Economic Development Committees at work, dealing with most of the country's major industries; they are listed in Appendix P. In 1973 the fifteen EDCs then in existence covered close on eleven million people at work.

Each Committee includes representatives of management, unions, the Government department(s) concerned with the industry and of the National Economic Development Office. The chairman is selected for his capacity for leadership and is not usually drawn from the industry concerned. In addition to the independent chairman provision is made for a small number of independent members who represent, with the Chairman, a critical component within the Committee, and who can bring a fresh view to bear on the industry's problems with no allegiance to any of the three parties.

In forming the Committee for each industry, the Office, acting for the Council, follows the principle that the management organizations, the trade unions and the sponsoring Government departments concerned must have a real sense of responsibility for the establishment of their Committee and of involvement in the success of its work. The three parties must, therefore, have freedom to put forward names of representatives in whom they have confidence. Members are not delegates of sectional interests but jointly agreed after consideration within the trade associations or unions. The Chairman is appointed by the Chancellor of the Exchequer after consultation with the three sides.

The National Economic Development Office, working under an independent Director General, provides the secretariat for the Council and for the Committees. The staff are drawn partly from industry, partly from trade unions, universities, the Civil Service and elsewhere. The independence of the Office is an essential part of the concept.

The Economic Development Committees have no executive powers and no powers of compulsion. Their function has been described as being 'to know and to inquire, to initiate and to prod, to advise and to seek to influence'. More specifically their terms of reference are in two parts.[2] First, to assess the economic progress of the industry for purposes of national economic planning; secondly, to examine and evaluate the whole field of activities of the industry and to

---

Swallow, Sir W., *Work of the Hotel and Catering Economic Development Committee*, Economic Planning Council for the South West Region, Exeter, September 24, 1968.

Further information was derived from Beach, S. T., The Little Neddy for Hotels and Catering, *HCIMA Review*, Volume 1, Number 4.

[2] The remit of the International Freight Movement EDC is somewhat different because it is not concerned with a particular industrial sector.

encourage the means of improving its efficiency. In other words, each Committee examines the prospects and plans of the industry, assesses from time to time its progress, and provides information and forecasts to the NEDC; it seeks to identify the problems within the industry, and to devise and to recommend ways of putting them right. Having agreed on the course of action and who should be taking it, it is the task of the EDC to persuade the relevant bodies – management, trade associations, trade unions, Government departments or other agencies – to take action.

The Committees operate mainly through working groups. Neither the chairman nor the members of working groups need be members of the EDC itself but usually at least the chairman is. It is through these groups that the resources of the whole industry can be called upon as necessary to deal with particular problems.

Since November 1975, the system of Committees has been extended as a result of the agreement by the NEDC on an approach to an industrial strategy. Forty key sectors of manufacturing industry have been selected for detailed study as a part of the strategy. Where EDCs already existed, these studies are being carried out under their auspices. Where there was no EDC, Sector Working Parties composed of representatives of the Government, employers and unions were set up. By 1976, forty sectors were being studied by EDCs and Sector Working Parties.

The Hotels and Catering Economic Development Committee was established in June 1966. In 1976 it comprised 19 members. Six of them were drawn from the two principal trade associations in the industry, the Brewers' Society and the British Hotels, Restaurants and Caterers' Association. The smaller independent hotelier and the self catering sector were also represented. Five were from trade unions: GMWU, NUPE, NUR, TGWU and USDAW. Government nominees were from the two 'sponsor' departments of the industry, the Ministry of Agriculture, Fisheries and Food and the Department of Trade. There was also a representative from the Department of Education and Science and of the tourist boards. There were two independent members, one representative of the National Economic Development Office and an independent chairman who had no direct involvement in the industry.

At its inception three standing working groups were established: Economics and Finance, Manpower, and Marketing. To these were later added the Statistics and Forecasting Working Group and several *ad hoc* Groups and Advisory Committees, including the Advisory Committee on Uniform Accounts, the Computer Group (in co-operation with the National Computer Centre), the Advisory Joint Committee on Convenience Foods (in conjunction with the Food Manufacturing EDC) and the Parity of Treatment Study Group. A Catering Industry Study Group and a Catering Supplies Study Group have also been established to examine aspects of the catering industry.

From its beginning the Economic Development Committee for Hotels and Catering provided a major catalytic influence on the industry and a focal point for development in the industry. It has contributed significantly to an identification of hotel and catering activity as an industry through the improvement of statistical and other data. It has highlighted the role of the industry in its contribution to the balance of payments, to regional economic development and to the business and social life of the community, against the background of developing awareness of the growing importance of the service sector in an advanced economy. It has stimulated a better understanding in the industry of the factors involved in the more efficient use of resources. It has promoted the importance of the marketing approach in solving the industry's problems, and in the realization of market opportunities. Last, but not least, it has provided information about current and future trends in demand, profitability and capacity, giving a useful management tool on the basis of which decisions can be taken on future marketing and investment policy.

Since its establishment, the industry's Little Neddy has influenced the thinking in the industry itself, the Government as well as informed public opinion more than any other agency, and could be said to have paved the way for the development of the industry into a progressive force in the British economy of the 1970s. Many of its efforts have not resulted in spectacular achievements; others have been essentially more long-term in their impact.

Industrial Training Boards

The White Paper on Industrial Training published in December 1962 highlighted the Government concern with the state of industrial training in Britain at the beginning of that decade.[3] Early in 1964 the Government's proposals for the setting up of statutory boards to be responsible for all aspects of training in individual industries were embodied in the Industrial Training Act 1964, which had three main objectives:

(*a*) to ensure an adequate supply of properly trained men and women at all levels in industry;
(*b*) to secure an improvement in the quality and efficiency of industrial training;
(*c*) to share the cost of training more evenly between firms.

As a result of the 1964 Act a number of Industrial Training Boards were set up covering various sectors of industry, each Board consisting of a chairman, a person with industrial or commercial experience, an equal number of employer and trade union members, and a number of educational members.

The main duties of each Board were to ensure that sufficient training was provided, and to publish recommendations on such matters as the nature, content and length of training for occupations in its industry.

Each Board's income was drawn from a levy on employers in the industry concerned. This finance was used to meet the costs of the Board's operations, including advisory and direct training services, and to provide grants to employers for specific training activities. In the levy and grant system in

[3] Ministry of Labour, *Industrial Training: Government Proposals*.

particular the Boards had a very powerful incentive to encourage firms to undertake approved training.

By 1976 there were twenty-seven Industrial Training Boards covering 15 million workers. The list of the Boards in operation in March 1976, with their dates of establishment and coverage of establishments and employees, is shown in Appendix Q.

A number of significant changes to the powers, finance and organization of the Boards were introduced by the Employment and Training Act 1973.[4]

First, the Act set up the Manpower Services Commission (MSC) and its two executive arms, the Employment Services Agency (ESA) and the Training Services Agency (TSA). The Commission was given responsibility for many of the education and training functions carried out previously by the Department of Employment itself. Its main duties can be summarized as assisting people to select, train for, obtain and retain suitable employment, and to assist employers to obtain suitable employees. It was also given the duty to make recommendations to the Secretary of State for Employment on employment and training matters including the setting up or abolition of Training Boards.

A second important change brought about by the Act was that the Commission was made responsible for co-ordinating the work of the Industrial Training Boards, for meeting their administration costs, and for providing funds for selective grants to stimulate key training activities. These duties are carried out by the Training Services Agency, which has also responsibility for providing training in sectors of employment not covered by the Boards.

A third significant change was that the Act relieved the Boards of the statutory duty to raise a levy on employers. Since 1973 the Boards have retained the powers to raise levies, but they now also have powers to give exemption where, in the Board's opinion this is considered appropriate.

The Hotel and Catering Industry Training Board (HCITB) came into existence in November 1966 as the eighteenth Board to be established, and one of the first to cover a service industry. According to its 1970 Annual Report its register included some 75,000 employers with about 106,500 establishments and 664,000 employees.

The original Order establishing the HCITB covered the bulk of hotel and catering services in Britain with few specific exclusions. Following a judgement in the House of Lords on May 13, 1969 in the case between the Board and Automobile Proprietary Limited (RAC), the scope of Industrial Training Boards was restricted to activities undertaken by way of trade or business carried on for the purpose of gain; it was held that activities subject to the Industrial Training Act were confined to the activities of persons engaged in industry or commerce. The effect of the judgement has been to rule out of scope of the Board catering activities not only in members' clubs but also in universities, colleges of education and the school meals service. In July 1969 the Secretary of State for Employment and Productivity announced her intention of returning the 200,000

[4] A full summary of these changes is given in the *Department of Employment Gazette* in March 1973.

employees in institutional and local authority sectors into the scope of the HCITB as soon as possible and this was re-affirmed in the House of Commons in December 1969. A Bill to amend the 1964 Act was introduced by the Government in January 1970. Its purpose was to restore to the scope of the Act activities excluded as a result of the House of Lords decision, and it also included a provision to enable Boards to provide training for self-employed employers. The Bill was abandoned as a result of the dissolution of Parliament in May 1970.

In 1976 the Hotel and Catering Industry Training Board consisted of the chairman, seven employer representatives, seven employee representatives and four educational members, and began to operate with a total staff of 268 (188 in training and 80 in administration) under a new Five Year Plan. By that time the Board had completed the first ten years of its activity, in which it made a pronounced impact on its industry in spite of the magnitude of its task; of an initial hostility on the part of many in the industry; and of the setback to its work in the welfare sectors as a result of the House of Lords judgement.

Following its establishment in 1966 the Board adopted a flexible 'Task Approach' in developing the training recommendations for the industry's main occupations. The recognition of the special problem of the small employers in the industry who are not in a position to organize training themselves, led to a major development of group training schemes, in which a number of employers in an area could share the services of a group training officer, thus achieving the benefits of a large company with its own training division. As training activity was gathering momentum in the industry, the Board was engaged in training its own training advisers, group training officers, and training officers in industry. As much training in the industry is conducted by departmental supervisors, the Board paid considerable attention to instructor training for on-the-job trainers, instructors and instructor trainers. The impending introduction of decimal currency in Britain in 1971, which was of much importance to the industry, found an expression in a massive nationwide training plan by the Board, and the introduction of metrication by 1975 provided scope for a similar approach. In parallel with the above activities there has proceeded the development of training advisory services to the industry through the Board's regional offices, the setting up of training centres, and the creation of channels for consultation and liaison between the Board and the industry nationally and regionally.

The Board's initial statutory levy was fixed at 1 per cent of the employer's payroll with a total exemption for employers with a payroll of less than £4,000, and a further exemption of the first £2,000 of the payroll from the levy for employers with a payroll of £4,000 or more. Subsequently the levy was raised to 1·25 per cent, and then gradually reduced to 1, 0·8 and finally 0·7 per cent by 1974–1975, where it has since remained. Concurrently the raising of the level at which employers became liable to levy proceeded and this reached £40,000 in 1975–1976. In 1975 in-scope employers remaining liable to levy numbered about 1,500, employing between them approximately two-thirds of the industry's in-scope employees.

There is no doubt that the upsurge of training consciousness and activity in the industry has been the direct result of the establishment and rapid initial progress of the Board. However, its success can be only judged by the extent to which it meets the objectives of the Industrial Training Acts in ensuring that the industry has manpower which is adequate in quantity and quality, at a cost acceptable to the employer.

In the early 1970s some doubts about the approach of the HCITB were apparent. Growing industry criticism of its training and financial policies led to the Board's three-year plan, with grants based on the need for incentives rather than cost recovery, on a simplified scheme and, as a consequence, of grant claim procedures, and on the need to contain total costs within a reduced levy. The Board's subsequent plans and activities came to be based increasingly on consultation with industry and the Training Services Agency under the new arrangements, which made the whole of the Board's levy income available for training grants, and which enable the Board to offer services and grants to all in-scope employers, whether leviable or not.

In May 1976 the HCITB published its Five Year Plan, the second under the 1973 Act, covering the period from April 1976 to March 1981.[5] The Board's declared objective under the Plan is 'to assist the hotel and catering industry to develop and implement training relevant to and effective for its short- and long-term operational needs'. To pursue this overall objective the Plan comprises four programmes: services to leviable employers; services to employers excluded from levy, services to the industry as a whole, and the management of the Board. The Board's training grant and levy schemes came to be based on the following premises:

(a) Only the 1,500 or so largest employers in the industry (as measured by size of payroll) should be liable to levy;
(b) Training grants for these leviable employers should be determined by the extent to which they plan and implement systematic training;
(c) Employers training systematically to meet their own needs should be eligible for exemption from levy;
(d) In addition to exemption and grants for systematic training there should be specific grants to encourage training in certain key areas;
(e) Appropriate key training area grants should be made available to non-leviable employers.

These provisions are set in the broader context of the Board's activities outlined in the Five Year Plan, which include a range of training advisory services, direct training, training aids and publications, and research and development.

Wages Boards and Wages Councils

Thirty-four years after the first direct intervention of the state for the fixing of

[5] Hotel and Catering Industry Training Board, *Five Year Plan 1976–1981*.

minimum wages in Britain in industries where wages were unreasonably low, and twenty-five years after the scope of the Trade Boards (which became Wages Councils in 1945) was extended generally wherever no adequate machinery existed for the regulation of wages, statutory regulation of wages and holidays was introduced in the hotel and catering industry by the Catering Wages Act 1943.

In accordance with the provisions of the Act the Minister of Labour and National Service established the Catering Wages Commission with the following powers:

1. to make such inquiries as they may think fit or may be directed by the Minister to make into existing methods of regulating the remuneration and conditions of employment in the catering trades, to report where they are adequate or can be made adequate, and to make proposals for the establishment of Wages Boards where the arrangements are inadequate and cannot be made adequate, or do not exist–
2. to make recommendations to any Government Department on any matters affecting the remuneration, conditions of employment, health or welfare of the workers; and
3. to make such inquiries as they think fit or may be directed by the Minister to make into means for meeting the requirements of the public, including in particular the requirements of visitors from overseas and for developing the tourist traffic, and make recommendations to any Government Department with regard to such matters.

The Catering Wages Commission consisted of not more than three independent persons, one of whom was chairman, together with not more than two persons representing employers and two representing workers, but none of them directly connected with the industry. Some of the Commission's reports on a variety of matters are mentioned elsewhere in this study. With regard to methods of regulating the remuneration and conditions of employment in the industry, the Commission found few instances of existing arrangements, which it considered adequate, or which it thought could be made adequate. The main ones were in the case of workers employed by the Crown who were covered by the Whitley machinery, and those employed by local authorities in establishments within the scope of the National Joint Councils for Local Authorities; the Commission found a limited form of joint voluntary machinery in existence in railway companies and it considered arrangements covering workers employed on railway trains to be adequate. Outside these spheres where some joint voluntary machinery existed, as it did, e.g. in some districts in Scotland where workers in public houses were covered by collective agreements, or in railway hotels and in refreshment-rooms at railway stations, the Commission regarded the joint voluntary machinery as a very useful complement to statutory regulation, but was unwilling to recommend that those establishments should be exempt from the scope of the Wages Boards, which it eventually recommended to be set up for the greater part of the industry.

The Commission recommended to the Minister that five separate Wages Boards be established for different sectors of the industry and outlined the scope of each; the Minister accepted the recommendations and set up the Wages Boards to cover various sectors of the industry as follows:

(a) The Industrial and Staff Canteen Undertakings (ISC) Wages Board to cover workers in canteens, but canteens in schools and hospitals were excluded from its scope.
(b) The Unlicensed Place of Refreshment (UPR) Wages Board for workers in cafés, coffee stalls, snack bars, unlicensed restaurants and catering contracting businesses.
(c) The Licensed Residential and Licensed Restaurant (LR) Wages Board for workers in licensed hotels and clubs with four or more letting bedrooms or accommodation for at least eight guests (whichever less), unlicensed hotels with the same minimum accommodation and with a registered club on the premises, and licensed restaurants.
(d) The Licensed Non-Residential Establishment (LNR) Wages Board for workers in public houses, clubs and other licensed establishments with less than four bedrooms or accommodation for less than eight guests or lodgers.
(e) The Unlicensed Residential Establishment (UR) Wages Board for workers in unlicensed hotels, boarding-houses and similar establishments with the same minimum accommodation as in the case of the LR Wages Board.

The Wages Boards operation proceeded at the outset as follows (Table 64).

Table 64

Catering Wages Act, 1943: Initial Stages of Wages Boards

Wages Board	ISC	UPR	LR	LNR	UR
Set up by Minister	13.3.44	14.12.44	24.2.45	22.3.45	3.12.45
Members appointed	14.8.44	10.7.45	10.12.45	5.12.45	8.7.46
First meeting	6.9.44	28.8.45	8.2.46	15.1.46	14.8.46
First Wages Order in force	15.11.45	11.8.47	1.3.48	2.2.47	

Source: Elwes, V., Catering Wages Regulations, *Journal of the Hotel and Catering Institute*, Spring, Summer, Autumn 1958.

As can be seen from that table, the UR Wages Board had not introduced Wages Regulation Orders into effective operation. After two and a half years of negotiation its first set of proposals was issued in February 1949, only to be followed by another set of proposals in August 1949; these were not placed before the Minister because the possibility of a special inquiry to include the UR section of the industry had by then been announced. The Minister of Labour directed the Catering Wages Commission to hold an inquiry into the operation of the Catering Wages Act in the hotel industry in December 1949, and the Commission under the chairmanship of Sir John Forster reported in 1950.

The Report,[6] in addition to suggesting minor amendments to the LR Wages Regulations, which were in the main adopted by that Board, made three major recommendations: first, that the UR Wages Board be abolished and a single Board set up to cover both licensed and unlicensed residential establishments, secondly, that the new Board should with the help of special committees make recommendations for large London establishments, large provincial establishments and small establishments wherever situated and, thirdly, that a national joint committee be appointed to examine the problem of tipping.

The UR Wages Board was subsequently not re-appointed, but a legal obstacle was discovered to the proposed merger of the two sectors of the industry under one Board. The special committee proposal contained in the Report was adopted in a very different form by the LR Wages Board; four special committees set up by the Minister at the Board's request were designed to consider the establishments within the scope of the Board according to type but, except for minor amendments, have not produced proposals for separate differential regulations. The recommended committee on tipping was not established.

In 1959 the Terms and Conditions of Employment Act 1959 repealed the Catering Wages Act 1943, abolished the Catering Wages Commission, and converted the four active Wages Boards into Wages Councils under the Wages Councils Acts of 1945–48. The whole Wages Councils legislation was subsequently consolidated in the Wages Councils Act 1959. In structure the Wages Councils are identical with the former Wages Boards, which they replaced, and with very minor changes, they have the same powers and functions. The change was, therefore, at first sight more one of nomenclature than of substance. The real significance of the new Act for the hotel and catering industry, however, lay in the possibility of a solution to the dilemma presented by unlicensed residential establishments, in which no statutory minimum wages existed; the Wages Councils Act of 1945–48 made it possible for a commission of inquiry to be set up to consider whether a Wages Council should be established for that sector of the industry.

The Wages Councils, like the former Wages Boards, consist of equal numbers of members representing employers and members representing workers in relation to whom the Council operates, and of not more than three independent members, one of whom is appointed by the Minister to act as Chairman and one as Deputy Chairman. A Wages Council has power to make proposals for the fixing of minimum remuneration, and of holidays to be allowed to the workers in relation to whom the Council operates. It may also make recommendations to any Government Department with respect to any matter affecting the remuneration, conditions of employment, health or welfare of the workers

---

[6] Catering Wages Commission, *Report on an Enquiry into the Operation of the Catering Wages Act, 1943, in the Hotel Industry*.

covered by the Council, or with reference to the industrial conditions affecting the workers and employers in relation to whom the Council operates.

When a notice of proposal has been agreed by a Wages Council the Council makes a Wages Order. The Wages Orders have legal force and are read into every existing contract of employment. They specify, however, only the minimum remuneration and conditions of employment to be complied with by any employer within the scope of the Council; an employer is free to employ workers on more favourable terms.

The composition of the three Catering Wages Councils in operation in 1976 is shown in Appendix R. The table in Appendix S gives the number of establishments on the list of the four original Wages Boards (now Wages Councils) from the beginning of their operation to 1975. A comparative table in Appendix T indicates the Wages Councils' approach to the fixing of minimum remuneration and of holidays and sets out the principal features of recent Wages Orders of the three existing Councils.

It can be seen from Appendix S that remuneration and holidays for hotel and catering workers were until 1976 regulated through the four wages councils in some 130,000 establishments, although some 200,000 establishments were within the scope of the Catering Wages Act. These numbers represent more than one-half and about four-fifths of the industry's establishments respectively. It appears that the majority of units not covered by statutory wage regulations are small units with no workers within the scope of the Act. The principal category of workers whose conditions of employment are still not safeguarded are those in unlicensed residential establishments. The Catering Wages Commission estimated that the number of workers in this substantial sector of the industry was in the region of 100,000, and repeatedly expressed its concern that workers in the least organized section should remain without the protection of the Catering Wages Act. Undoubtedly, this was one of the principal reasons for the repeal of the Act, under which no workable solution could be found to the situation, which has existed since the Forster Report. No steps to remedy the situation have been taken.

A significant change occurred with the exclusion from the field of operation of the LR Wages Council of workers employed by the hotel and catering services of the nationalized railways, following the Report of a Commission of Inquiry in 1964.[7]

The reference of the hotel and catering industry to the Commission on Industrial Relations in November 1969 and its three published Reports have been noted in Chapter 16. The abolition of one of the four catering Wages Councils in 1976 and the recommended extension of voluntary collective bargaining in the industry may represent the most important development in the sphere of the catering Wages Councils since their beginning. In the meantime the three Councils with an estimated coverage of 900,000 workers rank as a very significant element in the total of forty-three Wages Councils, with an estimated coverage of just under three million.

[7] Ministry of Labour, *Report of a Commission of Inquiry on the Licensed Residential Establishment and Licensed Restaurant Wages Council.*

Summary

The principal features and characteristics of the three industry organizations discussed in this chapter may be compared as shown in Table 65.

Table 65

Hotel and Catering Industry
Comparison of the EDC, ITB and Wages Councils in 1976

	Economic Development Committee	Industrial Training Board	Wages Councils (formerly Wages Boards)
Number	One	One	Three
Established	1966	1966	1944–45
Scope	Whole industry	Most of the industry	Three defined sectors
Establishments[a]	200,000+	100,000	104,000
People[a]	1 million+	650,000	900,000
Function	Economic development	Training	Wages and holidays[b]
Composition	Management, trade unions, Government, independents	Employers, employees, educationalists, (+Govt assessors)	Employers, employees, independents
Powers	Persuasive	Statutory	Statutory

[a] Very approximate estimates.
[b] Also other unspecified terms and conditions of employment.

20. Conclusion: The Future of the Hotel and Catering Industry

Much of this book has been devoted to the hotel and catering industry as it has been and to the way it has developed to what it is today, in order to provide a greater understanding of the present state of this vast field of commercial hospitality, and to bring up-to-date a similar but more modest work with the same objectives, which appeared in 1961. This last part looks ahead. It is not an exercise in economic and social forecasting, for the problems of forecasting are dealt with and forecasts of various aspects of the industry are made by others. This look ahead discusses some of the changing background to the environment, in which the hotel and catering industry operates, and some of the main aspects of the changing industry itself, as they may develop in the years to come. Such forecasts as are included have been used in the main to illustrate. The purpose of the chapter is to increase awareness and to stimulate imagination.

The approach begins with a view of some aspects of Britain, in which the industry has been and will be earning its living, and this is extended beyond, to form the basis for a view of the market for hotel and catering services in Britain in the years to come. Meeting the market needs calls for adequate resources, in particular investment capital and labour, and the next part is devoted to a brief consideration of the requirements and influences which may determine the availability of resources for the future development of the industry. The prosperity and standing of the industry will depend in part on the way the available resources are organized, and a view of the changing structure and organization of the industry concludes the consideration of the shape of the industry in the years to come. In this the approach is to describe what could, or perhaps should happen, rather than what necessarily will.

The Market in the Eighties

Two major studies of the future demand for hotel and catering services in Britain were completed recently, both by consultants commissioned by the Hotels and Catering Economic Development Committee.[1] Much of the assessment of the future market which follows is based on these studies.

The starting point in the study of economic and social development of any society is an understanding of trends in the size and structure of the population. In looking at the United Kingdom population in the past and at the projections to the end of the century, the first striking feature is the rate of growth. In the

---
[1] Hotels and Catering EDC, *Hotel Prospects to 1980*.
Hotels and Catering EDC, *Hotel Prospects to 1985*.

thirty-five years to 1975 the total population increased by 8 million or over 16 per cent; in the thirty-five years to 2011 it is expected to increase by 3 million or 5 per cent. This poses important physical planning implications facing the Government and the community: where and how will people live, work and find recreation by the end of the century?[2] It also provides an indication of the size of the market for goods and services, including hotel and catering services.

The second important feature is the changing age structure of the population.[3] The main increase of the last thirty-five years had been in the dependent age groups (children and retired), particularly in the older age groups, and there had been a corresponding decrease in the proportion of the population of working age. In the next five years there will be little difference, but from 1981 the proportion of the working population over 30 is expected to grow at the expense of the younger and older age groups. These long-term changes have major economic significance: the propensity to consume goods and services is affected by the whole population, but the tendency to stay away from home and to eat out is higher in the younger age groups and in the working population and lower in the older age groups. In the last few decades the trend to later school leaving and the increased proportion of young people going into higher education, as well as the reducing population of working age, tended to reduce the propensity to consume. While future population projections reveal little growth in the younger age groups, the considerable increase in the working population over 30 have important implications for the demand for hotel and catering services.

The third important factor in the demand for accommodation and eating out is the life cycle and the family circumstances. The marital status, size of the family, the number of children and the age structure of the family are particularly important, both for the level of demand and for the type of demand exercised. Although difficult to predict, the awareness of the actual family pattern at a particular time provides an indication of the potential market: on the whole single people tend to have a higher expenditure and children a deterrent effect on expenditure.

The fourth important influence on demand is income, which determines the standard of living of the population. The main indication of the standard of living is the growth of the Gross National Product, which has varied in Britain between a 7 per cent annual increase and a 2 per cent decrease in recent years. Equally important is its distribution, as an increase in lower income groups has a greater overall effect on most demand than in higher income groups; at the highest levels, expenditure on accommodation and eating out may reach saturation. The higher the average income, the greater the tendency for demand for most goods and services to increase, although the demand for particular expenditure competes with others in the discretionary range of disposable income. But generally, in most studies, demand for hotel and catering services has been found to be most strongly correlated with income.

[2] Central Statistical Office, *Social Trends,* No. 7, 1976. pp. 62–7.
[3] Central Statistical Office, ibid.

Income tends to be associated with occupation. In recent years there has been a steady growth in non-manual occupations, in professional and service occupations and in managerial occupations. Most of these changes tend to be conducive to higher participation in travel and other leisure activities and have a bearing on the type of demand exercised. There is evidence to suggest that these changes are likely to continue.

Similarly the level of terminal education affects both income and occupation and is closely correlated with them. As a broad indication, the number of students in British Universities increased almost 50 per cent in the last decade, in colleges of education by almost 40 per cent and in further education by 140 per cent; this trend is likely to continue albeit at a diminished rate. Similarly a higher proportion of pupils have been staying longer at school. The terminal level of education tends to increase the level of holidays, their type and the type of accommodation used, as well as the extent of eating out.

Higher incomes lead to increased car ownership, which is also conducive to the use of the car for holidays and other leisure activities. In Britain car ownership increased from 9·5 million to nearly 14 million in the last decade and this growth is expected to continue at an only slightly reduced rate.

The business of the British hotel and catering industry depends partly on the extent to which the nation chooses leisure rather than work. The extent is reflected in trends towards a shorter working week and longer holidays. The willingness to choose leisure rather than work is evident in the weekly pattern in the gradual reduction of the basic working week of men from 44–45 in the late 1940s, to 42–44 hours in the late 1950s and early 1960s, to below 40 hours in 1975. But the reluctance to substitute leisure for income is also prominent in the actual hours worked, which decreased only from 48 to 44 over the same period.[4] It seems that on the one hand managerial and professional groups will continue to work long hours; on the other hand a growing number of manual workers will have second jobs. But between we are likely to see a gradual introduction of the two-and-a-half-day weekend.

The annual leisure pattern finds an expression in the annual holidays of the population. In recent years there has been a rapid growth of holidays with pay. By the end of 1966 63 per cent of manual workers were estimated to have 2 weeks' paid holiday, 33 per cent 2–3 weeks, 4 per cent 3 weeks. Ten years later, at the end of 1975, the corresponding proportions were 1, 1, 15 per cent and 81 per cent had more than 3 weeks.[5] Between 1950 and 1974 British residents' holidays increased from 26·5 million to 47 million.[6] The major growth was in second and third holidays, and in holidays abroad. There was a marked decline in all holidays after 1973, particularly in second holidays, short holidays and holidays abroad. However, much of this decline appears to have been temporary and growth has been resumed in part.

The above factors, which affect mainly non-business demand for hotel and

[4] Central Statistical Office, *Social Trends*, No. 7, 1976, pp. 173–4.
[5] Central Statistical Office, ibid.
[6] British Tourist Authority, *Digest of Tourist Statistics*, No. 5.

catering services, point to some growth in demand in the years to come, assuming a sustained improvement in the Gross National Product and living standards of the population.

Business and Conference Demand

The tendency for an individual to stay and to eat away from home is related to the nature of his occupation, i.e. the sphere of activity in which he is engaged and his occupation and status within that employment. Future demand is likely to be influenced by the overall level of business activity, trends in the structure of industry and the tendency for businessmen to travel accompanied, all of which point to an increased demand for accommodation and, in particular, for higher quality accommodation. Improved communications and changes in world trading patterns, which may encourage businessmen to spend more time abroad, point in the opposite direction. The level of demand for meals and refreshments may be particularly influenced by the Government fiscal policies on business entertainment.

The demand for hotel and catering services generated by conferences depends on their nature, on the number of conferences, their duration and attendance. Social conferences are stimulated by most of the factors relating to pleasure travel discussed earlier, other conferences particularly by increasing specialization and professionalism in business activity, as well as by changing structure of industry and commerce. All conferences appear to be influenced by increasing professionalism among conference organizers and improved facilities. These factors all point to the growth of conference demand in the future, and the only likely decrease in Britain is from domestic conferences held overseas.

Overseas Markets

In the post-war period Britain has shared fully in the growth of international travel, brought about by rising standards of living and increasing holidays with pay in many countries, a high level of industrial and commercial prosperity and the development of means and organization of travel.

The particular success of Britain has been due to its attractions as a tourist destination. Common language, racial ties and current family ties have generated a particularly large volume of Commonwealth and United States visitors. History, pageantry, culture and education have been strong attractions for most foreign visitors. Conferences, meetings, exhibitions and other events in Britain stimulated more specialist travel, as did industry and commerce. Some of this has been also due to the effective promotion of the country as a tourist destination by the British Tourist Authority (and its predecessor the British Travel Association) and various other organizations, including providers of tourist services. The decline in the relative value of sterling gave Britain a significant price advantage over most of its competitors in the 1970s.

Further growth of tourist traffic is likely to be sustained by the attractions, but prospects depend also on continuing peace in the world, prosperity in the countries of origin, on the facilities – transport and accommodation in particular – and on the quality of overseas promotion. In economic terms the growth of non-business traffic depends primarily on the population and on the real *per capita* incomes in overseas countries, on the distance to Britain as reflected in the cost of fares, on the prices of tourist services in Britain, and on the promotion expenditure by Britain in overseas countries.

The growth of overseas business travel to Britain is less price-elastic, and depends on the level and pattern of trade between Britain and other countries, the growth of international companies and British participation in them, distance and communications. Overseas travel to Britain for conferences depends largely on the share of Britain of international conferences, which is influenced by availability of facilities, and for non-business conferences by most of the factors which affect non-business travel to Britain.

The importance of overseas visitors to Britain has led to a much greater effort in forecasting likely future developments in this field than in the field of domestic travel. On the basis of extrapolation of past trends, modified by socio-economic factors in the countries of origin, the British Tourist Authority expects the number of visitors to Britain to increase from 8·9 million in 1975 to 13 million in 1979, and their expenditure in the country from £1,114 million in 1975 to £2,450 in 1979.[7] Table 66 summarizes the outcome of this forecast. By 1985 the British Tourist Authority forecasts that the number of visitors may increase to 17·2 million and their expenditure to £7,200 (£3,200 at 1976 prices).[8]

Table 66

Overseas Visits and Expenditure in Britain 1975–1979 by Major Market Areas

	Visits (million) 1975	Visits (million) 1979	Expenditure (£ million) 1975	Expenditure (£ million) 1979
USA	1·4	2·0	201	386
Canada	0·5	0·7	66	134
Western Europe	5·5	7·8	471	1,040
Other	1·5	2·5	376	890
Total	8·9	13·0	1,114	2,450

Source: British Tourist Authority.

The prospect of 17 million overseas visitors in 1985, spending more than £7,000 million in the country means that on the basis of the present division of their expenditure, the hotel and catering industry may increase sixfold the

[7] British Tourist Authority, *International Tourism and Strategic Planning*.
[8] British Tourist Authority, *Tourism Intelligence Quarterly*, Vol. 1, No. 2.

value of its services from nearly £400 million in 1975 to more than £2,400 million in 1985.

The study of *Hotel Prospects to 1985* commissioned by the Hotels and Catering Economic Development Committee produced a forecast of demand for all accommodation and for hotel accommodation away from home, and of its distribution between different types of accommodation in 1980 and 1985. The data in Table 67 have been based on this forecast.

Table 67

Forecast Demand for Accommodation in Britain[a] 1980 and 1985
(million bednights)

		Domestic			Overseas			Total		
		Non-business	Business & conference	Total	Non-business	Business & conference	Total	Non-business	Business & conference	Total
Hotel and catering industry	1980	98	33	131	61	11	72	159	44	203
	1985	109	41	151	77	14	91	187	55	241
Other accommodation	1980	508	18	526	76	3	79	584	21	605
	1985	544	22	566	92	4	96	635	26	663
Total[b]	1980	606	51	657	137	14	151	743	65	808
	1985	653	63	717	169	18	187	822	81	904

Source: Based on Hotels and Catering EDC, *Hotel Prospects to 1985*.
[a] Based on 'most likely' outcome figures.
[b] Totals may not agree with the sum of individual items due to rounding.

The forecast represents an increase from 663 million to 904 million bednights between 1975 and 1985 in total accommodation demand, and an increase from almost 170 million to over 240 million bednights for the hotel and catering industry. The demand from overseas visitors is expected to increase by about 65 per cent and from domestic visitors by about 30 per cent. It is of particular importance to the hotel and catering industry that overseas demand for accommodation provided by the industry is expected to increase by 175 per cent, as compared with an increase of only 12 per cent in home demand.

Eating Out in the Eighties

The Catering Supplies Study Group, established in 1973 by the Hotels and Catering Economic Development Committee to examine the relationship between suppliers and caterers in the public and private sectors of the industry, identified six main factors likely to affect the development of the catering market,[9] as follows:

(*a*) The rate of growth of the UK economy.

[9] Hotels and Catering EDC, *The Catering Supply Industry*.

(b) The overall growth in real disposable income.
(c) Trends in catering prices relative to general price movements.
(d) Future prospects for the growth in tourism.
(e) World commodity prices and relative movements in exchange rates.
(f) Movements in the relative prices of food consumed at home as compared with that eaten out.

Other factors were identified that would affect certain sectors only. For instance, population changes would clearly have a significant impact on the school meals' sector, and the changing level of employment would affect demand in works' canteens.

Based on the likely changes in these factors, in particular on the basis of an average 2·5 per cent annual growth in the economy and a slower rate of growth in real disposable income as a result of counter-inflationary measures, the Study Group suggested that the potential for growth in the catering market was limited. The Group's assessment was that the overall growth of the market would be about 1·5 per cent a year in real terms during the period 1973–1980. This compares with an actual annual growth of 2·5 per year estimated by the Group for the period 1968–1973, as shown in Table 68.

This prediction is broadly similar to that of M. Bryn Jones in his study *Food Services in Britain 1970–1980*. Bryn Jones predicted a likely rate of growth of 5 per cent during the period. The experience of the mid-1970s, particularly the decline in real disposable income, which Bryn Jones established as the major influence on the level of eating out, suggests that both the predicted growth rates may be optimistic.

Within the EDC Study Group forecast a higher than average rate of growth is expected in the commercial sector, with particularly rapid growth in food purchases in pubs and clubs. In addition to those already outlined, another important factor here may be the Government fiscal policy on business entertainment. In the industrial and welfare sector a lower than average growth rate is expected, although the increase in catering in homes, mainly local authority establishments, is predicted to be above the average.

Investment in the Eighties

During the early 1970s there was a very high level of investment in the industry, mainly as a result of the Hotel Development Incentives Scheme. The high level of demand for the services of the industry, the increasing interest in hotel investment by the private capital market, the continuing capital requirements for the modernization of facilities, and the need to economize on the use of labour, also encouraged investment in the industry.

During the second half of the decade investment in most sectors has been at a much lower level. However, the forecast prepared for the Hotels and Catering Economic Development Committee indicates that further investment will be required in the accommodation sector to meet the forecast demand for accommodation in the 1980s, and that additional 65,400 bedrooms will be needed by 1985, as shown in Table 69.

Table 68
Food Purchases by the Catering Market 1973–1980

Sector	Value of food purchased at 1973 prices £million			% change per year	
	Actual 1968	Actual 1973	Forecast 1980	1968–1973	1973–1980
Commercial	660	750	860	+2·5	+2
Pubs/clubs	110	140	185	+5	+4
Restaurants	310	340	380	+2	+1·5
Hotels	100	120	135	+2·5	+1·5
Others	15	20	20	Nil	Nil
Take away	125	130	140	+0·5	+1
Institutional	295	330	360	+2	+1·25
Education	140	160	170	+2·5	+1
Homes	45	55	70	+3	+3·5
Hospitals	65	70	70	+0·5	Nil
Services	40	40	45	Nil	+1
Prisons	5	5	5	Nil	Nil
Industrial Works/offices	215	230	250	+1·5	+1
Total/average	1,170	1,310	1,470	+2·5	+1·5

Source: Hotels and Catering EDC, *The Catering Supply Industry.*

Table 69
Forecast Additional Bedroom Capacity Required in Great Britain 1976–1985

Tariff at 1974 prices	1976	1980	1985
Under £2·50	1,000	2,700	14,700
£2·50–£4·99	1,700	7,200	25,300
£5·00 and over	700	7,600	25,400
Total	3,400	17,500	65,400

Source: Hotels and Catering EDC, *Hotel Prospects to 1985.*

Much of this new investment will be required in London and in rooms in lower price brackets. However, another EDC study[10] demonstrated that it was not possible to build conventional hotels and operate them profitably at those tariffs. Possible solutions to this dilemma might lie with extensions to existing premises and with non-conventional hotel facilities, particularly self-catering.

However, the need for a high level of investment will continue with continuing physical and economic obsolescence, the latter of which may arise irrespective of the physical condition of the assets, as the industry needs to re-locate itself to meet changes in demand. Changes in customer tastes, the pattern of transport and communications and other factors, including higher customer expectations and increased competition, are also conducive to a high rate of investment. So are two particular demands which are making themselves felt with growing vigour – the demand for safety and the demand for cleanliness. An increasingly demanding consumer wants to be reassured, that it is safe to stay in an hotel, that it is safe to eat out – that clean food has been handled by clean people in clean kitchens.

Other stimulus to investment is likely to be provided increasingly by technological change, partly as a result of the need to improve working conditions, to economize in the use of scarce labour and to control labour costs. More widespread introduction of labour-saving equipment, increased use of convenience foods, with their special capital requirements, and moves towards central production systems are likely to call for substantial new investment, as the industry becomes gradually less labour intensive. The growth of large firms, with their special needs for communication and control, results in fixed capital expenditure in transport, in offices and even in computer installations. No one can fail to be impressed by the technical progress of the suppliers to the hotel and catering industry. In the 1950s few food and equipment manufacturers differentiated between the domestic and catering markets – between the needs of the housewife and between the needs of the hotelier and caterer; few food suppliers, for example, had separate companies to serve the hotel and catering markets. There are few who do not have them now. Thus the suppliers are forcing the pace of change in the industry generally and making it also more capital intensive in the process.

In the last few years the buoyant overseas visitor market and the successful record of many hotel and catering companies have contributed much to a change in investment attitudes on the part of lending institutions. The continuation of these trends is gradually producing a more favourable investment climate, in which an adequate supply of capital should be available for continued expansion and modernization of the industry in the 1980s.

But one uncertainty remains – in the Government attitude to the industry and, in particular, in its fiscal policies to investment in the industry. There are signs that the importance of the industry is being realized and that the doctrine of differentiation between manufacturing and service industries is losing ground.

[10] Hotels and Catering EDC, *Accommodation for the Lower Priced Market*.

If selective assistance in favour of particular industries is rejected, most hotel and catering firms should find it possible to finance their investment from their cash flow and by attracting loan finance, providing that they are treated for investment purposes on the same footing as other industries. The problems of the small firm and of the need to stimulate activity in Development Areas remain but these are not unique to the hotel and catering industry.

Manpower in the Eighties

We have seen earlier that the propensity to consume goods and services is affected by the whole population; the propensity to produce depends in the first place on the population of working age. From that population is drawn the labour force, and its size and productivity make up the growth of the economy. When the proportion of dependent population rises, the output of a given labour force has to be shared among a larger number of consumers. In the last few decades, the trend to late school leaving, the increasing proportion of young people going into higher education, and the growing numbers of retired people tended to reduce the propensity to produce. Economic progress rested largely on drawing to work an increasing proportion of women and on increased productivity. The main aspect of long-term future population projection is an increase in the population of working age, increasing the relative productive potential of the economy – a more favourable outlook for many industries. But its effects will not be very pronounced before the 1980s. Between 1971 and 1981 the population of the United Kingdom is expected to remain fairly constant and the working population to increase slightly,[11] which suggests only some loosening of the tight labour market in which the industry operated in the 1960s. However, as Britain faces the highest unemployment of the post-war period, the prospects of labour supply do not impose a short-term restraint on growth.

In the period to the 1980s the total labour supply will be, in fact, reduced with the possible further reduction in basic hours, widespread introduction of the 5-day week, and with longer holidays. The cost of labour will increase with all these developments, further moves to higher pay and the implementation of equal pay for men and women. The 5-day basic week of 40 hours and three weeks' annual holiday is virtually universal in Britain. The next phase – a basic week of 35 hours and four weeks' holiday may be not further away than 1980. Whilst the hotel and catering industry may view these developments with approval as far as its customers are concerned, because they provide them with higher disposable incomes and more time in which to spend them on its services, the industry is faced with their implementation with its own employees.

There are conflicting assessments of manpower requirements between different sectors of the industry and between different types and sizes of hotel and catering operations. As a broad generalization, larger hotel and catering companies tend to adopt a more rational approach to their operations than smaller

[11] Central Statistical Office, *Social Trends*, No. 7, 1976, p. 62.

ones, to offer a more standardized product and to be more economical in their use of labour. Smaller firms tend to be more individualistic and personal in their marketing and operation, and more wasteful in their use of labour. But a number of trends are unmistakable for the industry as a whole.

The marketing concept results in a closer match between market needs and their fulfilment, with subsequent effect on the range and standard of services provided. There has been a growing tendency to eliminate services for which there is no economic demand, to simplify others and to provide some by non-personal methods.

The traditional demarcation between departments and jobs, which is not conducive to efficient deployment of staff in hotels and restaurants with alternating work loads during the day and in the course of a week, has begun to give way to a new concept of staffing, in which traditional departments are merged or re-organized, thereby reducing the number of occupations and increasing the range of tasks undertaken by an individual employee.

There has been a growing recognition of the contribution of mechanization to the saving of staff through the increased use of modern equipment, and of the techniques of work study in eliminating wasteful practices.

The increased use of convenience foods has been contributing to the reduction of skilled kitchen staff by transferring food production from the individual kitchen to a central production unit, commissary, or to the food manufacturer.

Last but not least, the growing awareness of the importance of training has been resulting in more efficient staff producing a higher output of more consistent quality.

All these trends and others reduce the manpower requirements and are likely to continue with high intensity during the 1970s, but there are others which generate demand for additional manpower; new establishments, higher occupancies in hotels and improved employment conditions. On balance it is unlikely that the total manpower requirements of the industry will change significantly, as the rising productivity can be expected to be offset by these additional demands for labour. We may, therefore, see a relatively static total manpower in the industry for some time to come but producing higher output in better conditions than in the past.

Higher pay, better terms of employment and improved working conditions will continue to be established in the hotel and catering industry as a result of growing professionalism, of better quality of management and of pressures of the labour market. These influences will be re-inforced by an increase in organized labour, and by the development of joint consultation and of collective bargaining in all parts of the industry.

The impetus of the Industrial Training Board may be consolidated in the late 1970s within a comprehensive framework of job and career schemes of education and training, a rationalization of courses in the higher and further education sectors and a further development of the personnel and training functions in the industry.

It is unlikely that seasonal problems of employment in the industry will be completely resolved in those sectors and locations where they are most pressing. But a further growth of additional holidays and conferences, and area and group co-operative, as well as individual marketing schemes, should further increase the level of activity in the off-season and promote a higher stability of all-year-round employment. A more sophisticated approach to determining manpower requirements, and investigation of the most appropriate sources of additional manpower should result in improved manpower utilization.

Although the hotel and catering industry cannot ever expect an effortless staffing of its operations, the general manpower prospect of the late 1970s is an encouraging one. Against the background of the general labour market and of the influences whose primary concern is the quantity and quality of manpower of the industry, there is enough evidence of the quality of thought and action within the industry itself to suggest that manpower need not be an obstacle to growth to the 1980s. The hotel and catering industry should be more attractive to recruits and a more stable industry, in which higher costs can be met by reductions in labour turnover and improved manpower utilization.

Structure and Organization in the Eighties

Against the background of the market and resources the performance of the hotel and catering industry in the 1980s will be largely determined by its structure and organization.

In this first a major conflict remains to be resolved between disparate objectives of the whole industry on the one hand and of individual operators on the other hand, between those to whom the industry represents a commercial activity which makes use of scarce national resources, and those for whom it is little more than a way of life. For the former and for the industry as a whole, normal business criteria of profit, cost and efficiency represent the yardstick by which their performance is measured.

But for many providers of hotel and catering services their personal goals are different. For them the industry may be a source of livelihood, but they do not see the maximization of profit and return on capital either as their objectives or as the criteria to be applied to them. Instead they may regard their involvement in the industry as satisfying other objectives, such as the pursuit of an interesting life which provides economic freedom and independence, and other non-monetary benefits.

Their services contribute to the total output of the industry, a significant proportion of it in some locations and at times of peak demand, and may be, therefore, indispensable at present. But it must be also realized that these attitudes are not fully compatible with the aspirations and requirements of the industry, if it is to achieve the status and to reap the benefits of an important industry. Their expression may have an unfavourable effect on the image of the industry in the eyes of the Government, of the public and of other industries. It may impede progress towards co-operation in the industry. It may also lead to a waste of scarce resources when they can be employed in alternative uses.[12]

It seems that this situation will prevail and no means exist or, indeed, should be contemplated to eradicate it in a democratic society. But much remains to be done to draw a clear distinction between hotel and catering services provided in the pursuit of these different objectives in legislation and in the conduct of the affairs by the industry.

Growth of Specialization

Growing specialization in the hotel and catering industry continues to find an expression in the emergence of new types of establishment and in the adaptation of existing ones to changing market needs.

In the accommodation sector, the main growth outside population centres will be the British concept of a motel with more extensive services than the original American concept, but equally stimulated by the needs of the motorist and by the lower cost of land, and with a highly developed standard form as part of a chain, seeking to project a brand image. In the holiday market, the move to self-catering holidays is likely to continue, and the main developments will be in the creation of and in the conversion of existing facilities to self-catering units. In London and in large towns the long-overdue move will be towards the hotel garni – the bed and breakfast hotel – in response to tourist demand but also as a further symptom of the rising labour costs. On the other hand we may also expect new comprehensive developments of leisure and recreation centres with a wide range of activities and with hotels and restaurants as part of them.

Franchises are only one example of growing specialization in the catering sector. Speciality restaurant chains can be expected to increase in number and variety as both existing catering companies and others seek to diversify further and increasingly apply the marketing concept to catering markets. At the other extreme small quality restaurants will continue to cater for the more discriminating market as the standard of the middle and higher income groups rises. But the sharp distinction between the ale-house and the tavern, the public house and the restaurant, may become further blurred, as the publican continues to increase his involvement in serving food in the public house. In the same way as new holiday centres will seek to cater more or less comprehensively for the holiday maker, the weekly pattern of leisure will provide a growing market for various combinations of catering and entertainment in areas of high market density, some of them for all comers, others as a club activity. It is not so easy to see what form of innovation will be brought about by catering contractors except to say that they are likely to follow similar lines as the less captive markets and that, in fact, contractors may increasingly operate commercial catering establishments, rather than confining themselves as much to welfare catering as they have done up to the present.

---

[12] Cf. Pickering, J. F., *et al.*, op. cit., pp. 3–4.

Growth in Size and Concentration

The trend to larger units and to increasing concentration in the hotel and catering industry will continue. In recent years the main exodus from the industry has been in smaller units, and relatively little new investment has found its way into the building of small units. Most new investment is undertaken by the larger firms, in locations with sufficiently large and growing markets, and with large units. Although this trend will only very gradually change the size structure of the industry, it is clear that the industry of the remainder of this century is moving towards fewer and larger establishments. In particular, it will be composed of larger hotels and larger public houses.

Much of what has been said also points to the larger firm as the viable organization of the future. Progressive approach to hotel and catering management is not the prerogative of the big firms. But the availability of capital and the know-how necessary to exploit modern techniques on a significant scale are. The balance of advantages of the second half of the twentieth century belongs to the large organization.

This is not to say that we are ever likely to see the disappearance of the small, individually-owned unit, but it will inevitably compete against heavy odds. Its future lies in concentrating on what it can do best and what it alone can do, on the high-quality, individual and personal approach operations, in which the customer and the staff find an alternative to the large unit and large company. Its future also lies in a higher degree of alignment of its objectives and approach with that of the industry as a whole, and in adopting some of the advantages of the big to its needs.

We are, therefore, likely to see a further growth in co-operative groups of independent operators, which will enable individually-owned units to compete with large firms in marketing, purchasing and other common services to members of the groups. We are also likely to see an expansion in franchising, which provides to individual operators similar advantages, as well as advantages in financing, in more standard product markets.

In order to prosper, the small individually-owned unit will have to improve its management skills, not all of which are the prerogative of size. As the range of opportunities widens in the industry, equal opportunities are available for management development to the smaller firm.[13] It would be a pity if they failed to take advantage of them through the lack of realization of the need or through their own inertia.

Some profound changes are also taking place in ownership in the hotel and catering industry as a result of mergers and acquisitions, of the entry or expansion in the industry of other than hotel and catering companies, and of overseas companies.

---

[13] A wide range of short residential courses in all aspects of catering management, hotel management and tourism is offered each year by the Department of Hotel, Catering and Tourism Management of the University of Surrey, which may be taken individually or combined towards the award of University Certificates.

In 1970, as a result of the merger between Forte's and Trust Houses and of many others in recent years, Trust Houses Forte and Grand Metropolitan Hotels emerged clearly as the two largest hotel and catering companies; in early 1977 Trust Houses Forte became by far the largest hotel operator with the acquisition of most hotel interests of J. Lyons and Company; concentration of ownership in the industry has come to resemble more closely that in other industries, with a small number of companies increasing their share of the market, the remainder being shared by a large number of smaller firms. The proportions are likely to change further in favour of the large firms in the 1970s.

Major development plans of brewery and property companies in hotels and of food firms in restaurants suggest an acceleration of their involvement in the industry. Similarly, further joint ventures between hotel operators and airlines and ownership of hotels by airlines, directly or through hotel subsidiaries, continues to change the ownership pattern in hotels in Britain as well as in other countries. Further integration may also continue to develop between hotel companies and tour operators and travel agents.

Foreign influence on the ownership of the hotel and catering industry in Britain has been slow but is gathering momentum, as the profitability of the British industry continues to exceed that of other countries, particularly the United States, the main overseas operator in Britain. At the same time leading British companies are expanding their interests abroad and are likely to be increasingly international in the future.

Towards a Mature Industry

The vision of a united industry took a major step forward in 1971 when the two professional bodies, the Hotel and Catering Institute and the Institutional Management Association merged to form a new professional body, and when the two major trade associations, the British Hotels and Restaurants Association and the Caterers' Association, formed a new trade association for the industry in 1972. New strong representative bodies have emerged to bring together the management and the firms in the industry whose needs they should be able to serve better as a result of pooling their resources. But it may take many more years before all the remaining personnel associations which took part in the initial discussions for the formation of a single professional body become part of it, before the remaining trade associations become one, and before complete unity is achieved within the industry. It may also take several years before the new trade association moves decisively from protection to development as its main orientation.

The Reports of the Commission on Industrial Relations brought a step nearer the acceptance and growth of trade unions in the industry. If the unions seize the opportunity a new framework of industrial relations may develop, leading to the abolition of the remaining three Wages Councils and to the emergence of an industry which needs little State intervention in the conduct of its affairs.

The Industrial Training Act and the industrial training parts of the 1973 Act may be expected to achieve their purpose in a number of industries in the 1980s, and it is not impossible to envisage a similar approach to Industrial Training Boards as has been the case with Wages Councils – a gradual abolition of the Boards in industries, in which it can be shown that the quantity and quality of training is adequate to ensure a sustained supply of trained manpower for the future requirements of particular industries. If this is to happen, the hotel and catering industry may be out of the scope of a Training Board in the foreseeable future.

But one need is likely to remain, for the three estates of industry – management, unions and Government – to have a common platform and a planning instrument in the context of national economic planning. Even when the new professional body, the new trade association and the trade unions will have assumed much of the role of the Hotels and Catering Economic Development Committee, the need will remain for a 'Little Neddy' for the hotel and catering industry.

We have seen a growing sensitivity on the part of the industry to customer needs, and a ready response to meet them. The 1960s marked the beginning of a transition from a production-orientated towards a marketing-oriented industry; this will accelerate in the future. Market information about available facilities, services and prices will be more readily available with the introduction of a country-wide registration and classification system of accommodation, which will also make, for the first time, accurate planning data available on capacity. The growth of the industry in a growing market will be increasingly the product of a partnership between the organizations of the industry, statutory tourist boards and Government Departments in the interests of the consumer.

Appendixes

APPENDIX A
Table 70
Department of Trade and Industry/Business Statistics Office Analysis of Catering Turnover 1969

MLH (a)	Kind of Business	Organiza-tions	Establish-ments	Turnover	Sales of Meals and Refresh-ments	Sales of Alcoholic Drinks	Receipts for Residential Accom-modation	Receipts for other Services	Sales of Cigarettes and Tobacco	Sales of other Goods
		Number	Number	£ million	£ million	£ million	£ million	£ million	£ million	£ million
884 (part)	Licensed hotels, motels, guest houses and holiday camps Total	6,795		407·5	100·2	100·2	173·7	16·6	11·1	4·7
	Multiple licensed hotels etc.[b]	29		118·5	37·2	26·2	42·2	8·9	2·9	1·1
	Other licensed hotels etc.	6,659		257·0	61·3	70·1	111·1	5·9	7·0	1·6
	Holiday camps	107		32·0	2·7	3·9	20·4	1·8	1·2	2·0
885	Restaurants, cafes, snack bars and fish and chip shops Total	42,201		623·4	490·7	67·0	2·0	3·0	37·8	22·9
	Multiple restaurants etc.[b]	49		97·3	60·1	21·1	0·5	0·7	6·8	8·1
	Other restaurants etc.	27,978		402·3	315·7	45·9	1·5	2·2	24·6	12·4
	Fish and chip shops	14,174		123·8	114·9			0·1	6·4	2·4
886	Public houses Total	97		1,349·0	82·9	1,071·2	13·2	9·2	161·0	11·5
	Managed public houses[c,d]		43,641	531·0	32·8	435·4	7·6	4·2	46·7	4·3
	Brewery owned houses run by tenants		4,343	719·2	40·3	558·5	4·5	4·5	104·7	6·7
	Free houses			98·8	9·8	77·3	1·1	0·5	9·6	0·5
887	Licensed clubs Total	2,488		64·2	13·8	38·7	1·2	6·5	3·7	0·3
	Registered clubs[e] Total	23,367		371·8	10·5	276·8			40·6	44·0
888 (part)	Catering contractors/canteens Total	203		152·7	124·2	7·4	0·5	0·8	15·3	4·5
	Catering contractors			68·9	54·1	4·5	0·5	0·6	7·2	2·0
	Canteens operated by non-manufacturing companies		3,145	25·8	21·6	0·7		0·2	2·5	0·8
f	Canteens operated by manufacturing companies[g]		11,107	58·0	48·5	2·2			5·6	1·7
	Total			2,968·6	823·3	1,561·3	190·6	36·1	269·5	87·9

[a] Minimum List Heading of the Standard Industrial Classification (1968 edition). [b] Organizations with 10 or more establishments. [c] Includes licensed hotels, motels and licensed guest houses managed for brewery companies. [d] Sales on their own accounts by managers of brewery owned public houses have not been included. These are estimated as £3·1 million for sales of meals and refreshments, and £0·9 million for sales of other goods. [e] Total subscriptions received of £20·8 million excluded; last column includes all other sales and receipts. [f] Canteens run by industrial establishments for their own employees are classified with the main establishment. [g] Figures obtained from 1969 Census of Production.

Source: Department of Trade and Industry, Business Statistics Office, Catering Trades 1969, Statistical Inquiry, London, HMSO, 1972.

APPENDIX B
Table 71
Department of Industry (formerly Trade and Industry)/Business Statistics Office Annual, Quarterly and Monthly Statistics of Catering Trades 1969–1975

Index Numbers of Turnover Per Week 1969=100

Kind of Business (Turnover in 1969)	Year	1st qtr	2nd qtr	3rd qtr	4th qtr
Total all caterers (£2,533 million)	1969	100	85	102	115	99
	1970	108	92	110	124	108
	1971	118	100	120	135	119
	1972	131	110	131	150	134
	1973	148	125	150	169	148
	1974	170	140	169	195	175
	1975	201	166	201	233	206
Licensed hotels & holiday camps (£408 million)	1969	100	69	105	136	90
	1970	111	78	115	149	101
	1971	123	86	130	162	115
	1972	140	96	147	185	133
	1973	162	113	170	215	151
	1974	186	128	194	250	174
	1975	216	149	226	292	202
Restaurants, cafes, snack bars & fish and chip shops (£623 million)	1969	100	85	102	117	95
	1970	106	90	109	126	100
	1971	113	96	115	130	110
	1972	124	103	124	147	123
	1973	140	117	141	165	137
	1974	157	129	155	186	157
	1975	178	149	176	210	178
Public houses (£1,349 million)	1969	100	87	101	110	102
	1970	109	96	110	118	113
	1971	121	106	122	132	125
	1972	134	116	132	146	140
	1973	150	132	151	163	154
	1974	174	149	171	189	186
	1975	211	180	209	234	222
Canteens including all catering contractors (£153 million)	1969	100	103	99	92	105
	1970	103	104	102	97	110
	1971	105	107	103	98	111
	1972	111	109	109	103	121
	1973	123	124	123	115	132
	1974	143	137	142	134	157
	1975	166	161	166	156	179

This series has been fully rebased on the detailed results of the large scale inquiry into the cateri

Appendix B 237

The monthly periods consist of four weeks except those marked * which are five weeks

Jan.	Feb.	Mar.*	Apr.	May	June*	July	Aug.	Sept.*	Oct.	Nov.	Dec.*
86	81	86	96	99	109	118	120	108	100	92	103
88	90	96	100	112	117	129	128	117	108	101	114
98	99	103	113	119	127	140	136	129	119	110	125
107	106	114	122	129	139	153	154	145	133	125	140
121	123	129	141	146	160	171	174	164	147	142	154
138	138	143	160	167	178	194	200	191	174	166	183
162*	164	173	180	202	216	238	246	218	204	192	218
65	65	75	88	100	123	140	146	124	102	83	86
71	76	86	95	117	130	155	157	138	114	94	98
82	82	93	107	126	152	168	168	152	130	105	110
90	91	105	122	143	170	187	190	179	152	121	127
104	110	122	141	162	198	218	222	208	169	141	144
118	126	137	161	187	226	245	257	247	197	162	165
134*	150	164	182	223	264	288	313	279	232	184	192
86	82	87	95	98	110	120	126	109	99	94	94
88	89	94	98	110	116	132	133	116	102	97	101
94	95	98	107	113	122	132	137	124	112	106	110
102	100	106	114	122	133	146	155	143	122	121	126
114	115	121	132	136	151	164	171	161	134	137	139
126	126	134	148	154	161	181	190	186	155	160	157
146*	145	155	159	180	187	216	217	200	176	175	182
90	83	87	99	98	105	113	112	105	100	92	112
93	94	99	102	113	115	123	121	113	108	103	126
104	106	107	118	121	125	139	131	128	119	113	139
114	114	120	128	131	137	151	148	140	134	128	154
130	131	134	147	147	158	166	168	158	148	145	166
151	147	149	167	170	175	191	194	183	177	172	204
178*	177	184	190	210	222	242	249	215	211	204	247
98	104	108	97	103	97	93	90	94	108	110	100
99	105	108	106	100	100	96	95	98	114	113	105
102	106	113	103	107	98	101	96	98	113	115	106
105	104	116	110	113	106	105	99	104	123	124	116
215	121	134	121	128	119	115	112	116	132	135	130
122	135	151	141	145	139	136	131	135	157	159	156
149*	155	177	171	172	158	158	156	156	179	182	177

…des for 1969.   *Source: Business Monitor SD5.*

APPENDIX C
Table 72
Overseas Visitors[a] to Britain 1937 and 1946–1968
(000s)

Year	USA[b]	Common-wealth	Other, mainly W. Europe[c]	Total[c]
1937	103	85	300	488
1946	23	21	158	203
1947	51	55	290	396
1948	75	80	349	504
1949	105	122	336	563
1950	128	135	355	618
1951	128	162	422	712
1952	164	167	402	733
1953	186	186	446	819
1954	203	202	497	902
1955	239	229	569	1,037
1956	255	245	607	1,107
1957	263	255	663	1,180
1958	325	275	659	1,259
1959	357	307	731	1,395
1960	426	384	859	1,669
1961	424	443	957	1,824
1962	455	480	1,020	1,955
1963	509	457	1,193	2,159

	USA	Other	W. Europe[c]	Total[c]
1964	603	650	1,342	2,595
1965	713	710	1,472	2,895
1966	833	794	1,643	3,270
1967	904	831	1,822	3,557
1968	963	959	2,123	4,045

Source: Before 1964 Home Office, for arrivals of foreign visitors classified by nationality; Board of Trade, for estimates of arrivals of Commonwealth Nationals. From 1964 International Passenger Survey.

Note: Totals may not agree with the sum of individual items due to rounding.

[a] An overseas visitor to Britain is a person who, being permanently resident outside the United Kingdom, visits the United Kingdom for purposes other than employment and who stays for less than a year.

Immigrants and persons coming to the United Kingdom with employment as their main purpose, including military, merchant seamen and airline personnel on duty are excluded.

[b] US citizens only; British residents in the USA are excluded.

[c] Visitors from the Irish Republic excluded.

APPENDIX D

Hotel and Catering Industry
Some Major Events I:1945–1959

1945 The LR and LNR Wages Boards set up under the Catering Wages Act.
1946 A major strike took place in some London hotels.
1947 British Tourist and Holidays Board set up.
The first Town and Country Planning Act passed.
1948 British Hotels and Restaurants Association formed.
British Transport Commission took over railway hotels and catering.
National Society of Caterers to Industry joined the Caterers' Association.
Overseas visitor arrivals to Britain reached half a million.
1949 Hotel and Catering Institute founded.
1950 British Travel and Holidays Association established.
Census of Distribution and Other Services covered restaurants and canteens.
Forster Report on wages regulation in hotels published.
Meals in Establishments Order revoked.
1951 Festival of Britain brought a boom to hotels and restaurants.
Spirits consumption in UK exceeded ten million proof gallons.
1952 National Joint Apprenticeship Council for the industry set up.
1953 First Graham Lyon motel opened at Hythe.
New Licensing Act consolidated licensing law in England and Wales.
1954 Beer consumption in UK reached the lowest post-war level.
1955 First Hygiene Regulations introduced.
The Westbury, first new large post-war London hotel, opened.
Overseas visitor arrivals to Britain reached one million.
1956 Hotel Proprietors Act defined certain rights and obligations of hotels.
1957 Grand Hotels (Mayfair), now Grand Metropolitan, became quoted company.
Wine consumption in UK reached twenty million gallons.
1958 New Standard Industrial Classification published.
1959 Associated Hotels took over Kensington Palace Hotel in London.
Forte's acquired Fullers and Quality Inns.
Spiers and Pond acquired Chicken Inns.
A new Licensing Act consolidated licensing law in Scotland.
A new national diploma in hotel-keeping and catering established.

APPENDIX E

Hotel and Catering Industry
Some Major Events II: 1960–1975

1960 Courage and Barclay and H. and G. Simonds merged.
Express Dairy acquired Spiers and Pond.
Skyway Hotel, first major hotel at London Airport, opened.
Catering Teachers Association founded.
1961 Ariel Hotel at London Airport, first circular hotel in Britain, opened.
Carlton Tower, first skyscraper hotel in London, opened.
Mount Pleasant, first large economy hotel in Britain, opened.
New Licensing Act for England and Wales was passed.
1962 Civic Catering Association formed.
First casino in Britain in the Hotel Metropole opened.
The President, largest post-war London hotel, opened.
Trust Houses acquired the Lockhart Group.
1963 Forte's acquired Kardomah.
Grosvenor House merged with Trust Houses.
John Gardner acquired Staff Caterers.
London Hilton opened.
Overseas visitors arrivals to Britain reached two million.
1964 First University degree course began at the proposed University of Surrey.
Hotel Sales Managers Association formed.
John Gardner acquired by Trust Houses.
1965 Business entertainment disallowed for tax purposes.
Grand Metropolitan Hotels took over Gordon Hotels.
National Association of School Meals Organizers formed.
Trust Houses took over Queen Anne's Hotels and Properties.
1966 Aviemore Centre in Scotland opened.
Government experimental hotel loan scheme announced.
Grand Metropolitan Hotels acquired Levy and Franks.
Hotel and Catering Economic Development Committee established.
The Hotel and Catering Industry Training Board established.
Investment allowances withdrawn from hotels and restaurants.
Prestige Hotels, first major co-operative marketing group, formed.
Selective employment tax introduced.
1967 Bass, Mitchell and Butler and Charrington merged.
Committee on Invisible Exports published a major report.
Forte's took over Frederick Hotels.
Grand Metropolitan Hotels took over the Bateman Catering Organization.
Overseas visitors arrivals to Britain exceeded four million.
1968 Association of Hotel and Catering Training Executives formed.
Government announced a new grants and loans scheme for hotels.

Interchange Hotels, second major co-operative marketing group, formed.
Selective Employment Tax increased by 50 per cent.
Torquay hotels were engaged in a major trade union dispute.
1969 British Association of Hotel Accountants formed.
Development of Tourism Act came into force.
Higher and Ordinary National Diplomas introduced in England and Wales.
Several industry sectors excluded from the Training Board scope.
Inter Hotels, third major co-operative marketing group, formed.
Monopolies Commission Report on Beer published.
Selective employment tax was increased by 28 per cent.
1970 *Standard System of Hotel Accounting* published by Little Neddy.
Grand Metropolitan Hotels acquired Berni Inns and Mecca.
Trust Houses and Forte merged.
British residents took more than 40 million holidays.
UK consumption of spirits reached 20 million proof gallons.
1971 Hotel, Catering and Institutional Management Association formed.
Fire Precautions Act passed.
Commission on Industrial Relations published first two reports.
Standard System of Catering Accounting published by Little Neddy.
Selective employment tax rates halved.
Grand Metropolitan Hotels acquired Truman, Hanbury, Buxton.
1972 British Hotels Restaurants and Caterers Association formed.
Eight national associations formed the National Catering Federation.
Erroll Committee report on liquor licensing published.
Imperial Tobacco Group acquired Courage.
Grand Metropolitan Hotels took over Watney Mann.
The boardroom battle for the control of Trust Houses Forte ended.
Hotel Prospects to 1980 published by Little Neddy.
The Golden Egg Group was taken over by EMI.
Bass Charrington took over Esso Motor hotels.
1973 Clayson Committee report on liquor licensing in Scotland published.
Food and Beverage Managers Association formed.
The London Penta, largest post-war London Hotel, opened.
Employment and Training Act passed.
Selective employment tax and purchase tax abolished.
Value added tax introduced.
UK consumption of spirits reached 30 million proof gallons.
1974 First Michelin Guide to British hotels and restaurants published.
Report on hotels and Government policy published by Little Neddy.
Little Neddy initiated Trends in Catering study.
UK consumption of wines exceeded 80 million gallons.
Overseas visitors arrivals to Britain approached 8 million.
1975 Little Neddy manpower policy report published.
UK consumption of beer reached 40 million bulk barrels.
Overseas visitors spent more than £1,000 million in Britain.

APPENDIX F

Standard Regions in England and Conurbations in Great Britain 1971

Standard Regions in England
These are regions generally used for regional organization purposes by Government departments and others. England is divided into eight such regions. The list below shows the areas covered by each region. Counties, etc. are defined by reference to local government administrative boundaries.

North	Cumberland, Durham, Northumberland, Westmorland, Yorkshire North Riding.
Yorkshire and Humberside	Part of Lincolnshire (Parts of Lindsey), Yorkshire East Riding, Yorkshire West Riding.
North West	Cheshire, Part of Derbyshire (Buxton MB, Glossop MB, New Mills UD, Whaley Bridge UD, Chapel en le Frith RD), Lancashire.
East Midlands	Remainder of Derbyshire, Leicestershire, Part of Lincolnshire (Parts of Holland, Parts of Kesteven, Lincoln CB), Northamptonshire, Nottinghamshire, Rutland.
West Midlands	Herefordshire, Shropshire, Staffordshire, Warwickshire, Worcestershire.
East Anglia	Cambridgeshire and Isle of Ely, Huntingdon and Peterborough, Norfolk, Suffolk East, Suffolk West.
South East	Bedfordshire, Berkshire, Buckinghamshire, Part of Dorset (Poole MB), Essex, Greater London, Hampshire, Hertfordshire, Kent, Oxfordshire, Surrey, Sussex East, Sussex West, Isle of Wight.
South West	Cornwall, Devon, Remainder of Dorset, Gloucestershire, Somerset, Wiltshire.

Conurbations
The seven conurbation areas in Great Britain each consist of an aggregation of entire local authority areas. An indication of their geographical coverage is given below, but other sources should be consulted for details of their exact constitution.[1]

Tyneside	Parts of Durham and of Northumberland.
West Yorkshire	Part of Yorkshire West Riding.
South East Lancashire	Parts of Cheshire and of Lancashire.
Merseyside	Parts of Cheshire and of Lancashire.
West Midlands	Parts of Staffordshire, of Warwickshire and of Worcestershire.

[1] *Source:* Office of Population Censuses and Surveys London, General Register Office Edinburgh, *Census 1971, Great Britain, Economic Activity, Part III (10% Sample)*, London, HMSO, 1975.

Greater London	Great London County.
Central Clydeside	Part of Dumbarton County, Glasgow County of City, Part of Lanark County, Part of Renfrew County.

APPENDIX G
Table 73

Licensed Premises and Registered Clubs in England and Wales and Scotland 1899, 1904, and 1911–1975 (*see* Notes *a, b, c, d*)

Year	On-licences England and Wales	Certificates Hotels	Certificates Scotland Public houses	Certificates Total	Year	Registered Clubs England and Wales	Registered Clubs Scotland
1899[b]	102,189	–	–	–	1899	–	–
1904	99,478	–	–	–	1904	6,589	637
1911	89,939	–	–	–	1911	8,209	628
1912	88,739	1,604	5,223	6,827	1912	8,457	613
1913	87,660	1,584	5,175	6,759	1913	8,738	602
1914	86,626	1,578	5,130	6,708	1914	8,902	–
1915	85,889	1,569	5,088	6,657	1915	8,520	549
1916	85,273	1,533	5,024	6,557	1916	8,167	443
1917	84,644	1,502	4,930	6,432	1917	7,972	396
1918	84,038	1,482	4,893	6,375	1918	8,049	389
1919	83,432	1,464	4,870	6,334	1919	8,994	455
1920	82,739	1,458	4,825	6,283	1920	9,924	486
1921	82,054	1,430	4,618	6,048	1921	10,663	511
1922	81,480	1,413	4,595	6,008	1922	11,126	539
1923	80,987	1,411	4,572	5,983	1923	11,471	544
1924	80,420	1,407	4,550	5,957	1924	11,780	576
1925	79,860	1,401	4,531	5,932	1925	12,138	597
1926	79,330	1,415	4,538	5,953	1926	12,481	598
1927	78,803	1,410	4,519	5,929	1927	12,775	603
1928	78,307	1,412	4,503	5,915	1928	13,132	628
1929	77,821	1,410	4,481	5,891	1929	13,526	643
1930	77,335	1,416	4,450	5,866	1930	13,947	635
1931	76,886	1,419	4,417	5,836	1931	14,377	633
1932	76,418	1,421	4,383	5,804	1932	15,010	678
1933	75,955	1,441	4,328	5,769	1933	15,298	650
1934	75,528	1,446	4,288	5,734	1934	15,657	664
1935	75,062	1,460	4,257	5,717	1935	15,982	687
1936	74,681	1,478	4,222	5,700	1936	16,297	679
1937	74,326	1,491	4,214	5,705	1937	16,563	687
1938	73,920	1,506	4,203	5,709	1938	16,951	700
1939	73,572	1,524	4,177	5,701	1939	17,362	695
1940	73,365	1,517	4,155	5,672	1940	16,463	678
1941	73,210	1,509	4,125	5,634	1941	15,864	661
1942	73,092	1,501	4,101	5,602	1942	15,682	649
1943	73,005	1,501	4,099	5,600	1943	15,732	651
1944	72,965	1,499	4,101	5,600	1944	15,678	657
1945	72,960	1,506	4,070	5,576	1945	15,590	681
1946	71,094	1,565	4,092	5,657	1946	16,496	740
1947	71,431	1,646	4,102	5,748	1947	17,470	773
1948	71,639	1,690	4,111	5,801	1948	18,370	834
1949	71,730	1,709	4,115	5,824	1949	18,962	884
1950	71,814	1,740	4,118	5,858	1950	19,221	912

APPENDIX G

	On-licences	Certificates				Registered Clubs	
			Scotland				
Year	England and Wales	Hotels	Public houses	Total	Year	England and Wales	Scotland
1951	71,778	1,768	4,123	5,891	1951	19,508	944
1952	71,790	1,770	4,111	5,881	1952	19,903	966
1953	71,674	1,800	4,134	5,934	1953	20,348	990
1954	71,524	1,826	4,156	5,982	1954	20,767	1,021
1955	71,244	1,821	4,162	5,983	1955	21,164	1,056
1956	70,875	1,846	4,176	6,022	1956	21,438	1,132
1957	70,353	1,872	4,201	6,073	1957	21,988	1,169
1958	69,913	1,893	4,181	6,074	1958	22,567	1,219
1959	69,455	1,942	4,177	6,119	1959	23,232	1,245
1960	69,184	1,987	4,186	6,173	1960	23,773	1,297
1961	68,936	2,056	4,206	6,262	1961	24,418	1,326
1962	72,000	2,200	4,218	6.418	1962	21,459	1,379
1963	73,409	2,355	4,212	6,567	1963	20,663	1,421
1964	74,012	2,486	4,222	6,708	1964	21,010	1,497
1965	74,758	2,589	4,213	6,802	1965	21,405	1,554
1966	75,544	2,690	4,222	6,912	1966	21,872	1,607
1967	75,843	2,809	4,230	7,039	1967	22,368	1,686
1968	76,421	2,935	4,198	7,133	1968	22,705	1,793
1969	76,834	3,042	4,111	7,153	1969	23,176	1,890
1970	77,526	3,150	4,190	7,340	1970	23,521	1,938
1971	77,878	3,265	4,176	7,441	1971	23,985	2,073
1972	78,728	3,347	4,064	7,411	1972	24,368	2,148
1973	80,072	3,574	4,086	7,660	1973	24,593	2,214
1974	80,977	3,604	3,923	7,527	1974	24,665	2,214
1975	82,310	3,659	4,002	7,661	1975	24,931	2,404

Source: Home Office, *Liquor Licensing Statistics.*
Scottish Home and Health Department, *Civil Judicial Statistics.*

– not available.

[a] For England and Wales at December 31 until 1949, at June 30 from 1950, except for clubs registered in the County of London which relate to December 31 until 1954.

[b] Compensation provisions for redundant licences were introduced in England and Wales in 1905; figures for 1899 and 1904 are given for comparison with subsequent years.

[c] Licensed clubs in England and Wales are included in registered clubs until 1961 and in on-licences from 1962 onwards.

[d] From 1962 figures for Hotel Certificates in Scotland include Restricted Hotel and Restaurant Certificates.

APPENDIX H

Index of Retail Prices
Meals Bought and Consumed Outside the Home 1974–1976

The general index of retail prices compiled by the Department of Employment measures the change from month to month in the average level of prices of the commodities and services purchased by the great majority of households in the United Kingdom, including those of practically all wage earners, and most small and medium salary earners. The changes which were originally related to a base of 100 on January 16, 1962 are now related to a base of 100 on January 15, 1974. On the original base the general retail prices index had reached 191·8 by January 16, 1974.

The index is based on eleven groups of items ranging from food to services; one of the eleven groups represents meals bought and consumed outside the home. The total weights for all items, applied to the eleven groups, are 1,000; of these the meals-out index accounted for 51 weights in 1974, 48 in 1968 and 47 in 1976 implying that meals out represented over 5 per cent of total expenditure of the households concerned in 1974 which had declined to below 5 per cent in 1976. The equivalent figure for 1968 was 41 indicating that meals out represented an increasing proportion during the early 1970s.

The index series for meals bought and consumed outside the home with January 1974 taken as 100 is shown in Table 74.

Table 74
Price Index for Meals Bought and Consumed Outside the Home
(Jan. 1974 = 100)

Year	Jan.	Feb.	Mar.	Apr.	May	June	July	Aug.	Sept.	Oct.	Nov.	Dec.
1974	100	101·0	102·2	104·8	106·1	107·5	109·1	110·4	111·7	113·8	115·3	116·5
1975	118·7	120·5	122·1	128·0	129·9	132·3	135·4	136·6	139·2	140·8	142·1	143·6
1976	146·2	148·3	149·5	153·1	154·6	156·3	158·0	159·9	161·2	164·4	167·0	169·1

The meals-out index rose continuously throughout the three years 1974–1976. In January 1975 it was 19 per cent above the January 1974 level, whilst the general price level represented by all items rose by 20 per cent. Between January 1975 and January 1976 the meals-out index rose by 23 per cent as did the index for all items. In 1976 the meals-out index rose by 18 per cent as compared with a rise of 17 per cent for all items. In January 1977 the meals-out index stood at 172·3, the general index at 172·4.

APPENDIX I

British Travel Association/British Tourist Authority
Hotel Sleeper Occupancy Surveys 1962–1970

Table 75 has been compiled from five separate annual surveys of the British Travel Association and one of the British Tourist Authority, between 1962–70.

The first five inquiries were carried out by the British Travel Association Research Department. The first three covered periods of twelve months' October to September 1962/63, 1963/64 and 1964/65, the fourth and fifth, the calendar years 1966 and 1967. The inquiries were based on information supplied by a sample of hotels in the BTA guide *Hotels and Restaurants in Great Britain*. Because of the type of hotel included in the guide and of the level of response, the samples were not statistically representative of all British hotels, but the results are believed to give a general indication of the pattern of business in quality hotels in Britain. Because of changes in sample composition, the results are not directly comparable from year to year, although they show a similar occupancy pattern in the five surveys.

In the fifth inquiry, in respect of 1967, occupancy rates were calculated as medians and not as arithmetic averages as in previous years, the national figures of those responding were weighted in proportion to the mailed questionnaires, and figures for London hotels were shown separately.

The sixth inquiry covered the period April 1969 to March 1970, and the survey was carried out for the British Tourist Authority by a market research agency whose interviewers visited the participating hotels. It produced room occupancy data in addition to sleeper occupancy data, and much more detailed analysis than previous surveys.

In all surveys, sleeper occupancy represents the number of individual bed spaces occupied. A double bed was counted as two bed spaces, and a single person sleeping in a double room represented one sleeper occupancy of two bed spaces or a 50 per cent occupancy for that double bed. Occupancy rates were calculated on the basis of beds available and not beds offered; where hotels were closed during the winter, the beds in these hotels were still counted as available and nil occupancy was recorded.

All surveys produced in addition data on length of stay, proportion of nights spent by overseas visitors and other information.

Table 75

Hotel Sleeper Occupancy 1962–1970
(percentages)

	Year	Jan.	Feb.	Mar.	Apr.	May	June	July	Aug.	Sep.	Oct.	Nov.	Dec.	Annual
				LONDON	(included with town hotels to 1966)									
	1962													
	1963													
	1964													
	1965													
	1966													
	1967	36	37	43	55	71	72	79	77	76	72	51	42	57
	1968													
April	1969													}77
March	1970													
				TOWN HOTELS	(including London to 1966)									
	1962										52	44	32	
	1963	31	35	36	44	59	67	72	65	65	54	42	33	50
	1964	36	38	38	48	56	64	65	61	67	68	58	42	53
	1965	44	48	48	56	79	80	79	81	80				
	1966	42	44	51	55	63	72	74	71	74	61	49	38	58
	1967	43	45	48	48	50	57	58	57	61	53	47	38	52
	1968													
April	1969													}53
March	1970													
					COUNTRY HOTELS									
	1962										43	31	25	
	1963	26	26	31	46	47	59	55	60	62	37	20	17	41
	1964	17	18	29	42	54	61	72	80	74	40	21	18	44
	1965	16	20	26	44	49	73	70	77	73				
	1966	17	22	29	44	50	65	64	69	71	44	23	21	43
	1967	15	20	35	39	51	63	60	69	72	50	26	22	48
	1968													
April	1969													}41
March	1970													
					SEASIDE HOTELS									
	1962										40	17	14	
	1963	12	14	22	55	54	87	77	94	75	35	18	18	47
	1964	14	19	24	38	58	82	87	97	84	34	16	16	47
	1965	12	14	19	35	47	69	71	78	67				
	1966	15	19	24	36	47	68	73	76	74	43	20	19	43
	1967	16	19	33	36	51	66	69	75	72	42	22	21	43
	1968													
April	1969													}44
March	1970													
					ALL HOTELS									
	1962										52	44	32	
	1963	31	35	36	44	59	67	72	65	65	46	32	26	48
	1964	27	30	32	46	57	73	73	74	76	51	36	29	50
	1965	28	31	34	46	62	75	75	79	72				
	1966	31	34	40	48	57	70	72	72	73	54	37	30	52
	1967	27	33	39	42	50	62	60	66	66	51	37	30	49
	1968													
	1969				43	50	59	69	72	63	50	33	28	}50
	1970	29	33	41										

Source: British Travel Association/British Tourist Authority.

For explanatory notes *see* text.

APPENDIX J

English Tourist Board
English Hotel Bed Occupancy Surveys 1971–1975

The table below has been compiled from the English Hotel Occupancy Surveys commissioned by the English Tourist Board and carried out by A. C. Nielsen Co. Ltd. of Oxford, between 1971–1975.

Table 76
English Hotel Bed Occupancy 1971–1975
(percentages)

Year	Jan.	Feb.	Mar.	Apr.	May	June	July	Aug.	Sept.	Oct.	Nov.	Dec.	Annual
LONDON (Greater London Council Area)												
1971						73	82	74	70	63	49	40	
1972	41	36	49	58	65	73	75	69	72	63	49	43	58
1973	41	39	48	59	62	65	76	65	67	61	49	45	56
1974	42	36	43	51	54	58	77	70	70	61	44	40	54
1975	36	36	47	46	58								
LARGE TOWNS (population of over 100,000 excluding London)												
1971						55	54	51	54	51	47	35	
1972	41	46	43	48	51	54	56	49	54	56	48	34	48
1973	44	47	48	47	52	52	53	50	55	57	47	36	49
1974	40	44	47	47	48	52	55	50	51	54	49	31	47
1975	35	46	42	50	45								
SMALL TOWNS (population of between 10,000–100,000)												
1971						51	55	55	56	47	38	32	
1972	34	35	40	45	52	54	58	59	60	52	44	33	47
1973	38	41	43	47	55	56	63	63	60	51	39	32	49
1974	33	40	46	53	53	55	64	66	65	57	42	33	51
1975	35	40	42	46	53								
COUNTRYSIDE (remainder of England excluding seaside)												
1971						53	57	62	58	46	28	24	
1972	21	25	29	40	47	54	59	58	60	45	26	24	41
1973	23	27	32	40	42	49	57	62	61	46	30	24	41
1974	22	25	33	42	44	51	56	63	61	48	31	25	42
1975	27	30	36	38	47								
SEASIDE (coastal areas not predominantly industrial)												
1971						66	72	81	70	47	26	24	
1972	21	22	29	39	49	61	73	80	71	46	27	23	45
1973	19	25	28	39	45	59	73	80	69	44	27	22	44
1974	18	24	28	43	49	66	77	86	71	41	28	25	46
1975	21	25	33	32	47								
ALL ENGLAND												
1971						60	65	67	63	50	35	30	
1972	29	30	36	44	51	59	65	66	65	50	36	30	47
1973	31	34	38	44	49	56	64	67	63	50	37	30	47
1974	29	32	38	46	49	57	66	72	66	49	36	30	48
1975	29	33	39	39	49								

Source: English Tourist Board, Hotel Occupancy Surveys 1971–1975.

The sample for the surveys is comprised of hotels in England with at least five bedrooms which are listed in one or more of the major national, regional or local accommodation guides. The lists from which the sample is drawn include a high proportion of the larger, higher-priced and group-owned hotels, but have a far smaller coverage of the smaller, lower-priced and independent hotels. The results provide a useful guide to occupancy of English hotels.

APPENDIX K
Table 77
British Hotels by Size and Location 1 January, 1974

	\multicolumn{6}{c}{Bedrooms}
	4–10	11–15	16–25	26–50	51–100	Over 100	Total
\multicolumn{7}{c}{LICENSED HOTELS}
London	51	62	21	69	107	135	445
Large towns[a]	330	175	111	182	117	100	1,015
Small towns[b]	2,435	669	513	416	197	54	4,284
Countryside	1,793	428	291	154	38	10	2,714
Seaside	1,590	1,140	1,093	941	377	69	5,210
Total	6,199	2,474	2,029	1,762	836	368	13,668
\multicolumn{7}{c}{UNLICENSED HOTELS}
London	163	488	92	68	26	10	847
Large towns[a]	1,177	440	99	36	—	2	1,754
Small towns[b]	2,143	480	87	16	5	2	2,733
Countryside	1,028	163	23	7	1	—	1,222
Seaside	9,997	2,653	620	151	12	2	13,435
Total	14,508	4,224	921	278	44	16	19,991
\multicolumn{7}{c}{ALL HOTELS}
London	214	550	113	137	133	145	1,292
Large towns[a]	1,507	615	210	218	117	102	2,769
Small towns[b]	4,578	1,149	600	432	202	56	7,017
Countryside	2,821	591	314	161	39	10	3,936
Seaside	11,587	3,793	1,713	1,092	389	71	18,645
Total	20,707	6,698	2,950	2,040	880	384	33,659

Source: Hotels and Catering EDC, *Hotel Prospects to 1985.*

[a] With population of over 100,000 excluding London.
[b] With population of under 100,000.

APPENDIX L

Table 78
Bedroom Capacity of British Hotels by Size and Location of Hotels
1 January, 1974

	\multicolumn{7}{c}{*Bedrooms*}
	4–10	*11–15*	*16–25*	*26–50*	*51–100*	*Over 100*	*Total*

LICENSED HOTELS

	4–10	11–15	16–25	26–50	51–100	Over 100	Total
London	350	791	433	2,711	7,576	40,873	52,734
Large towns[a]	2,475	2,164	2,228	6,557	8,199	15,961	37,584
Small towns[b]	17,186	8,468	10,062	14,182	13,611	7,453	70,962
Countryside	12,225	5,443	5,677	5,157	2,710	1,126	32,338
Seaside	12,131	14,743	22,351	33,216	25,856	8,938	117,235
Total	44,367	31,609	40,751	61,823	57,952	74,351	310,853

UNLICENSED HOTELS

	4–10	11–15	16–25	26–50	51–100	Over 100	Total
London	1,132	6,304	1,756	2,336	1,729	1,347	14,604
Large towns[a]	8,371	5,402	1,960	1,264	—	370	17,367
Small towns[b]	13,839	5,921	1,674	500	284	350	22,568
Countryside	5,996	1,990	439	209	80	—	8,714
Seaside	71,834	33,051	12,508	4,905	854	244	123,396
Total	101,172	52,668	18,337	9,214	2,947	2,311	186,649

ALL HOTELS

	4–10	11–15	16–25	26–50	51–100	Over 100	Total
London	1,482	7,095	2,189	5,047	9,305	42,220	67,338
Large towns[a]	10,846	7,566	4,188	7,821	8,199	16,331	54,951
Small towns[b]	31,025	14,389	11,736	14,682	13,895	7,803	93,530
Countryside	18,221	7,433	6,116	5,366	2,790	1,126	41,052
Seaside	83,965	47,794	34,859	38,121	26,710	9,182	240,631
Total	145,539	84,277	59,088	71,037	60,899	76,662	497,502

Source: Hotels and Catering EDC, *Hotel Prospects to 1985.*

[a] With population of over 100,000 excluding London.
[b] With population of under 100,000.

APPENDIX M

Table 79
Leading Hotel Operators in Britain 1976

	Organization	Bedrooms	Hotels	Location	Notes
1	Trust Houses Forte	16,600	199	National	Includes Ireland, also hotels abroad
2	Grand Metropolitan	9,500	81	National	24 in London, 31 County Hotels 26 Steak House division
3	J. Lyons	7,900	38	National	Strand Hotels and Falcon Inns, also hotels abroad
4	Bass Charrington	7,000	104	England and Wales	Crest Hotels including Europe, and some smaller hotels
5	Centre Hotels	5,300	24	National	Includes Holland
6	Scottish & Newcastle Breweries	3,600	66	National	41 Thistle Hotels and 25 Ofer House Inns
7	British Transport	3,500	28	National	British Rail
8	Rank Organisation	3,000	12	National	Also hotels abroad
9	Imperial London Hotels	2,400	6	London	Private company
10	Allied Breweries	2,200	42	England and Wales	Ind Coope Hotels also some smaller hotels
11	Norfolk Capital Hotels	2,200	18	London and provinces	
12	De Vere Hotels and Restaurants	1,800	16	England	
13	Whitbread	1,800	98	England and Wales	Includes tenanted and leased hotels
14	Cunard	1,700	4	London and Cambridge	
15	Reo Stakis Organization	1,700	26	National	
16	Vaux Breweries	1,700	48	N. England and Scotland	Includes Lowlands of Scotland Hotels
17	Adda International	1,600	7	London	Also one in Amsterdam and one in Paris
18	EMI Hotels and Restaurants	1,600	17	London, Birmingham, Scotland	Royal London Hotels
19	Mount Charlotte Investments	1,500	22	England	Nuthall and Ocean Hotels
20	North Hotels	1,300	12	London and South	Unlicensed
21	Courage	1,200	38	England	Anchor Hotels and Taverns
22	Lex Hotels	1,200	3	London and airports	Also hotels in US
23	Greenall Whitley	1,000	30	Midlands, Wales, N. England	Compass Hotels and Red Rose Grills and Inns
24	Rowton Hotels	900	4	London and Suffolk	Townor Hotels, also hostels
25	Queen's Moat Houses	800	17	England and Wales	
26	Savoy Hotel	800	4	London	Also hotel in Paris
27	Scottish Highland Hotels	800	15	Scotland and Yorks	
28	Travco Hotels	800	9	England	Also 3 holiday centres
29	Leisure and General Holdings	700	11	National	Mercury Motor Inns
30	North British Trust	700	14	Scotland and N. England	

The table is intended to provide a broad indication of bedroom capacity concentration and includes organizations with at least 1,000 beds. Numbers of bedrooms and hotels are in some cases estimates.

Source: Pacesetters 1976–1977 and miscellaneous.

APPENDIX N

Table 80
Leading Restaurant Operators in Britain 1976

	Organization	Restaurants	Location	Notes
1	Trust Houses Forte	500	National	Includes 173 Little Chefs, 51 Henekey Inns and also other catering activities
2	Allied Bakeries	420	National	Associated British Foods. 20 restaurants, 400 light-bites and grills
3	British Transport	380	National	At railway stations. Also other British Rail catering
4	Grand Metropolitan	300	National	282 steak house restaurants, 18 Mecca restaurants
5	Whitbread	150		Includes Dutton's, Trophy Taverns and Britannia Inns
6	J. Lyons	120	National	40 Jolyon restaurants, 34 London Steak Houses, 46 other restaurants. Also Wimpy and other catering
7	D. S. Crawford	119	National	Includes 48 Crawford's of Edinburgh and others
8	Banquets Group of Companies	83	National	Also overseas units
9	EMI Hotels and Restaurants	80	National	Includes 24 Angus Steak Houses, 35 Wimpy, Golden Egg and Tennessee Pancake Houses. Also other catering
10	Allied Suppliers	75	National	Includes popular restaurants in supermarkets
11	R. V. Goodhew	60	London and Home Counties	Includes some public houses
12	Reo Stakis Organization	50	National	
12	Goodhews	50	London and Home Counties	Includes some hotels and public houses
14	British Home Stores	49	National	Self-service store restaurants
15	F. W. Woolworth	46	National	Stores
16	Centre Hotels	36	National	9 Centre Restaurants, 3 Centre Inns, 24 Old Kentucky Restaurants
16	Finch	36	London	
18	Associated Restaurants	30	England	Pizzaland and several other restaurants and pubs
19	Rank Organisation	30	National	
20	Bass Charrington	27	National	5 restaurants and 22 Toby Inns
21	Owen Owen	26	England and Wales	Stores
22	Associated Fisheries	25	England	Seafarer and Bumbles restaurants
23	John Lewis Partnership	23		Department stores and supermarkets
24	Mount Charlotte Investments	20	London and Resorts	
24	Corrett Holdings	20	London	Includes 10 Bistingo Group, 8 Alpino Group
26	Brent Walker	17	England	Includes Peter Evans restaurants and various other units
27	Wheeler's Restaurants	13	London and South England	
28	Fortes Quality Foods	12	South England	
29	Galleon Roadchef	11		6 motorway service areas, 5 roadside restaurants

The table is intended to provide a broad indication of restaurant concentration. It includes mainly operators of commercial restaurants with more than ten units. Hotel, cinema and other types of restaurant associated with other activities are in the main excluded, unless stated otherwise. Number of units are in some cases estimates.

Source: Pacesetters 1976–1977.

APPENDIX O

The tables that follow are intended to provide a broad indication of ownership concentration in three sectors of the hotel and catering industry. Numbers are in some cases estimates.

Table 81
Leading Public House Operators in Britain 1976

Organization	Houses	Location	Notes
1 Bass Charrington	9,200	UK	Includes Tennent Caledonian
2 Whitbread	8,600	UK	Includes Brickwoods
3 Allied Breweries	8,200	UK	
4 Grand Metropolitan	7,500	England and Wales	Includes Watney Mann and Truman
5 Courage	6,000	England and Wales	Includes John Smith Tadcaster

Source: Companies and miscellaneous.

Table 82
Leading Holiday Camp and Centre Operators in Britain 1976

Organization	Beds	Camps	Location	Notes
1 Butlin	77,000	9	UK and Eire	Also 7 holiday centres and 4 hotels
2 Pontin	30,000+	23	UK	Also overseas
3 Ladbroke Holidays	30,000	12	East and South	
4 Warner	10,000	14	East and South	

Source: Pacesetters 1976–1977 and miscellaneous.

Table 83
Leading Catering Contractors in Britain 1976

Organization	Contracts	Location	Notes
1 Gardner Merchant Food Services (Trust Houses Forte)	1,800	UK	1,650 industrial/commercial 120 schools/colleges 37 hospitals/institutions
2 Sutcliffe Catering (Town and City Properties)	750	UK	
3 Bateman Catering (Grand Metropolitan)	500	England	
4 Midland Catering (Grand Metropolitan)	500	England and Wales	420 industrial/commercial 70 schools/colleges 13 hospitals/institutions
5 Taylorplan Catering	200	UK	180 industrial/commercial 14 schools/colleges 7 residential

Source: Pacesetters 1976–1977 and miscellaneous.

APPENDIX P

Table 84
Economic Development Committees 1973[a]

Date of first meeting[b]	Industry	Employment coverage[c,e] (000)	Of which employers & self-employed[c,d] (000)	Notes
15 Apr. 1964	Machine tools	65	0	Includes some activities not covered by EDC
20 Apr. 1964	Chemicals	428	1	
23 Apr. 1964	Electronics	535	2	
21 May 1964	Mechanical engineering	978	8	Includes some activities not covered by EDC
25 May 1964	Wool textiles	109	1	
26 May 1964	Electrical engineering	382	2	Includes some activities not covered by EDC
15 July 1964	Distributive trades	2,850	436	Includes some activities not covered by EDC
21 June 1965	Building	2,200	313	Includes estimate of 500,000 for construction materials, MLH 500 only for employees and self employed
21 June 1965	Civil engineering			
3 Mar. 1966	Clothing	366	13	Includes some activities not covered by EDC
20 June 1966	Hotels and catering	928	134	SIC coverage only
13 Oct. 1966	Motor vehicle distribution and repair	525	61	
21 Dec. 1966	Agriculture	666	258	
31 July 1967	Motor manufacturing	512	2	
Mar. 1974	Shipbuilding and ship repairing	159	1	
Total	15	10,703	1,232	

Source: National Economic Development Office.

[a] This table has been compiled to show the proportion of UK labour force covered by EDCs collectively, and to provide estimates of the employment coverage of individual EDCS. The estimates relate to 1973 except for shipbuilding and repairing which was established in 1974. Since 1974, four further EDCs have been established covering Mechanical and Electrical Engineering Construction, International Freight Movement, Ferrous Foundries and Food and Drink Manufacturing.

Also since 1973 the EDC covering motor manufacturing has been disbanded. The EDC for printing and publishing was disbanded in 1972.

[b] The EDCs are listed in the order in which they first met.

[c] Department of Employment data have been used to compile estimates of UK employees in employment, including temporarily stopped, for June 1973. These data are based on the Standard Industrial Classification 1968. Estimates for parts of Minimum List Headings are not generally included.

[d] Estimates of the numbers of employees and self-employed obtained from 1971 Census of Population (1% sample). These refer to Great Britain only and not the United Kingdom.

[e] A part-time employee is counted as one employee

APPENDIX Q

Table 85
Industrial Training Boards 1976[a]

	Established[b]		Industry	Establishments[c]	Employees	Notes
1		1935*	Merchant Navy	350	120,000	*Reconstituted 1941, 1964 and September 1971
2	June	1964	Wool, jute and flax	1,589	116,523	
3	July	1964	Iron and steel	550	273,000	
4	July	1964	Engineering	25,239	3,174,989	
5	July	1964	Construction	37,750	1,100,000	
6	Nov.	1964	Shipbuilding	1,084	108,000	
7	Mar.	1965	Foundry Industry Training Committee	1,439*	137,407*	*August 1974 figures
8	June	1965	Electricity supply*	16	170,000[f]	*The Electricity Supply ITB was disbanded in Dec. 1973, its functions being taken over by the Electricity Supply Industry Training Committee
9	June	1965	Gas*			*The Gas ITB was disbanded in December 1972, its functions being taken over by the British Gas Corporation
10	June	1965	Water supply*	58	85,000[f]	*The Water Supply ITB was disbanded in March 1974 its functions being taken over by the National Water Council Training Division
11	July	1965	Ceramics, glass and mineral products	2,180	322,200	
12	Dec.	1965	Furniture and timber	5,253	223,272	
13	Feb.	1966	Man-made fibres producing	41*	43,054	7 companies
14	Mar.	1966	Carpet	260	46,896	
15	Mar.	1966	Knitting, lace and net	1,500	135,000	
16	July	1966	Cotton and allied textiles	1,650	181,000	
17	Aug.	1966	Agricultural*	236,734[d]	509,550[d]	*Called the Agricultural, Horticultural and Forestry until April 1974
18	Sep.	1966	Road transport	53,000	905,000	
19	Nov.	1966	Hotel and catering	100,000*[e]	650,000	*Leviable establishments 1500
20	Mar.	1967*	Air transport and travel	2,000	110,000	*First as Civil Air Transport ITB and reconstituted March 1970 and March 1973
21	May	1967	Petroleum	1,700	90,000	
22	Aug.	1967	Rubber and plastics processing	2,201	288,485	
23	Oct.	1967	Chemical and allied products	3,408	443,000	
24	Sept.	1967	Local government	456*	2,450,000	*Local authorities in England and Wales
25	May	1968	Printing and publishing	10,700	369,000	
26	May	1968	Paper and paper products	1,767	213,740	
27	July	1968	Distributive	98,000	1,600,000	
28	July	1968	Food, drink and tobacco	19,702	925,878	
29	Nov.	1968	Footwear, leather and fur skin	1,798	124,799	
30	Oct.	1969	Clothing and allied products	6,200	290,000	
31	Dec.	1969	Hairdressing and allied services*			*Disbanded in 1971
Total			27 ITBs[g]		14,950,793[g]	

Source: BACIE, *Industrial Training Boards, Progress Report, No. 7*, March 1976.

[a] At March 1976.
[b] The Boards are listed in the order in which they were established.
[c] Many figures throughout are approximate.
[d] Source: Agricultural Training Board.
[e] Source: Hotel and Catering ITB.
[f] Establishments, and employees not included in the totals.
[g] Not including electricity supply, gas, water supply.

APPENDIX R
Table 86
Wages Councils in the Hotel and Catering Industry
Constitution of Employers' and Workers' Sides 1976

Employers	LNR	LR	UPR	Total
Association of Conservative Clubs	1	–	–	1
Association of London Clubs	–	1	–	1
Association of Metropolitan Authorities	–	–	1	1
Brewers' Society	8	2	–	10
British Hotels, Restaurants and Caterers Association	–	15	11	26
(in consultation with the Retail Distributors Association)	–	1	–	1
Cinematograph Exhibitors Association	–	–	1	1
Council of Voluntary Welfare Work	–	–	1	1
National Association of Master Bakers etc	–	–	1	1
National Federation of Fish Friers	–	–	1	1
National Association of Holiday Centres Ltd	–	2	–	2
National Golf Clubs Advisory Association	1	–	–	1
National Union of Liberal Clubs	1	–	–	1
National Union of Licensed Victuallers	7	1	–	8
Parliamentary Committee, Co-op Union	–	–	1	1
Royal British Legion	1	–	–	1
Scottish Licensed Trade Association	3	1	–	4
Working Men's Club and Institute Union	3	–	–	3
	25	23	17	65
Workers				
Bakers Union	–	–	1	1
General and Municipal Workers Union	4	18	6	28
National Association of Licensed House Managers	2	–	–	2
National Union of Public Employees	–	–	1	1
Transport and General Workers' Union	4	4	1	9
Union of Shop, Distributive and Allied Workers	13	1	7	21
United Federation and National Union of Club Stewards and Hotel Managers	2	–	–	2
Unorganized	–	–	1	1
	25	23	17	65

Source: Department of Employment.

APPENDIX S

Wages Councils in the Hotel and Catering Industry:
Establishments and Scope

Table 87
Establishments[a] on the List of Wages Councils 1946–1975[b]

	ISC	LNR	LR	UPR
1946	24,379	–	–	–
1947	26,396	60,899	–	36,181
1948	28,551	59,823	9,090	35,495
1949	29,302	60,139	9,307	36,015
1950	29,917	60,482	9,629	37,997
1951	30,361	60,467	9,853	38,865
1952	30,421	60,453	9,916	38,776
1953	30,326	59,854	9,982	38,614
1954	29,799	59,379	10,053	37,173
1955	29,615	59,330	10,099	35,651
1956	29,450	59,082	10,134	33,944
1957	29,160	58,869	10,198	32,577
1958	28,962	58,405	10,333	31,304
1959	29,143	58,101	10,437	30,358
1960	28,856	57,740	10,808	29,382
1961	29,076	57,863	11,166	28,836
1962	28,849	59,176	12,886	27,777
1963	28,887	58,826	14,132	27,214
1964	29,212	59,557	14,962	26,808
1965	29,599	59,563	15,715	26,352
1966	29,814	60,046	16,477	25,656
1967	29,864	59,755	17,313	24,868
1968	30,086	59,539	18,093	24,238
1969	30,058	59,375	18,911	23,959
1970	30,076	59,200	19,729	22,821
1971	29,861	58,143	20,419	22,753
1972	29,411	58,632	21,432	21,506
1973	29,404	59,223	22,515	21,352
1974	29,192	59,514	23,188	20,783
1975	28,790	60,004	23,913	20,171

Table 88
Scope and Wages Orders of Wages Councils 1976[c]

Wages Council		Covers	Wages Order	
			Number	Operational
LNR	Licensed Non-residential Establishment	public houses and non-residential clubs	LNR 117 LNR 118	22.12.75 23.2.76[d]
LR	Licensed Residential Establishment and Licensed Restaurant	licensed hotels, residential clubs, licensed restaurants	LR 51	20.10.75
UPR	Unlicensed Place of Refreshment	unlicensed restaurants, cafés, snack bars	UPR 48	21.6.76

Source: Department of Employment.

[a] The numbers of establishments relate only to units having workers in respect of whom the Wages Councils operate, and do not denote the total number of establishments of a particular type in existence. Proprietors working on their own account without outside employees are not covered. Excluded are also establishments operated directly by the Crown or by a local authority, and certain other units. The appropriate Wages Orders should be consulted as to the exact scope of each Council.

[b] In November 1946 and 1947, December 1948, October 1 from 1949 onwards; Wages Boards until 1959, Wages Councils since 1959.

[c] In force on June 30, 1976.

[d] There are separate Orders for managers and club stewards and other workers.

APPENDIX T
Table 89
Principal Features of Wages Orders at 30 June, 1976

	LNR	LR	UPR
Employees excluded from provisions of Wages Orders.	Club secretaries, entertainers, some other ancillary workers, certain PT workers.	Managers and manageresses, assistant managers and manageresses, wives of managers. No rates fixed for chef, head waiter, housekeeper.	
Special provisions for following groups.	Managers and manageresses, club stewards and stewardesses, relief managers and manageresses, trainee managers and manageresses.	Service workers, apprentice and trainee cooks, extra waiting staff, late entrant waiters.	Managers and manageresses, occasional workers.
Basic rates for a week of	40 hours.	40 hours.	40 hours.
Area differentiation.	Differential rates for all workers in London and other areas.	Differential rates for 3 defined areas.	Differential rates for 3 defined areas.
Treatment of payments in kind.	8 differential rates according to the extent to which meals and/or lodging provided by employer.	Differential rates for those supplied with (a) full board and lodging (b) meals when on duty (c) neither.	Differential rates for those supplied with (a) full board and lodging (b) meals when on duty (c) neither.

Guaranteed remuneration payable to	Workers ordinarily working not less than 40 hours per week.	Workers ordinarily working not less than 32 hours per week.	Workers ordinarily working not less than 36 hours per week.
Increments or special provisions in respect of		Uniform and protective clothing, their laundering and cleaning. Emergency duty Night work.	
	Spreadover of hours.	Spreadover of hours. Higher grade work. Rest day work.	Work at different times of day. Rest day work. Sunday work.
	Overtime including rest day work. Public holidays.	Overtime. Customary holidays. Intervals of rest.	Overtime. Customary holidays.
Holidays with pay and accrued holiday pay (with exceptions).	For workers with minimum 4 weeks' service during qualifying period.	For workers with minimum 3 weeks' service during qualifying period.	For workers with minimum 8 weeks' service during qualifying period.
Special provisions.	Some provisions differ as between England and Wales and Scotland.	In respect of small and seasonal establishments.	In respect of Jewish undertakings.
Notes.	Weekly rates for regular workers. Hourly rates for other than regular workers.	Weekly rates.	Hourly rates for various categories of worker, weekly rates for managers and manageresses.

Source: Wages Orders in Force at June 30, 1976 (*see* Appendix S).

APPENDIX U

Table 90
New Hotel Construction in Great Britain 1970–1973

Year	New Hotels Number	New Hotels Bedrooms	Extensions Number	Extensions Bedrooms	All constructions Number	All constructions Bedrooms	All constructions % Number	All constructions % Bedrooms
				LONDON[a]				
1970	12	1,689	16	451	28	2,140		
1971	11	1,698	21	684	32	2,382		
1972	21	3,786	23	968	44	4,754		
1973	34	10,448	18	1,128	52	11,576		
Total	78	17,621	78	3,231	156	20,852	13·5	33·1
				REST OF ENGLAND[a]				
1970	40	1,670	54	1,123	94	2,793		
1971	44	1,872	118	2,397	162	4,269		
1972	90	5,164	121	2,797	211	7,961		
1973	96	7,822	86	2,528	182	10,350		
Total	270	16,528	379	8,845	649	25,373	56·2	46·3
				SCOTLAND[b]				
1970	5	346	13	223	18	569		
1971	7	433	14	433	21	866		
1972	7	576	22	694	29	1,270		
1973	15	1,304	15	264	30	1,568		
Total	34	2,659	64	1,614	98	4,273	8·5	7·8
				WALES[b]				
1970–71	10	111	17	150	27	261		
1971–72	11	135	33	314	44	449		
1972–73	67	2,521	113	1,043	180	3,564		
Total	88	2,767	163	1,507	251	4,274	21·8	7·8
				GREAT BRITAIN				
1970–73	470	39,575	684	15,197	1,154	54,772	100·0	100·0

Source: Hotels and Catering EDC, *Hotel Prospects to 1985*.

[a] New hotels or extensions of 10 or more bedrooms.

[b] New hotels of 25 or more bedrooms and extensions of 10 or more bedrooms–the figures include hotels built under grants from the HDI Scheme and the Highlands and Islands Development Board Scheme. They also include some establishments which did not receive any financial assistance.

Table 91
Changes in the Hotel Population of Great Britain between 1 January, 1970 and 1 January, 1974

	4–10	11–25	26–50	51–100	Over 100	All hotels
			HOTELS			
1970	24,554	7,790	1,913	740	262	35,259
1974	20,707	9,648	2,040	880	384	33,659
% change	– 16	+ 24	+ 7	+ 19	+ 47	– 5
			BEDROOMS			
1970	164,485	118,999	66,388	50,873	50,034	450,779
1974	145,539	143,385	71,037	60,899	76,662	497,502
% change	– 12	+ 20	+ 7	+ 20	+ 53	+ 10

Source: Hotels and Catering EDC, *Hotel Prospects to 1985*.

Bibliography

Amulree Report, *Report of the Royal Commission on Licensing (England and Wales) 1929–31*, London, HMSO, 1932.

Balsom, E., Trends in Catering: the history of a market research project, *HCIMA Review*, Vol.2, No.1, London, HCIMA, 1977, pp. 82–102.
Beach, S. T., The Little Neddy for Hotels and Catering, *HCIMA Review*, Vol.1, No.2, London, HCIMA, 1976, pp. 248–259.
Board of Trade, The Catering Trades in 1964, *Board of Trade Journal*, May 13, 1966.
Bootle, V., and Nailon, P., *A Bibliography of Hotel and Catering Operation*, London, New University Education, 1970.
British Association for Commercial and Industrial Education, *Industrial Training Boards, Progress Report Number 7*, London, BACIE, 1976.
British Hotels and Restaurants Association, The Story of the Association, *BHRA Journal*, London, BHRA, November 1957–May 1958.
British Hotels and Restaurants Association, *Annual Reports 1949–1971*, London, BHRA, 1950–1972.
British Hotels, Restaurants and Caterers Association, *Annual Reports 1972–1976*, London, BHRCA, 1973–1977.
British Tourist Authority, *Annual Reports for the Years Ended 31 March 1970–1976*, London, BTA, 1970–1976.
British Tourist Authority, *British Travel News*, London, BTA, quarterly.
British Tourist Authority, *Digest of Tourist Statistics, Nos. 5 and 6*, London, BTA, 1975 and 1976.
British Tourist Authority, *International Tourism and Strategic Planning*, London, BTA, 1976.
British Tourist Authority, *The British on Holiday 1951–1970*, London, BTA, 1971.
British Tourist Authority, *Tourism Intelligence Quarterly*, Vol.1, No.2, London, BTA, 1977.
British Tourist Boards, *British Home Tourism Survey, 1972–1975*, London, English Tourist Board, 1973–1976.
Brunner, E., *Holiday-Making and the Holiday Trades*, London, Oxford University Press, 1945.
Bryn Jones, M., *Food Services in Britain 1970–1980*, London, New University Education, 1970.
Bull, F. J., and Hooper, J. D. G., *Hotel and Catering Law*, London, Barrie & Jenkins, 1975.
Burkart, A. J., and Medlik, S., *Tourism: Past, Present, and Future*, London, Heinemann, 1974.
Burkart, A. J., and Medlik, S. (editors), *The Management of Tourism*, London, Heinemann, 1975.
Burke, T., *English Inns*, Britain in Pictures, London, Collins, 1944.
Burke, T., *The English Inn*, London, Herbert Jenkins, 1947.

Campbell-Smith, G., *Marketing of the Meal Experience*, London, University of Surrey, 1967.
Caterer & Hotelkeeper and Staff and Welfare Caterer, *Pacesetters 1976/77*, London, IPC Consumer Industries Press, 1976.
Caterers Association of Great Britain, *Annual Reports 1960–1971*, London, CA, 1961–1972.
Catering Wages Commission, *Catering Wages Act 1943, Report of the Catering Wages Commission on the Recommendation for the Establishment of a Wages Board for Industrial Catering*, London, HMSO, 1944.
Catering Wages Commission, *Catering Wages Act 1943, Report of the Catering Wages Commission on the Recommendation for the Establishment of a Wages Board for Unlicensed Catering Establishments*, London, HMSO, 1944.
Catering Wages Commission, *Catering Wages Act 1943, Report of the Catering Wages Commission on the Recommendation for the Establishment of a Wages Board for Licensed Non-Residential Establishments*, London, HMSO, 1945.
Catering Wages Commission, *Catering Wages Act 1943, Report of the Catering Wages Commission on the Recommendation for the Establishment of a Wages Board for Licensed Residential Establishments and Licensed Restaurants*, London, HMSO, 1945.
Catering Wages Commission, *Catering Wages Act 1943, Report of the Catering Wages Commission on the Recommendation for the Establishment of a Wages Board for Unlicensed Residential Establishments*, London, HMSO, 1946.
Catering Wages Commission, *Report on an Enquiry into the Operation of the Catering Wages Act, 1943, in the Hotel Industry*, London, HMSO, 1950.
CBD Research, *Directory of British Associations, Edition 5 1977–8*, London, CBD Research, 1977.
Central Statistical Office, *Standard Industrial Classification, Revised 1968*, London, HMSO, 1968.
Central Statistical Office, *Monthly Digest of Statistics*, Nos. 306, 342, 366, June 1971, June 1974, June 1976, London, HMSO, 1971, 1974, 1976.
Central Statistical Office, *Standard Industrial Classification*, London, HMSO, 1956.
Central Statistical Office, *Standard Industrial Classification, Revised 1958*, London, HMSO, 1958.
Central Statistical Office, *Standard Industrial Classification, Revised 1968*, London, HMSO, 1968.
Central Statistical Office, *Standard Industrial Classification, Revised 1968, Alphabetical List of Industries*, London, HMSO, 1968.
Central Statistical Office, *National Income and Expenditure 1965–1975*, London, HMSO, 1976.
Central Statistical Office, *Social Trends No. 7 1976*, London, HMSO, 1976.
Central Statistical Office, *United Kingdom Balance of Payments 1965–1975*, London, HMSO, 1976.
Clayson Committee, *Report of the Committee on Scottish Licensing Law*, Edinburgh, HMSO, 1973.
Colam, E. E. F., *Practical Milk Bar Operation*, 1946.
Commission on Industrial Relations, *Report No.23, The Hotel and Catering Industry, Part 1, Hotels and Restaurants*, London, HMSO, 1971.
Commission on Industrial Relations, *Report No. 27, The Hotel and Catering Industry, Part 2, Industrial Catering*, London, HMSO, 1972.
Commission on Industrial Relations, *Report No. 36, The Hotel and Catering Industry, Part 3, Public Houses, Clubs and Other Sectors*, London, HMSO, 1973.

Committee on Invisible Exports, *Britain's Invisible Earnings, Report of the Committee on Invisible Exports*, London, British National Export Council for the Financial Advisory Panel on Exports, 1967.

Curtis-Bennett, Sir N., *The Food of the People, being the History of Industrial Feeding*, London, Faber and Faber, 1949.

Customs and Excise, *1st to 66th Reports of the Commissioners of Her Majesty's Customs and Excise for the years ended 31st March 1910 to 1975*, London, HMSO, 1910–1975.

Department of Employment, *DE News, Department of Employment Newsletter*, monthly.

Department of Employment Gazette, Vols. 79–85, London, HMSO, 1970–1977; monthly.

Department of Employment, *Manpower Studies No. 10, Hotels*, London, HMSO, 1971.

Department of Employment, *Manpower Studies No. 11, Catering*, London, HMSO, 1972.

Department of Employment, *Report of the Commission of Industry on the draft Order to abolish the Industrial and Staff Canteen Undertakings Wages Council*, London, HMSO, 1975.

Department of Employment, *Wages Regulation (Licensed Residential Establishment and Licensed Restaurant) Order 1975*, London, HMSO, 1975.

Department of Employment, *Wages Regulation (Licensed Non-residential Establishment) Order 1975*, London, HMSO, 1975.

Department of Employment, *Wages Regulation (Licensed Non-residential Establishment) (Managers and Club Stewards) (No. 2) Order 1975*, London, HMSO, 1975.

Department of Employment, *Wages Regulation (Unlicensed Place of Refreshment) Order 1975*, London, HMSO, 1975.

Department of Employment, *Wages Regulation (Unlicensed Place of Refreshment) (Amendment) Order 1975*, London, HMSO, 1975.

Department of Trade, *Bankruptcy, General Annual Report for the Year 1975*, London, HMSO, 1976.

Department of Trade, *Trade and Industry*, London, HMSO, monthly.

Department of Trade, Business Statistics Office, *Catering Trades 1969, Statistical Inquiry*, London, HMSO, 1972.

Drummond, J. C., and Wilbraham, A., *The Englishman's Food, A History of Five Centuries of English Diet*, London, Jonathan Cape, 1957.

Ellis, A., *The Penny Universities, A History of the Coffee Houses*, London, Secker and Warburg, 1956.

Elves, V., Catering Wages Regulations, *Journal of the Hotel and Catering Institute*, Spring, Summer, Autumn 1958.

English Tourist Board, *Annual Report for the Year Ended 31 March 1976*, London, ETB, 1976.

English Tourist Board, *The Hotel Development Incentives Scheme in England*, London, ETB, 1976.

Erroll Committee, *Report of the Departmental Committee on Liquor Licensing*, London, HMSO, 1972.

French, R. V., *Nineteen Centuries of Drink in England*, London, Longmans, Green, 1884.

General Register Office London, General Register Office Edinburgh, *Sample Census 1966, Great Britain, Economic Activity Tables Part I*, London, HMSO, 1968.

George, K. D. *Industrial Organization*, London, Allen & Unwin, 1971.

Government Statistical Service, *Business Monitor M6, Overseas Travel and Tourism*, London, HMSO, 1971–1977.
Government Statistical Service, *Business Monitor SD5, Catering Trades*, London, HMSO, 1974–1976.
Government Statistical Service, *New Earnings Survey 1974, Part F Hours, Holidays with Pay, Earnings of Part-time Workers*, London, HMSO, 1975.
Government Statistical Service, *New Earnings Survey 1975, Part C, Analyses by Industry*, London, HMSO, 1976.
Guillebaud, C. W., *The Wages Councils System in Great Britain, Economic Monograph*, London, James Nisbet, 1958.
Gluecksman, R., *Das Gaststaettenwesen*, Stuttgart, C. E. Poeschel Verlag, 1927.

Hammond, J. R., *History of the Second World War, United Kingdom Civil Series, FOOD, Volume I, The Growth of Policy*, and *Volume II, Studies in Administration and Control*, London, HMSO & Longmans, Green, 1951.
Harrison, W., *Description of England*, London, Truebner, 1877–8.
Home Office, *Liquor Licensing Statistics for England and Wales for the years 1899 to 1975*, London, HMSO, 1890–1976.
Home Office, *Report of Her Majesty's Chief Inspector of Fire Services for the years 1974–1976*, London, HMSO, 1975–1977.
Home Office/Scottish Home and Health Department, *Guide to the Fire Precautions Act 1971, No. 1, Hotels and Boarding Houses*, London, HMSO, 1972.
Hotel and Catering Economic Development Committee, *Your Market*, London, HMSO, 1966.
Hotel and Catering Economic Development Committee, *Visitors to Britain*, London, HMSO, 1967.
Hotel and Catering Economic Development Committee, *Your Manpower*, London, HMSO, 1967.
Hotel and Catering Economic Development Committee, *More Hotels?* London, NEDO, 1967.
Hotel and Catering Economic Development Committee, *Investment in Hotels and Catering*, London, HMSO, 1968.
Hotel and Catering Economic Development Committee, *Service in Hotels*, London, HMSO, 1968.
Hotel and Catering Economic Development Committee, *Your Manpower Supplement*, London, NEDO, 1969.
Hotel and Catering Economic Development Committee, *The First Two Years 1966–68*, London, NEDO, 1969.
Hotel and Catering Economic Development Committee, *Staff Turnover*, London, HMSO, 1969.
Hotel and Catering Economic Development Committee, *Is Staff Turnover Your Problem?* London, NEDO, 1969.
Hotel and Catering Economic Development Committee, *Staff Turnover Conference Report*, London, NEDO, 1969.
Hotel and Catering Economic Development Committee, *Why Tipping?* London, NEDO, 1969.
Hotel and Catering Economic Development Committee, *The Use of Computers*, London, NEDO, 1969.
Hotel and Catering Economic Development Committee, *A United Kingdom Hotel Reservation System*, London, NEDO, 1969.

Hotel and Catering Economic Development Committee, *Hotel Accounting: Introduction to a Standard System*, London, HMSO, 1969.
Hotel and Catering Economic Development Committee, *A Standard System of Hotel Accounting*, London, HMSO, 1969.
Hotel and Catering Economic Development Committee, *Value Added Tax: Points for Discussion*, London, HMSO, 1969.
Hotel and Catering Economic Development Committee, *Economic Assessment to 1972*, London, HMSO, 1970.
Hotel and Catering Economic Development Committee, *Marketing in a Small Business*, London, HMSO, 1970.
Hotel and Catering Economic Development Committee, *Hotels and the Business Traveller*, London, HMSO, 1970.
Hotel and Catering Economic Development Committee, *A Standard System of Catering Accounting*, London, HMSO, 1971.
Hotel and Catering Economic Development Committee, *Convenience Foods in Catering*, London, NEDO, 1971.
Hotel and Catering Economic Development Committee, *Your Market 1971*, London, NEDO, 1971.
Hotels and Catering Economic Development Committee, *Hotel Prospects to 1980*, Vols. 1 and 2, London, NEDO, 1972.
Hotels and Catering Economic Development Committee, *Hotels and Government Policy*, London, NEDO, 1974.
Hotels and Catering Economic Development Committee, *Trends in Catering: A Study of Eating Out*, Annual and Quarterly Reports April 1974–March 1977, London, NEDO, 1974–1977.
Hotels and Catering Economic Development Committee, *Accommodation for the Lower Priced Market*, London, NEDO, 1975.
Hotels and Catering Economic Development Committee, *Manpower Policy in the Hotels and Restaurant Industry, Research Findings*, and *Summary and Recommendations*, London, NEDO, 1975.
Hotels and Catering Economic Development Committee, *The Catering Supply Industry: Some Key Problems and Proposals for Action*, London. NEDO, 1976.
Hotels and Catering Economic Development Committee, *Hotel Prospects to 1985, Research Findings*, London, NEDO, 1976.
Hotels and Catering Economic Development Committee, *A Report to the NEDC*, January 1977, London, NEDO, 1977.
Hotels and Catering Economic Development Committee, *Employment Policy and Industrial Relations in the Hotels and Catering Industry*, London, NEDO, 1977.
Hotel and Catering Industry Training Board, *Report and Statement of Accounts for the years ended 31st March 1970–1976*, London, HMSO, 1970–1976.
Hotel and Catering Industry Training Board, *Service, Newsletter of the Hotel and Catering Industry Training Board*, Nos. 1–60, November 1967 – September 1977.
Hotel and Catering Industry Training Board, *Five Year Plan 1976 – 1981*, London, HCITB, 1976.
Hotel and Catering Institute, *Annual Reports for the years ending 30 November 1960–1970*, London, HCI, 1961–1971.
Hotel and Catering Institute, *Interim Report of the professional associations' working party set up to explore the possibility of establishing a wider professional body*, London, HCI, 1969.
Hotel, Catering and Institutional Management Association, *Annual Report for the years*

ending 30 November 1971–1976, London, HCIMA, 1972–1977.

Hotel, Catering and Institutional Management Association, *The Corpus of Professional Knowledge in Hotel, Catering and Institutional Services, HCIMA Research Fellowship Final Report*, London, HCIMA, 1977.

Hotel, Catering and Institutional Management Association, *The Profile of Professional Management*, London, HCIMA, 1977.

Hotel, Catering and Institutional Management Association, *Tomorrow's Managers*, London, HCIMA, 1974.

Housden, J., Brewers and Tenants: A Changing Relationship, *HCIMA Review*, Vol.2, No.1, London, HCIMA, 1976, pp. 5–23.

Howley, M., The Market for Wine in Hotels and Restaurants, *HCIMA Review*, Vol. 1, No.1, London, HCIMA, 1974, pp. 10–19.

Industrial and Commercial Finance Corporation, *Annual Review 1977*, London, ICFC, 1977.

Institutional Management Association, *Annual Reports and Accounts 1959/60 – 1969/70*, London, IMA, 1960–1970.

International Labour Office, *Year Book of Labour Statistics*, Geneva, ILO, 1975.

Johnson, P. W. R., *Professional Development and the Corpus of Knowledge in Hotel, Catering and Institutional Services*, Guildford, University of Surrey, Unpublished PhD thesis, 1977.

Jusserand, J. J., *English Wayfaring Life in the Middle Ages*, Translated from the French by Smith, L. T., London, Ernest Benn, 4th Edition, 1950.

Kotas, R., *Labour Costs in Restaurants, A Study of Labour Costs in Catering Establishments in the Greater London Area*, London, Intertext Books, 1970.

Kotas, R., *Management Accounting for Hotels and Restaurants*, London, Surrey University Press, 1977.

Kotas, R. (editor), *Market Orientation in the Hotel and Catering Industry*, London, Surrey University Press, 1975.

Koudra, M., Industrial and Welfare Catering 1970–1980, *HCIMA Review*, Vol.1, No.1, London, HCIMA, 1974, pp. 29–38.

Koudra, M., Catering Contractors: A Study in Industrial Concentration, *HCIMA Review*, Vol.1, Number 2, London, HCIMA, 1975, pp. 97–111.

Lecky, W. E. H., *A History of England in the Eighteenth Century, Vol. II*, London, Longmans, Green, 1892.

Lennard, R., The Watering Places, in Lennard, R. (editor), *Englishmen at Rest and Play, Some Phases of English Leisure 1558–1714*, Oxford, Clarendon Press, 1931.

Levy, H., *Drink, An Economic and Statistical Study*, London, Routledge & Kegan Paul, 1951.

Lewes, F. M. M. et.al., *The Holiday Industry of Devon and Cornwall*, London, Ministry of Housing and Local Government, 1970.

Licensing Commission, *Report of the Royal Commission on Licensing (Scotland)*, Edinburgh, HMSO, 1931.

Lickorish, L. J. and Kershaw, A. G., *The Travel Trade*, London, Practical Press, 1958.

Ludy, R. B., *Historic Hotels of the World Past and Present*, Philadelphia, David McKay, 1927.

Manpower Services Commission, *Annual Report 1975–76*, London, HMSO, 1976.
Medlik, S., *The British Hotel and Catering Industry, An Economic and Statistical Study*, London, Pitman, 1961.
Medlik, S., Catering Labour under Technological Influence, in Fuller, J., *Catering Management in the Technological Age*, London, Barrie and Rockliff, 1967, pp. 95–107.
Medlik, S., *Britain – Workshop or Service Centre to the World?* University Lecture, Guildford, University of Surrey, 1977.
Middleton, V. T. C., Changing Patterns in Hotel and Other Holiday Accommodation in Britain, *HCIMA Review*, Vol.1, No.3, London, HCIMA, 1975, pp. 160–174.
Ministry of Labour and National Service, *Catering Wages Commission, Catering Wages Act 1943, First to Eleventh Annual Reports 1944 to 1954*, London, HMSO, 1945–1955.
Ministry of Labour and National Service, *Catering Wages Commission, The Rehabilitation of the Catering Industry, Report to the Minister of Labour and National Service on an Enquiry by the Catering Wages Commission under Sect.2 of the Catering Wages Act, 1943*, London, HMSO, 1945.
Ministry of Labour and National Service, *Catering Wages Commission, Development of the Catering, Holiday and Tourist Services, Report to the Minister of Labour and National Service on an Enquiry by the Catering Wages Commission under Sect. 2(1)(b) of the Catering Wages Act, 1943*, London, HMSO, 1946.
Ministry of Labour and National Service, *Catering Wages Commission, Training for the Catering Industry, Report to the Minister of Labour and National Service, Secretary of State for Scotland and the Minister of Education, on an Enquiry by the Catering Wages Commission under Sect. 2 of the Catering Wages Act, 1943*, London, HMSO, 1946.
Ministry of Labour and National Service, *Catering Wages Commission, Report on an Enquiry under Sect. 2(1) of the Catering Wages Act into the Problems Affecting the Remuneration of Catering Workers which Result from the Practice of Giving Tips*, London, HMSO, 1947.
Ministry of Labour, *Report of a Commission of Inquiry on the Licensed Residential Establishment and Licensed Restaurant Wages Council*, London, HMSO, 1964.
Ministry of Labour, *Industrial Training: Government Proposals*, London, HMSO, 1962.
Mitchell, P. and Ashton, R. K., Wages Councils: Do They Matter? *HCIMA Review*, Vol.1, No.1, London, HCIMA, 1974, p.20–28.
Monopolies Commission, *Beer, A Report on the Supply of Beer*, London, HMSO, 1969.
Moryson, F., *An Itinerary*, 4 vols., Glasgow, James MacLehose, 1907–8.
Meunch, T., *Das Hotelunternehmen im Lichte Betriebswirtschaftlicher Lehre und Praxis*, Zurich, Leipzig, Orell Fuessli Verlag, 1930.
Munthe, P., *Freedom of Entry into Industry and Trade*, Paris, The European Productivity Agency of the OEEC, 1958.

National Caterers' Federation, *The Golden Jubilee of the National Caterers' Federation 1900–1950*, London, John Morris (Publicity), 1950.
National Institute of Economic and Social Research, *The United Kingdom Economy*, London, Heinemann, 1976.
Nightingale, M. A., Catering Education in the Seventies, *HCIMA Review*, Vol.1, No.2, London, HCIMA, 1975, pp. 82–96.
Norval, A. J., *The Tourist Industry, A National and International Survey*, London, Pitman, 1936.

Office of Population Censuses and Surveys, *Classification of Occupations 1970*, London, HMSO, 1970.

Office of Population Censuses and Surveys London, General Register Office Edinburgh, *Sample Census 1966, Great Britain, Economic Activity Sub-regional Tables*, London, HMSO, 1970.
Office of Population Censuses and Surveys London, General Register Office Edinburgh, *Census 1971, Great Britain, Economic Activity, Part I (100%), Part II (10% Sample), Part III (10% Sample), Sub-Regional Tables (10% Sample)*, London, HMSO, 1973, 1975, 1975, 1976.
Ogilvie, F. W., *The Tourist Movement, An Economic Study*, London, Staples Press, 1933.

Pickering, J. F., Greenwood, J. A., Hunt, Diana, *The Small Firm in the Hotel and Catering Industry*, London, HMSO, 1971.
Pimlott, J. A. R., *The Englishman's Holiday, A Social History*, London, Faber and Faber, 1947.
Political and Economic Planning, *Industrial Trade Associations, Activities and Organisation*, London, George Allen and Unwin, 1957.
Powers, T. F., The Competitive Structure of the Hotel/Motel Market, A paper to the *Council on Hotel, Restaurant and Institutional Education*, December 28, 1969, pp. 1–27.
Prest, A. R., and Coppock, D. J. (editors), *The UK Economy, A Manual of Applied Economics*, London, Weidenfeld & Nicolson, 1976.

Richardson, A. E., *The Old Inns of England*, The British Heritage Series, London, Batsford, 6th Edition 1952.
Richardson, A. E., and Eberlein, H. D., *The English Inn Past and Present, A review of its history and social life*, London, Batsford, 1925.
Robinson, J., *Economics of Imperfect Competition*, London, Macmillan, 1946.
Robinson, E. A. G., *The Structure of Competitive Industry*, Cambridge, James Nisbet, 1953.
Royal Hotel Guide and Advertising Handbook containing a list of the Hotels, etc., of the United Kingdom, London, Smith, 1854.
Ruff's Hotel Guide and Railway Travellers' Companion and Vade Mecum, London, Hotel and General Advertising Company, 1902.

Sarkies, E. L., *The Importance of the Hotel Industry*, Doctorate Thesis Leiden, Leiden, N.V. Boek-en Steendrukkerij Eduard Ijdo, 1933.
Scottish Home and Health Department, *Civil Judicial Statistics (Including Licensing and Bankruptcy) for the years 1912 to 1975*, Edinburgh, HMSO, 1913–1975.
Scottish Home and Health Department, *Her Majesty's Inspector of Fire Services for Scotland, Reports for 1974 and 1975*, Edinburgh, HMSO, 1975 and 1976.
Scottish Tourist Board, *Annual Report for the Year ended 31 March 1976*, Edinburgh, STB, 1976.
Seldon, A., The British Brewing Industry, in *Lloyds Bank Review*, London, October 1953.
Stehle, J., *Gaststaetten in aller Welt, Eine geographisch – historische Plauderei*, Lindenberg in Allgau, J. A. Schwarz, 1926.
Stehle, J., *Der Hotel-, Restaurations- und Kaffehausbetrieb*, 2 vols., Nordhausen am Harz, Heinrich Killinger, 1928.
Stokes, H. G., *The very first history of the English Seaside*, Sylvan Press, Undated.
Stuart, M. W., *Old Edinburgh Taverns*, London, Robert Hale, 1952.

Trevelyan, G. M., *History of England*, London, Longmans, Green, 1926.

Vaizey, J., *The Brewing Industry 1886–1951, An Economic Study for the Economic Research Council*, London, Pitman, 1960.

Wales Tourist Board, *Annual Report for the Year Ended 31 March 1976*, Cardiff, WTB, 1976.

Young, Sir G., *Accommodation Services in Britain 1970–1980*, London, New University Education, 1970.

Index

ABC tea shops, 38
Accounting, 206
Adda International, 252
Air transport, 41, 50
Airline catering, 4
Airports, 50, 240
Ale-House Act (1828), 38–9
Ale Houses, 22, 23, 28, 29, 39
  closed in 14th century, 24
  early licensing regulations, 31
  Roman, 21
  Scottish, 26, 30
Allied Bakeries Ltd., 143, 253
Allied Breweries Ltd., 252, 254
Allied Suppliers, 253
Alpino Group, 253
Amulree Commission, 64, 65, 76, 144
Amusements, 21, 23
Anchor Hotels and Taverns, 252
Angus Steak Houses, 253
Aqua vitae, 35
Ariel Hotel, 240
Armed forces canteens, 61n
Assets, 120
Associated British Foods, 253
Associated Fisheries, 253
Associated Hotels Ltd., 239
Associated Restaurants, 253
Association of Hotel and Catering Training Executives, 240
Attwood Survey (1965), 140
Aviemore Centre, 240

Bank loans, 131
Bankruptcy, 89
Banquets Group, 253
Bar service, 167–8
Barclay. *See* Courage Barclay and Simonds Ltd.
Barry, Edward Myddleton, 36
Bass Mitchell, Butler and Charrington Ltd., 240, 241, 252, 253, 254
Bateman Catering Organization, 143, 240, 254
Bath, 30, 32, 37
Battersea College of Technology, 162
  See also Surrey University
Beatachs, 21
Beer, 39, 68, 241
  consumption, 113, 239, 241
Beerhouses, 39, 63, 75
Berni Inns, 241
Bibulium, 21
Bistingo Group, 253
Blackpool, 37
Board of Trade
  Catering Inquiry, 8, 70, 73, 111, 139
  Catering Inquiry (1964), 4, 6
  Catering Inquiry (1969), 10, 75, 79, 140, 141, 143
    hotel groups, 142–3
    restaurant chains, 143–4
  Monthly Inquiries, 4, 10, 236–7

Boarding houses, 3, 5, 43, 70, 97
  introduction, 34
Bognor Regis, 34
Bournemouth, 37, 65
Brent Walker, 253
Breweries
  provision of finance, 87, 131
  rationalization of outlets, 63
  See also Tied house system
Brewers' Society, 199, 206
Bridging loans, 131
Brighton, 34
Bristol, 29–30
Britain's Invisible Earnings, 12
Britain—Workshop or Service Centre to the World, 16n
Britannia Inns, 253
British Association of Hotel Accountants, 241
British Federation of Hotel and Guest House Associations, 198
British Home Stores, 253
British Home Tourism Survey, 96, 99, 100, 103
British Hotels, Restaurants and Caterers' Association, 199, 201, 206, 230, 239, 241
British Motel Federation, 197, 199
British National Travel Survey, 96, 97
British Restaurants, 44
British Tourist and Holiday Board, 239
British Tourist Authority, 13, 104, 111, 125, 219
  hotel occupancy surveys, 247–8
  See also British Travel Association
British Transport Commission, 253
British Transport Hotels, 143, 252
British Travel and Holidays Association, 239
British Travel Association
  hotel occupancy surveys, 247–8
  See also British Tourist Authority
Brughnibhs, 21
Bruighs, 21
Bryn Jones, M., 107, 110, 222
Building societies, 131
Buildings, 120, 129
Bumbles Restaurants, 253
Burkart, A. J., viin
Business Statistics Office Inquiries, 4n, 11
Butler. *See* Bass Mitchell, Butler and Charrington Ltd.
Butlin (Rank Organization), 42, 143, 252, 254
Buxton, 30, 37

Cafés, 3, 4, 5, 38, 73–4
Cambridge, 29
Camping, 42
Canadian visitors, 101, 102
Canteens, 4, 78
  armed forces, 6, 61
  colliery, 45
  industrial, 2, 3, 4, 5, 6, 40–1, 44–5, 79–80, 106
  NAAFI, 3
  school, 3, 4, 5, 44, 79, 106
  seamen's, 61n
  staff, 2, 3, 6, 79n

Capital expenditure, 4
Carlton Hotel, 37
Carlton Tower Hotel, 240
Carpets, 27
Cars, 39, 41, 218
Caterers Association of Great Britain, 79n, 197, 199, 230, 239
Catering
 and travel, 106
 costs, 123, 127
 effects of rationing, 40
 expenditure, 107–10
 industrial and welfare, 80
 investment, 118
Catering contractors, 5, 51, 70, 78–80, 143–4
 statistics, 81
Catering establishments, 140
Catering Managers Association, 193
Catering Teachers Association, 240
Catering Trades Inquiries, 4, 75
Catering Wages Act (1943), 2–3, 6, 7
Catering Wages Commission, 2, 7, 43, 70, 161, 211–12
 estimate of requisitioned hotels, 42–3
Census of Distribution, 239
Census of Population, 51, 151–4, 167
Centre Hotels, 252, 253
Centre Inns, 253
Centre Restaurants, 253
Charles I, 30
Charles II, 29
Charrington. *See* Bass Mitchell, Butler and Charrington Ltd.
Chefs, 163–5
Cheltenham, 32
Chester, 21, 28
Chicken Inns, 239
Chief Inspector of Factories, 40
Church, 31
 See also Monasteries
Cigarettes. *See* Tobacco sales
Cinque Ports, 28
City and Guilds of London Institute, 164, 165, 166, 167, 170, 172
Civic Catering Association, 240
Civil Judicial Statistics, 62
Claridges Hotel, 37
Classification of Occupations, 160
 See also Standard Industrial Classifications
Clayson Committee, 59, 68, 241
Clerkenwell, 32
Closing time. *See* Opening hours
Clubs, 5, 38, 70, 77–8
 admission of women, 38
 development from coffee houses, 34
 employees, 77
 increase in numbers, 63–4
 licensed, 4, 51, 59, 60
 luncheon, 3
 members, 66
 political, 3
 proprietary, 38, 66
 ratio to public houses, 64–8
 registered, 4, 59, 61–2, 91–2, 244–5
 residential, 3, 38
 social, 3
 sports, 4

 statistics, 62–3, 77–8, 81
 turnover, 141
Coaching inns, 32–3
Coffee bars, 5, 73–5
Coffee-houses, 29–30, 34–5, 77
Collective bargaining, 179, 180
Colleges, 161, 162
Commercial inns, 33
Commission on Industrial Relations, 79, 185, 203, 241
Committee on Invisible Exports, 240
Committee on Scottish Licensing Law, 59
Commonwealth visitors, 101, 102
Compass Hotels, 252
Competition, 92–4
 defined, 92
Conferences, 99, 100, 219
Cooks, 163–5
Co-operative groups, 146–7, 229
Co-operative Holidays Association, 39, 43
Cornwall, 87
Correct Holdings, 253
Cost of living index. *See* Retail price index
Costs
 accommodation, 121–3
 catering, 123, 127
 fixed, 124, 125–6
 labour, 123
 unit, 125
 variable, 124, 125–6
Council for National Academic Awards, 162
Council for Small Industries in Rural Areas, 132, 133
Courage Barclay and Simonds Ltd., 240, 241, 252, 254
Crawford, D. S., 253
Credit arrangements, 93
Crest Hotels, 252
Cumberland Hotel, 42
Cunard, 252
Curfews, 25, 43
Cyclists' Touring Club, 39

Danes, 21
Debentures, 130
Defoe, Daniel, 30
Department of Trade and Industry Catering Inquiry. *See* Board of Trade Catering Inquiry
Development areas, 90, 158
Development of Tourism Act (1969), 129, 132, 201, 241
De Vere Hotels and Restaurants, 252
Devon, 87
Diversoria, 21
Domestic staff, 168–9
Dorchester Hotel, 42
Dover, 28, 49
Drinks, 10
 expenditure, 111, 113–14
Droitwich, 32, 37
Druids, 21
Durham, 65
Dutton's, 253

Earnings. *See* Pay

Index

Eastbourne, 34
Eating out, 38, 106–7, 221–2
  price index, 246
Economic Development Committees, 255
  See also Hotel and Catering Economic Development Committee
Edinburgh
  coffee houses, 30
  hotels, 33
Elizabeth I, 27
EMI Hotels and Restaurants, 241, 252, 253
Employees, 14, 15–18, 151–9
Employment
  bar service, 167–8
  between 1966 and 1975, 153–4
  categories, 160–1
  conditions, 174–86
  domestic staff, 168–9
  future prospects, 225–7
  office staff, 170–1
  uniformed staff, 169–70
Employment and Training Act 1973, 208, 231, 241
Employment Services Agency, 208
English Tourist Board, 249
Epsom, 30, 32
Equipment, 120
Equities, 130
Erroll Committee, 68, 241
Evans, Peter, 253
Excise licenses, 61–2
Exeter, 28, 29
Expenditure
  on accommodation, 104, 105
  on drinks, 111, 113–14
  on food, 107–9
  on holidays, 97, 98
Exports. See Invisible exports
Express Dairy Ltd., 240

Factories (Canteens) Orders (1940 and 1943), 44
Falcon Inns, 252
Family inns, 33
Finance. See Investment
Finance Act (1959), 64
Finance Act (1967), 61
Finance Corporation for Industry, 132
Finch, 253
Fire Precautions Act 1971, 73, 132, 141
Fire Precautions (Hotels and Boarding Houses) Order 1972, 71
Fire Precautions (Loans) Act 1973, 132
Firms, 1, 119
Fish and chip shops, 4, 5, 6, 73, 74, 75
Food
  preparation, 163–5
  provision in public houses, 76
  rationing, 106
    in World War I, 40
    in World War II, 44
  service, 165–7
Food and Beverage Managers Association, 241
Foreign visitors. See Overseas visitors
Forster Report, 213
Forte. See Trust Houses Forte
Fortes Quality Foods, 253

Franchising, 133–4, 228
Frederick Hotels, 240
Free houses, 144, 145
Fullers Ltd., 239
Furnished apartments, 3

Galleon Roadchef, 253
Gardner, John, 240
Gardner Merchant Food Services, 140, 254
Gatwick Airport, 50
General Strike (1926), 41
George III, 34
George IV, 34
Gin, 35
Glamorgan, 65
Glasgow, 36
Golden Egg Group Ltd., 241, 253
Goodhews, 253
Goodhew, R. V., 253
Goods, v, 15–16
Gordon Hotels, 240
Graham Lyon Motel, 239
Grand Hotels (Mayfair), 239
Grand Metropolitan Hotels, 142, 143, 230, 239, 240, 241, 252, 253, 254
Gratuities, 122, 176, 180, 181
Greenall Whitley and Co. Ltd., 252
Grill-rooms, 38
Gross National Product, 8, 9
Grosvenor House Hotel, 42, 240
Guardian Wage Index, 179–80
Guest houses, 5, 70, 72, 97, 98
Guilds, 24

Hampstead, 32
Hardwick, Philip C., 36
Harrison, William, 27
Harrogate, 32
Hastings, 34
Heathrow Airport, 50, 129, 240
Henekey Inns, 253
Highlands and Islands Development Board, 132, 133
Hilton Corporation, 93
  See also London Hilton
Holiday camps, 5, 42, 70, 72, 98, 143
  requisitioned in World War II, 43
Holiday Inns, 133
Holidays, 45, 50, 95, 218
  conditions of employment, 181–3
  expenditure, 97
  facilities, 8
  of British people, 96–9, 241
  touring, 41
  with pay, 41–2
Hospital Caterers' Association, 193
Hospital catering, 4, 6
Hostels, 3, 5, 70
  distinguished from hotels, 72
  See also Youth hostels
Hotel and Catering Economic Development Committee, vi, 2n, 4, 6, 8, 107, 109, 129–30, 175, 206–7, 216, 231, 240
  Catering Supplies Study Group, 221, 222
  effect on the industry, 206–7
  forecasts, 216n, 222, 223

Hotel and Catering Economic Development Committee – *contd.*
Hotel Prospects to 1980, 241
Hotel Prospects to 1985, 72, 73, 121, 122
Investment in Hotels and Catering, 135
investment study, 134n, 135
investment survey, 138
Manpower Working Group, 186
members, 206
Supplies Study, 75, 221
surveys, 99, 110, 111, 182
Trends in Catering, 111, 113, 241
working groups, 206
See also Economic Development Committees
Hotel and catering industry
as ancillary activity, 7
as exporter, 13
as local employer, 158–9
chains, 141–2
chronology (1945–75), 239–41
demand forecasts, 216
development, 7–8
economic importance, 8
economies of scale, 146
effect of Depression, 41
effect of World War I, 40
effect of World War II, 42–5
emergence, 1
employees, 151–9
employment categories, 160–1
firms, 119
future prospects, 216–31
history, 21–45
importance, 7
index number, 10
location, 49–58
managers, 161–3
number employed, 16–17
organizations, 189–96
personnel associations, 192–5
professional bodies, 190–2
regions, 17–18, 52–3, 54, 242–3
relation to tourism, vi
role in national economy, v–vi, 14
sectors, 17–18, 69–81
size of establishments, 137–42, 250, 251
specialization, 228
structure in 1980s, 227–8
trade associations, 89–90, 197–203
trade unions, 195–6
turnover, 4, 11, 141, 235
unemployment, 155–6, 157
unfilled vacancies, 156, 157
Hotel and Catering Industry Committee (TUC), 195
Hotel and Catering Industry Training Board, vi, 2, 4–5, 6, 8, 162, 164, 204, 207–10
effect on the industry, 210
formation, 208, 240
members, 209
See also Industrial Training Boards; Training
Hotel and Catering Institute, 2n, 163, 166, 170, 190, 191, 193, 230, 239
Hotel, Catering and Institutional Management Association, 2n, 163, 190, 192, 194, 241
courses, 172
Hotel Cecil, 37

Hotel Development Incentive Scheme, 129–30, 132, 135, 222
Hotel Proprietors Act (1956), 71n, 239
Hotel Russell, 37
Hotel Sales Managers' Association, 240
Hotel Victoria, 37
Hotels, 5, 6, 70
bedroom capacity, 251
conversion for other uses, 89
co-operative groups, 146–7
definition, 70, 71
estimate of the number requisitioned, 42–3
introduction of, 33
investment, 120
leading operators, 252
licensed, 4
location, 250–1
new construction, 262
occupancy, 124–5, 247–9
optimum size, 139–40
private, 3, 34, 71, 72
purchase, 87
railway, 36, 49, 239
requisitioned
World War I, 40
World War II, 42–3
size, 139, 250–1
star classification, 71–2
statistics, 81
war damage, 43
See also names of individual hotels
Hotels garnis, 33
Hours of opening. *See* Opening hours
Hours of work, 174–6
Howley, M., 113
Hydros, 36
Hygiene Regulations, 239
Hythe, 239

Ice-cream parlours, 5
Imperial London Hotels, 143, 252
Imperial Tobacco Group, 241
Incomes, 217–18
Ind Coope Hotels, 252
Industrial and Commercial Finance Corporation, 132
Industrial Catering Association, 193
Industrial Training Act 1964, 207
Industrial Training Boards, 207–8, 231, 256
See also Hotel and Catering Industry Training Board
Industries, 1
Inn-keeper, 26
Inns, 27–8, 39
as early theatres, 27
coaching, 32–3
commercial, 33
family, 33
history, 22–3
superseded by hotels, 36
system developed, 25
Tudor, 27
Inspectors of Fire Services, 73
Institutional Management Association, 2n, 163, 169, 190, 191, 192, 230
Insurance companies, 131
Inter Hotels, 147

Index

Interchange Hotels, 147, 241
International Passenger Surveys, 13, 102, 103
Internment of aliens, 40
Investment, 119–23, 129–36, 224, 240
　in 1980s, 222–5
　studies, 134–5
Invisible exports, 12, 13–14
Ireland, 21
　visitors to Britain, 101, 102
Islington Spa, 32

James I, 30
Joint Committee for National Diplomas in Hotel Catering and Institutional Management, 172
Jolyon Restaurants, 253

Kardomah Ltd., 240
Kendal, 28
Knights Hospitallers, 27
Kotas, R., 123, 137, 140
Koudra, M., viin, 80, 111

Labour costs, 122
Ladbroke Holidays, 143, 254
Lancashire, 65
Lancaster, 28
Langham Hotel, 37
Laws. *See* Legislation
Leamington, 32
Leaseback of property, 130–1
Leeds, 36
Legislation, v
　Ale-house Act (1828), 38–9
　Catering Wages Act (1943), 2–3
　conduct of ale-houses, 31
　Development of Tourism Act (1969), 241
　dissolution of monasteries, 27
　Employment and Training Act (1973), 208, 231, 241
　Factories (Canteens) Orders (1940 and 1943), 44
　15th century Scottish, 26
　Finance Act (1959), 64
　Fire Precautions Act (1971), 73, 132, 241
　Fire Precautions (Hotels and Boarding Houses) Order (1972), 71, 73
　Fire Precautions (Loans) Act (1973), 132
　governing entry into market, 90–2
　historical, 24–5
　Hotel Proprietors Act (1956), 71, 239
　Hygiene Regulations, 239
　Industrial Training Act (1964), 207
　licensing, 38–9
　Licensing Act (1953), 239
　Licensing Act (1961), 59, 61, 66, 91, 240
　Licensing Act (1964), 59
　Licensing (Scotland) Act (1976), 59, 60n
　Licensing (Scotland) Act (1962), 66, 91
　Meals in Establishments Order (1942), 44
　Tippling Acts, 35
　Town and Country Planning Acts, 90, 239
　Wages Councils Act (1959), 3n
　Wages Regulation Orders, 177–8, 258–61
Leisure, 45, 218

Leisure and General Holidays, 252
Levy and Franks Ltd., 240
Lewes, F. M. M., 87
Lewis (John) Partnership, 253
Lex Hotels, 252
Licensed clubs, 4, 51, 59, 60, 61
Licensed premises, 59–61
　location, 51
　statistics, 62–3, 244–5
Licensed residential establishments, 2
Licensed restaurants, 2, 60
Licensed victuallers, 76
Licenses
　Excise, 61
　types in England and Wales, 59–60
　types in Scotland, 60
Licensing, 35
　beer houses, 39
Licensing Act (1953), 239
Licensing Act (1961), 59, 61, 66, 91, 240
Licensing Act (1964), 59
Licensing Laws. *See* Liquor licensing
Licensing (Scotland) Act (1976), 59, 60n
Licensing (Scotland) Act (1962), 66, 91
Liquor licensing, 38–9, 59–68, 169, 174
　effect on entry into market, 91–2
　history, 30–1
　opposition to new outlets in England and Wales, 91
　opposition to new outlets in Scotland, 91
Liquor Licensing Statistics for England and Wales, 62
Little Chefs, 253
Location factors, 51–2, 54
Location of industry, 49–58, 120, 128, 250–1
　advantages of concentration, 58
　economies of concentration, 58
　measurement of concentration, 51–8
Lockhart Group, 240
Lodging houses, 3, 72
　in seaside resorts, 34
London, 21, 129
　accommodation near airports, 50
　coffee houses, 29
　hotel occupancy, 125
　location of inns, 27
　tea gardens, 32
　watering places, 32
London Airport. *See* Heathrow Airport
London Hilton, 240
London Penta Hotel, 241
London Steak Houses, 253
Londoners' Meal Service Centres, 44
Lowlands of Scotland Hotels, 252
Luncheon clubs, 3
Lunn, Sir Henry, 39
Lyons, J. and Co., 252, 253
Lyons tea shops, 38

McAdam, Robert, 32
Mail coaches, 32
　See also Stage coaches
Maintenance staff, 171, 173
Malvern, 32
Managers, 161–3
Manors, 24
Manpower. *See* Employees

Manpower Services Commission, 208
Mansiones, 21
Market, 94
  cost of entry, 87
  definition, 85, 86
  density, 50
  entry, 86–7
  growth, 86
Matlock, 32, 37
Mayfair Hotel, 42
Meals in Establishments Order (1942), 44
Mecca Restaurants, 241, 253
Mercury Motor Inns, 252
Metcalf, John, 32
Middle Ages, 22
Midland Catering, 143, 254
Midlands, 65
Milk bars, 3, 5, 42, 73–5
Milk Bars Association, 197
Ministry of Food, 107
Mitchell. *See* Bass Mitchell, Butler and Charrington Ltd.
Monasteries, 22, 23, 25
  dissolution, 27
  See also Church
Monmouthshire, 65
Monopolies Commission, 65, 68, 144, 241
Monopoly value, 64
Mortgages, 130
Moryson, Fynes, 28
Motels, 5, 49, 70, 72, 239
Motor cars. *See* Cars
Mount Charlotte Investments, 252, 253
Mount Pleasant Hotel, 240

NAAFI canteens, 3
Napoleonic Wars, 38
National Association of Holiday Centres, 199
National Association of School Meals Organizers, 192, 240
National Brewer/Retailer Liaison Committee, 200
National Catering Federation, 241
National Cyclists' Union, 39
National Economic Development Office, 205, 206
National Examining Board for Supervisory Studies, 172
National Hotel Keepers' Association, 197
National Income, 8
National Income and Expenditure, 8, 104–5, 107
National Income Blue Book, 9, 10, 104, 107
National Joint Apprenticeship Council, 239
National Restaurants, 40, 123
National Society of Caterers to Industry, 79, 239
National Union of General and Municipal Workers, 184, 195, 206
National Union of Public Employees, 195, 206
National Union of Railwaymen, 195, 206
New Earnings Surveys, 175, 177, 180–1
Newcastle, 28
Nielsen Co. Ltd., A. C., 249
Norfolk Capital Hotels, 252
North British Trust, 252
North Hotels, 142, 252
Northumberland, 65
Nuthall and Ocean Hotels, 252

Ofer House Inns, 252
Off-licenses, 59, 60
Ogilvie, F. W., vn
Old Kentucky Restaurants, 253
Opening hours, 31, 174
  medieval, 25
Ordinaries. *See* Taverns
Overseas visitors, 100–4, 220, 221, 238, 239, 240
Owen Owen, 253
Oxford, 29

Paris, 33, 38
Park Lane Hotel, 42
Patronage, 34
Pay, 176–81
  collective bargaining, 183–4
  elements, 176–7
  statutory regulations, 183–5
Peel Commission, 144
Pensions, 72
Pilgrims, 22
Pizzaland, 253
Planning permission, 90
Plays, 27
  See also Theatres
Plymouth, 28
Political clubs, 3
Polytechnic Touring Association, 39
Pontins, 143, 254
Population, 28
President Hotel, 240
Prestige Hotels, 147, 240
Preston, 28
Prices, 92, 93
  See also Retail price index
Private hotels, 3, 34, 71, 72
Products, 1
Prohibition, 41
Public House Trust Companies, 39
Public houses, 4, 5, 6, 39, 70, 75–7
  leading operators, 254
  licensing, 76
  provision of food, 76
  ratio to clubs, 64–8
  statistics, 76–7, 81
  turnover, 138
Publicans, 35

Quality Inns, 239
Queen Anne's Hotels, 240
Queen's Awards, vi, 14
Queen's Moat Houses, 252

Railway catering, 3, 6
Railway hotels, 36, 239
Railways, 36–7, 61n
  hotels, 49
Rank Organisation, 252, 253. *See also* Butlin
Rationing. *See* Food rationing
Red Rose Grills and Inns, 252
Refreshment rooms, 5, 73–5
Refreshments, 10, 23
  See also Food
Regions. *See* Standard regions
Registered clubs, 4, 59, 61–2, 91–2, 244–5
  statistics, 62–3
Religious institutions. *See* Church; Monasteries

Index

Reo Stakis, 252
Reservation services, 93
Residential accommodation, 3, 10
Residential clubs, 5, 38
Residential establishments, 5, 6, 70–3
  licensed, 2, 60
  unlicensed, 3
  See also Hotels
Resorts, 50
  dependence on hotel and catering industry, 158–9
  Government Departments evacuated to, 42
  history, 30, 32
  influence of railways, 37
  seaside, 33–4, 37, 43
  troops garrisoned, 42
Restaurants, 3, 4, 5, 6, 38, 70, 73–5, 106
  chains, 143–4
  change of ownership, 89
  costs, 123–4
  fluctuation in numbers, 74–5
  leading operators, 253
  licensed, 2, 60
  new, 87
  statistics, 81
  turnover, 141
Retail price index, 246
Ritz, César, 37
Ritz Development Co., 37
Roads, 31, 32
  medieval, 22
  Roman, 21
Roman Britain, 21
Rowton Hotels, 252
Royal Household, 24
Royal London Hotels, 252
Royal Patronage, 34
Royal Progresses, 21, 27
Ruff's Hotel Guide (1902), 37
Russell, Dr. Richard, 33

S.E.T *See* Selective Employment Tax
Sadlers Wells, 32
Savoy Hotel, 37, 252
Saxons, 21
Scarborough, 32, 33, 34
School catering, 5, 6
Scotland, 25–6, 43
  ale-houses, 30
  Aviemore Centre, 240
  coffee-houses, 30
  consolidating Licensing Act, 239
  hotels introduced, 33
  licenses, 59, 60, 61
  winter sports facilities, 158
Scott, Gilbert, 36
Scottish and Newcastle Breweries Ltd., 252
Scottish Highland Hotels, 252
Sea transport, 61
Seafarer Restaurants, 253
Seaside resorts, 33–4
  evacuation of population, 43
  influence of railways, 37
  war damage, 43
Selective Employment Tax, 12, 16, 240, 241
Self-catering accommodation, 98

Services, v, 14–16
Shares, 131
Shawcross, Lord, 199
Shift work, 175
Shipping, 49–50
Simonds, H. and G. *See* Courage Barclay and Simonds Ltd.
Size of establishments, 137–42, 250–1
  economies of scale, 146
Skyway Hotel, 240
Small Industries Council for Rural Areas of Scotland, 132, 133
Snack bars, 3, 5, 73–5
Social clubs, 3
Soda fountains, 3
Southampton, 49
Southend, 34
Southport, 37, 65
Southwark, 36
Spas, 50
  Bath, 30
  Buxton, 30
  decline, 37
  Epsom, 30
  Government Departments evacuated to, 42
  troops garrisoned, 42
  Tunbridge Wells, 30
  See also Watering places
Spiers and Pond Ltd., 239, 240
Spirits, 35, 39
  consumption, 113, 239, 241
  price regulation in World War I, 40
Sports clubs, 3
Stabler, 26
Stabulae, 21
Staff Caterers Ltd., 240
Stage coaches, 28, 32
  See also Mail coaches
Standard Industrial Classifications, vi, 2n, 3–4, 5, 6, 7, 8, 69, 70, 79, 151, 239
  See also Classification of Occupations
Standard regions, 17–18, 52–3, 54, 252–3
Star classification, 71–2
Statistical bases, 7
Statistics, v, vi
  accommodation post-war, 43
  catering contractors, 81
  clubs, 62–3, 77–8, 81
  hotels, 81
  industrial canteens, 45
  licensed premises, 62–3, 244–5
  national income and expenditure, 8
  of inns (1577), 28
  public houses, 76–7, 81
  registered clubs, 62–3
  restaurants, 81
Steamships, 37
Stocks, 4
Strand Hotels, 252
Strand Palace Hotel, 42
Strathclyde University, 162
Superannuation funds, 131
Surrey University, vii, 162, 240
  See also Battersea College of Technology
Sutcliffe Catering, 143, 254
Swiss Hotel School, 161
Switzerland, 33

Tabard Inn, 27, 36
Tapestries, 27
Taverns, 23, 28, 29, 39, 106
  as providers of food, 35
  closed in 14th century, 24
  early licensing regulations, 31
  number in 14th century, 24
  Scottish, 25
Taylorplan, 143, 254
Tea gardens, 32
Tea shops, 3, 5, 38, 73–5
Technician Education Council, 163
Telford, William, 32
Tennessee Pancake Houses, 253
Theatres, 27, 61n
Thistle Hotels, 252
Tied house system, 39, 68, 76, 88, 133
  distinguished from free houses, 144–5
Tippling Acts, 35
Tobacco sales, 10
Toby Inns, 253
Toll roads, 31
Torquay, 34, 37
Torquay Leisure Hotels, 147, 241
Touring holidays, 41
Tourist boards, vi
Tourist trade, vi, 8, 12, 13, 14, 219, 241
Town and City Properties, 254
Towner Hotels, 252
Town and Country Planning Acts, 90, 239
Trade associations, 89–90, 197–203
  definition, 199
  functions, 200–2
Trade deficits, 12
Trade unions, 195–6
Training, 226, 239, 241
  food preparation and cookery, 164–5
  food service, 166–7
  in universities and colleges, 157–8
  managers, 161–3
  office staff, 170–1
  uniformed staff, 169–70
  See also Hotel and Catering Industry Training Board; Industrial Training Boards
Transport, 49
  air, 41, 50
  cars, 39, 49
  mail coaches, 32
  railways, 36–7, 49
  shipping, 49–50
  stage coaches, 28, 32
Transport and General Workers' Union, 195, 206
Travco Hotels, 143, 252
Travel, 8, 12–13, 14
  abroad, 219
  and catering facilities, 106
  between wars, 41–2
  business, 99
  end of 19th century, 37
  history, 21–4
  in 18th century, 32
  in 19th century, 32
  overnight, 95
  railway, 37
  16th century, 27
  steamship, 37

Trophy Taverns, 253
Truman Hanberry Buxton and Co. Ltd., 241
Trust Houses, 39, 240
Trust Houses Forte, 142, 143, 230, 239, 240, 241, 252, 253, 254
Tunbridge Wells, 30, 32
Turnover, 4, 11, 236–7
  clubs, 141
  public houses, 141
  restaurants, 141
Turnpikes, 31

Unemployment, 155–6
Union of Shop, Distributive and Allied Workers, 184, 195, 206
United Biscuits, 133–4
United States visitors, 101, 102
Universities. *See under names of individual universities*
Unlicensed premises, 2
Unlicensed residential establishments, 3

'Value added' contributions, 8, 10, 241
Vaux Breweries, 252
Victuallers, 35, 76

Wages. *See* Pay
Wages Board, 2–3, 7, 79n, 210–15, 239
Wages Councils, 73, 75, 177, 182, 185, 204, 210–15, 257–8
  Orders, 260–1
Wages Councils Act (1959), 3n
Wages Orders, 183, 260–1
Waiters, 166
Wales
  Sunday opening, 91
Warners, 143, 254
Watering places, 32, 34, 36
  See also Spas
Watney Mann Ltd., 241
West European visitors, 101, 102
Westbury Hotel, 239
Westminster Technical College, 161
Weymouth, 34
Wheeler's Restaurants, 253
Whitbread and Co. Ltd., 252, 253, 254
Wimpy Bars, 133–4, 253
Winchester, 28
Wine consumption, 113, 114, 239
Women
  in clubs, 38
  in restaurants, 38
Woolworth, F. W., 253
World War I, 40
World War II, 42–5
Worthing, 34

York, 21
  stage coach services, 28
Yorkshire, 65
Young, Sir George, 99
Youth hostels, 42
  requisitioned in World War II, 43
  See also Hostels